FORCE MULTIPLIERS

ALERT PRESS

Montréal, Québec, Canada
2015

FORCE MULTIPLIERS
THE INSTRUMENTALITIES OF IMPERIALISM

The New Imperialism, Volume 5

Edited by
Maximilian C. Forte

ALERT

PRESS
Montréal, Québec, Canada
2015

Library and Archives Canada Cataloguing in Publication

Force multipliers : the instrumentalities of imperialism / edited by Maximilian C. Forte.

(The new imperialism ; volume 5)
Includes bibliographical references and index.
Issued in print and electronic formats.
ISBN 978-0-9868021-7-1 (bound).-ISBN 978-0-9868021-6-4 (paperback).--ISBN 978-0-9868021-8-8 (pdf)

1. Imperialism. 2. United States--Foreign relations. 3. United States--Military policy. 4. World politics--1989-. 5. International relations. 6. Instrumentalism (Philosophy). I. Forte, Maximilian C., 1967-, editor II. Series: New imperialism (Montréal, Québec) ; v. 5

JC359.F67 2015   325'.32   C2015-906336-1
                                               C2015-906337-X

Cover design: Maximilian C. Forte

© 2015 Alert Press
1455 de Maisonneuve Blvd., W.,
Montreal, Quebec, Canada, H3G-1M8
www.alertpress.net

Printed in Canada

CONTENTS

FIGURES

PREFACE

Friends and allies, partners and protégés, extensions and prox-ies—the vocabulary of US power in the form of multiples of itself has become so entrenched that it rarely attracts atten-tion, and even less so critical commentary. Force multiplica-tion is about "leverage": using partners and proxies in an expand-ing network, but where power still remains centralized. Forces are conceptualized in multi-dimensional terms. Anything in the world of cultural systems, social relationships, and material production can become force multipliers for imperialism: food security, oil, electricity, young leaders, aid, social media, NGOs, women's rights, schoolgirls, democratization, elections, the G8, the European Un-ion, NATO, the IMF, the World Bank, the World Economic Fo-rum, AFRICOM, development, policing, borders, and epidemics, among others. This takes us to related conceptualizations of "full-spectrum dominance," "three-dimensional warfare," and "interop-erability," in what has become an imperial syndrome. Chapters in this volume present diverse examples of force multiplication, rang-ing from Plan Colombia to Bulgarian membership in NATO and the US-Israeli relationship, from the New Alliance for Food Secu-rity to charitable aid and the control of migration, to the manage-ment of secrecy.

Chapters in this volume represent a selection of the work that emerged from the New Imperialism seminar in 2014, in the De-partment of Sociology and Anthropology at Concordia University in Montreal. Each chapter has been carefully developed, revised, and extensively edited prior to publication. Given that the topics that are addressed by individual chapters are quite broad, the con-tributions to this volume should serve as useful complements to knowledge that readers may already have, interesting for their in-sights as much as the empirical side of research, or they may serve as invitations to do further research on the part of the members of the reading public.

This volume is timely on numerous fronts. The time spanning the production of this book, from late 2014 to late 2015, has wit-nessed several new and renewed US interventions overseas, from Ukraine to Venezuela, Iraq, Syria, Yemen, and Libya, and the non-withdrawal of US forces from Afghanistan, where a disastrous war stretches into its 14th year. On the academic front, and particularly in North American anthropology where the word "imperialism" is virtually unspeakable and the subject of deliberate or unconscious censorship, seminar participants have taken on a bold and unusual challenge. As it happens, this year is the first time that the contributors whose work was selected for this volume happen to all be anthropologists. Looking back over this and the past four volumes published since 2010, I believe that I detect a basic pattern that distinguishes the anthropologists from the sociologists: the former tend to prefer a case-study situated in a specific place, whereas the latter are more likely to study processes and broad phenomena that travel across numerous places, and are more likely to choose domestic phenomena when producing case-studies.

This is the fifth volume in the New Imperialism series published by Alert Press, and for the time being, the last. As always it has been my pleasure and honour to serve as the editor for such a collection, despite the fact that this year has been particularly challenging for personal reasons. Given the costly and time-consuming nature of these endeavours, and the fact that the seminar itself is not likely to be offered for the next couple of years at least, it will be a while before readers can hope to see a new volume in this series. Until next time then, I thank the reader for taking the time to study the contents of this volume.

FORCE MULTIPLIERS: IMPERIAL INSTRUMENTALISM IN THEORY AND PRACTICE

Maximilian C. Forte

"Force multipliers: Machines which allow a small effort to move a larger load are called *force multipliers*. Some examples of force multipliers include: a crowbar, wheelbarrow, nutcracker, and bottle opener. The number of times a machine multiplies the effort is called its *mechanical advantage*. *The mechanical advantage of a machine is the number of times the load moved is greater than the effort used. Mechanical advantage (MA) = load/effort*". (Avison, 1989, p. 109)

"Force Multiplier. A capability that, when added to and employed by a combat force, significantly increases the combat potential of that force and thus enhances the probability of successful mission accomplishment." (US Department of Defense [DoD], 2007, p. GL-11)

"Observation Number 9, *cultural awareness is a force multiplier*, reflects [*sic*] our recognition that knowledge of the cultural 'terrain' can be as important as, and sometimes even more important than, knowledge of the geographic terrain. This observation acknowledges that the people are, in many respects, the decisive terrain, and that we must study that terrain in the same way that we have always studied the geographic terrain." (General David H. Petraeus, 2006, p. 8)

"Gender issues aren't just personnel issues. They are intelligence issues! Gender is a force multiplier—if you understand how gender works in a particular society, you can control that society much more effectively!" (A senior US military lawyer speaking at a workshop on gender and international humanitarian law, in 2007. Quoted in Orford [2010, p. 335])

Whether it is smart (as in "smart bombs" or "smart power"), involves stealth ("stealth technology" like the B-2 bomber, or "leading from behind" as in the US-led NATO war on Libya), uses "leverage", employs "force multipliers," or engages in "full-spectrum operations," the political and military establishment of the US has produced a battery of terms having an aura of rationality and science. Added to the physics of dominance produced in rhetoric about "force-multipliers," there is a geometry of war ("asymmetric warfare" and "three-dimensional warfare") and even a quasi-biology of war ("hybrid wars"). Power is described by military leaders using concepts of time, energy, mass, and velocity. Just as the US Department of State (DoS) announces "smart, effective American leadership" (DoS, 2010, p. 14), so does the US Army proclaim "the science of control" (US Army, 2008a, p. 6-1). It is fitting then that the new US Secretary of Defense, Ashton Carter, is someone who received a PhD in physics. What lies behind the scientific-sounding certitude is both a deep anxiety about the increasingly precarious global grasp of the US, and a signal that many other nations will face greater peril as the US leans more than ever on social and cultural forces internal to those nations in order to advance its political and corporate interests.

US military spokespersons appear to have little trouble in speaking either plainly or in transparent euphemisms about the US' quest for control over other societies, through a variety of "force multipliers". Force multiplication means using leverage, proxies, cogs, and networks of collaborators. Force multipliers can also refer to mechanisms, processes, and institutions: trade treaties, military education, or the rule of law. Power relations are built into force multiplication, such as "leveraging debt": for example, structural adjustment policies have sought to reverse long-standing political principles and legal systems originating in anti-colonialism, national self-determination, and anti-imperialism, by eliminating the socio-economic supports of self-determination (such as tariffs, subsidies, wages, and support for national industries; see: Hickel & Kirk, [2014/11/20]). The concept—if we can call it that—of the "force multiplier" has itself been prone to multiplication, such that a force multiplier can refer to anything from military technology, to culture in the abstract, or culture in terms of news and entertainment communicated via radio, television, newspapers, and the Internet; gender and specifically relations between men and women; sexuality; law and legal enforcement systems; energy; food; education; "humanitarian aid" by non-governmental organizations (see Forte, 2014a, pp. 8-12; Lischer, 2007); and even induced mental states where according to retired US General Colin Powell, "perpetual optimism is a force multiplier" (Powell, 2006, slide 13). Simply showing images of potential force, by flying bombers over civilian areas with the expectation that crowds will post images to Twitter, is an act cast as a force multiplier designed to intimidate North Korea (Thompson, 2014/6/26). It seems that everything can or could be a force multiplier. The reason for this is due to the fact that in the West, militarization and securitization have reached such an extreme state of expansion (with practices following suit), that they are predicated on the potential recruitment of everything and everybody, manufacturing compliance with complicity as the desired by-product. That the *means* available may not produce "successful mission accomplishment," does not in any way deny either the *attempt* to secure control or the *desire* for totalizing forms of control.

Events during 2014-2015 alone, the period in which this volume was developed, seem to speak to the active use of force multipliers by the US in Ukraine, Venezuela, Russia, Iraq and Syria. For example, backing anti-government protesters in Ukraine and Venezuela, both having explicit aims of overthrowing their respective, democratically-elected governments, succeeding in Ukraine where the US had an active hand in selecting pro-US "leaders" (see O'Connor, 2014/2/7). In addition, as confirmed in a multitude of US government documents, there has been extensive US financing and training of dozens of Venezuelan opposition groups (see Johnston, 2014/2/21; Capote, 2014/3/25; Carasik, 2014/4/8; US Embassy-Caracas, 2006/11/9). The Obama administration also quietly admitted to supporting activists in the 2014 protests, along with providing current funding worth US $5 million, among other means of intervening to destabilize the legitimate government (Balluck, 2014/4/27; US Department of State [DoS], 2014a, p. 126; Busby, 2014; Weisbrot, 2014/2/18; Al Jazeera, 2014/3/14). Recently, Obama went as far as officially declaring in an Executive Order that Venezuela was an "unusual and extraordinary threat to the national security and foreign policy of the United States," a move typically used when imposing sanctions, and escalating intervention (Obama, 2015; White House, 2015a). In this same time period sanctions were imposed on Russia, support of NGOs in Russia was defended, and the US State Department appeared to be publicly adopting Pussy Riot, a supposed punk band that engaged in pornographic acts in Russian churches and museums, while also supporting LGBT rights in Russia, and this includes US and Western support for the "right" to spread information about "non-traditional" sex to *minors*—which Western corporate media (the state's private information contractors) typically denounced as a "draconian" law that was "anti-gay," without any mention of children or the fact that LGBT persons have legal protection in Russia; indeed, an argument has been made that Hollywood interests would be most affected by the passage of Russian Federation Federal Law № 135-FZ (Heiss, 2014, pp. 63, 66; also see Ossowski, 2013/10/22). In Syria, the US began to openly support armed rebels with military aid, plus training, and financing. In Iraq, the US launched new military attacks, while loudly lauding the supporting role of its allies and partners (Obama, 2014a). Add all of this to news from recent years about Pentagon "sock puppets" in social media, the US crackdown on whistle blowers, and the supportive role played by US academics, universities, professional associations, and philanthropies, and we have, even so brief, a robust picture of US force multipliers. Typically we find such US multipliers listed in US documents under the banners of "democracy promotion," "strategic communications," "humanitarianism," and "stabilization".

In addition to introducing the chapters contributed to this volume, all of which speak to one or more aspects of the concept of force multipliers, or more broadly the imperial "physics" of dominance, the aim of this chapter is to introduce and critically analyze the thinking and historical context implicated in the idea of force multipliers. This continues a project begun elsewhere (see Forte 2014a, 2014b) involving the critique of imperial ideology and its social and cultural practice. Specific to this chapter, we ask and address several questions: What is and what is not a force multiplier? What assumptions are at the root of the concept? Why does the US need force multipliers? What are the implied aims? What does the use of the term convey about how the US values its supposed partners and allies? What does the existence of social and cultural force multipliers, spread worldwide, suggest about the nature of US empire and its power? Since when has the US needed such multipliers? Does the possession and use of force multipliers suggest strength, weakness, or both?

One of my theses is that the resort to the language of science betrays a need for conceptual security on the part of political and military leaders, along with an attempt to provide assurance of clear thinking and successful outcomes to deeply fatigued and disgruntled masses at home, and elected officials tasked with making budget cuts. Linguistic scientism also creates an aura of order and neutrality, which helps to mask much uglier realities. Conceptual security, even just the "sound" of such security, is needed to offset the rising instability caused by US interventions around the globe, ranging from fighting up to eight international wars simultaneously (Afghanistan, Iraq, Yemen, Somalia, Libya, Syria, Pakistan, Colombia), the spread of militant resistance across Africa wherever the US engages in military intervention, to the outright creation of what the US itself alludes to as "failed states" (Iraq, Libya), and multiple productions of chaos and disorder on the streets of Kiev and Caracas. In the face of such rising instability, US planners and their corporate allies seek to reassure themselves of eventual success, thus gaining continued political and financial support in the form of new laws, and new weapons or consulting contracts. Everything, at home and abroad, is thus cast in terms of overt or implied destabilization. Thus US strategists and policymakers do abroad what they fear at home: protests are not about free speech or free assembly, but about destabilization—this is why protests are repressed at home, yet encouraged abroad, and the fig leaf of "human rights" is not meant to be taken at face value. The "fear of the masses," at the heart of democratic elitists, is now projected externally and turned into policy as "democracy promotion". Fear at home continues meanwhile, and is conveyed by an "all-threats, all-hazards" philosophy of enhanced national security awareness, with calls for more community policing and even the use of conservation officers as "force multipliers" in "counterterrorism" (Carter & Gore, 2013, p. 285).

Related to the above thesis, one cannot help but think that, at best, a spurious science is being generated by strategists, offering imprecision that is muted by the sound of conceptual precision. The idea of developing force multipliers is more useful when read as a statement of intent, a plan, as an index of actual and desired reach, rather than something certain, fixed, and unambiguous. What is also interesting to note is that such language refuses to reject or deflect conspiratorial views of power; instead, it actively promotes such views, thereby validating them.

A second thesis is that the force multiplier idea, premised on the definition of using a small effort to move a large load, involves recognition of limits while threatening expansion. In simple terms, it can mean that either the effort is getting smaller because resources are diminished (budget cuts, increased costs, rising debt, collapse in public support), or the load is getting larger because too many interventionist projects have been initiated, or both. In some sense, the idea masks a deeper anxiety about perceived weakness and strain. This anxiety about a diminished autonomous capacity is starting to come out in the open: "success will increasingly depend on how well our military instrument can support the other instruments of power and enable our network of allies and partners" (DoD, 2015, p. i). However, the danger comes in the desire to maintain the "large load," even to increase the size of the load, rather than scaling back to "small effort, small load," or "no effort, no load". "Force multiplier" implies projection at the same time as recognition of limits, of force that is insufficient on its own and thus requires extensions, that is, multiples of itself. However, we should also note some of the changing tone—more openly worried—that we find in very recent US military statements, such as those of the Chairman of the Joint Chiefs of Staff in the 2015 *National Military Strategy*: "control of escalation is becoming more difficult and more important…and that as a hedge against unpredictability with reduced resources, *we may have to adjust our global posture*" (DoD, 2015, p. i, emphasis added). While not going further and thus leaving much room for interpretation, the emphasized statement is still unusual in contrast with the normally assured tone of such documents.

A third thesis is that the use of partners and proxies highlights the role of collaborators in the imperialist project. As the load-bearing hands of US empire recede into the background, those of its local collaborators stand out on the front line. This shifts struggles for power from the international arena, between states, to the domestic arena within states. Inevitably then anti-imperialist violence becomes domestic, not international, which is exactly where US leaders want to move such violence—"Assad is killing his own people" can then become the opportunistic, expedient, and disingenuous claim fit for rhetorical contests about "human rights" at the UN Security Council, as a discredited US seeks to build up its "soft power" among the less-informed, the forgetful, and especially youths. No wonder then that doctrines like the "responsibility to protect" (R2P) are so popular among segments of the interventionist Western elite, as it allows them to treat opportunistically selected target states as if such states existed in a vacuum, and were not what they actually are: the new battlegrounds for the proxies of empire.

A fourth thesis is based on recognition of the simple fact that the force multiplier concept is ultimately rooted in military force. Problematically, the concept implies that if the multipliers fail, the hard force behind them will be brought closer to bear, creating a chain-link of connections that draw US intervention in more closely, turning indirect intervention into direct intervention. The force multiplier idea would thus appear to be a perilous, deceptive means of making a down payment on future US aggression against another nation, without wishing to telegraph such intentions too far in advance.

A fifth thesis is that the force multiplier idea reduces a complex world to a grid-like array, that is still based on ideas of "us" versus "them," masking what is still the basic doctrine of George W. Bush—you are either with us or against us—by encoding it into scientific-sounding, or scientistic, rhetoric. The world is thus reduced to force multipliers versus force "diminishers". By turning the term into a blob concept, US leaders make it seem that everything is open to intervention and manipulation, but likewise everything can also diminish US power. There has been obviously, painfully, little effort to clarify or elaborate on the concept, that is, little in the way of "deep thinking" that critically examines the concept, and what attempts there have been (e.g. Hurley, 2005), seem to obscure more than they explain by using sequences of mathematical equations with invented variables.

My sixth thesis is rather blunt: *that this is all fake*. By fake I mean that the attempt to produce a scientific effect around the idea of "force multipliers" is simply something intended as misdirection. The suggestion here is that those deploying the term are not taking their task seriously; they offer an underdeveloped concept as a gloss for a policy of destabilization—that is to say, *phony science* for *real policy*, masking internal uncertainty, confusion, and a refusal to logically think through the ramifications of policy. The scientism is for internal propaganda purposes, to impress peers, seniors, lawmakers, budget panels, and to convince the kinds of readers who might search and consult documents of state. The fakery also allows proponents of the use of proxies—like the Afghan collaborators identified in WikiLeaks documents whose safety, once exposed, caused much public fretting among US officials—to defer questioning of US assumptions about the nature of humans, the nature of its allies, and the potential for contradictions and reversals, let alone potential harm to human proxies. Ultimately, the real message about force multipliers is not partnership, it is domination.

The seventh thesis, for which this chapter provides some notes for further development, concerns force multiplication as another form of capital accumulation, namely, extraction. The need to "multiply" plus the need to *reduce* energy *expended*, are both meaningful primarily, even exclusively, as an expression of *cost*. What is thus directly implied is that the US seeks to minimize the cost of any intervention in the affairs of another nation-state, by passing those costs onto others. Those others thus effectively subsidize US intervention, either "literally" by paying for it, or in analogous terms of taking on risk and of doing the leg work. By using humans as strategic resources, and by using more of them and at the least possible expense, we have a relation of extraction. This is the equation that is hidden by that of the force multiplier—it is not so much about power *projection*, which could also connote ideas of power being spread abroad, and even less power *sharing*, as it is about *power extraction*—rendering all others less powerful, or even powerless, in the face of US global expansion. Moreover, by fixating on a concept which is expressed as a function of cost, US military planners and diplomats make calculations, and this calculating logic about the cost and utility of others is fundamentally an instrumentalist and transactionalist perspective. Such an approach was already abundantly evident in US theorizations of winning hearts and minds in Afghanistan by distributing *things* and offering *jobs*, in return for non-resistance or armed cooperation—reducing human social interaction and cultural meaning to a matter of strategic gain and rational choice on the part of individual "agents". The trick for an "overstretched" empire is, of course, how to minimize financial burdens by instead using cultural means— "shared values"—to win allegiance, acceptance, and acquiescence.

Instrumental Partners: An Imperial Science of Agency

For an empire whose imperialism is still denied by many, a striking number of terms and concepts have been generated by US leaders that nonetheless are premised on the root idea of "force" in achieving or securing US "global leadership". These terms command the language of US military, political, and corporate spokespersons, and they have been influential enough to be institutionalized in formal military doctrine. However, in order to acquire a varnish of respectability and credibility, and to project the image of likely success, these force-based terms are presented as scientific. In rendering domination in neutral *scientistic* terms, the processes involved are naturalized and thus depoliticized; or at least the undertone is that of mastery over nature, rather than the subjugation of others or their instrumentalization as "partners". Partners, as in coalitions and alliances, are presented as "force multipliers" in numerous documents produced by the State and Defense Departments. The amorphous concept of force multipliers is our focus, both for what it reveals as for what it obscures.

Limited resources occasioned by another reality that is stated in physics-like terms—overstretch—is a recurring concern for US strategists, as is the consequent demand for operating indirectly through chains of allied operatives, or force multipliers. Major David S. Powell, in a paper for the School of Advanced Military Studies at Fort Leavenworth, Kansas, stated that, "the concept of force multipliers is a key element of U.S. doctrine that asserts we can fight with limited resources and win" (Powell, 1990, p. 1). In addition, "there are several categories of force multipliers which include human, environmental, and organizational" (Powell, 1990, p. 2). The force multiplier concept is rooted in doctrines of "low-intensity conflict," the scientistic term for the US-directed counter-insurgencies in Central America in the 1980s (Powell, 1990, p. 3). In explaining the slippery concept of force multipliers, Powell (1990) makes reference to Honduras, the US invasion of Grenada in 1983, the US invasion of Panama in 1989, Costa Rica, and the US invasion of Dominican Republic in 1965—primarily Latin American and Caribbean cases, that is, the old laboratory of US imperialism. But what is, and what is not, a force multiplier? For Powell, "a force multiplier is a tangible or intangible variable that increases the combat value and overall capability of a military force" (1990, p. 5)—which could be anything. Indeed, since then the concept—if we can call it that—has expanded dramatically, to include virtually any *thing* and anyone, anywhere, who might advance US interests in any measure. Far from dispelling "conspiracy theory," US military and diplomatic strategists have in fact proceeded to fashion their plans in the most conspiratorial (even if unrealistic) terms.

In 2014 there was a surprising yet widely ignored admission from the White House that the use of force by the US had created "failed states": "We know from hard-learned experience that it is better to encourage and support reform than to impose policies that will render a country a failed state" (White House, 2014). This has not stopped the US from either using force or imposing policies. The recognition that force has its limits was preceded by the policy to lessen US costs by spreading the burden to other actors. As then US Secretary of State Hillary Clinton declared, "the problems we face today will not be solved by governments alone. It will be in partnerships—partnerships with philanthropy, with global business, partnerships with civil society" (Clinton, 2009). Adding to this, she spoke of "the three Ds of our foreign policy—defense, diplomacy and development" (Clinton, 2009). Clinton also spoke in terms of force multipliers: "by combining our strengths, governments and philanthropies can more than double our impact. And the multiplier effect continues if we add businesses, NGOs, universities, unions, faith communities, and individuals. That's the power of partnership at its best—allowing us to achieve so much more together than we could apart" (Clinton, 2009). There would be a "new generation of public-private partnerships" coordinated by the State Department, which Clinton hailed as "smart power"—the emphasis being on "collaboration" and the deployment of "the full range of tools available" (Clinton, 2009), with *tools* underscoring the degree to which the US government instrumentalizes the agency of others. The purpose of such tools is to advance US interests, to ensure "American leadership" in the euphemistic though nonetheless imperial language of government spokespersons. As Obama argued, "no nation should be better positioned to lead in an era of globalization than America—the Nation that helped bring globalization about," which he stated even as he denied any intent to build an empire (White House, 2010, pp. ii, iii).

US military strategists are keen to maximize the potential for US dominance in the context of "globalization," with some apprehension but also with a rising interest in working through the agency of others. The US Army's Field Manual for *Stability Operations* (FM 3-07), states these concerns in the following terms:

> "As the Nation continues into this era of uncertainty and persistent conflict, the lines separating war and peace, enemy and friend, have blurred and no longer conform to the clear delineations we once knew. At the same time, emerging drivers of conflict and instability are combining with rapid cultural, social, and technological change to further complicate our understanding of the global security environment. Military success alone will not be sufficient to prevail in this environment. To confront the challenges before us, we must strengthen the capacity of the other elements of national power, leveraging the full potential of our interagency partners". (US Army, 2008b, p. ii)

The level of apprehension has recently come into clearer public view, with the Chairman of the Joint Chiefs of Staff exclaiming in what is meant to be a staid document, "today's global security environment is the most unpredictable I have seen in 40 years of service" (DoD, 2015, p. i). The "complications," "challenges," and "opportunities" of globalization, have recently tended to be replaced by reference to "global disorder" which has "significantly increased," with the prediction being that, "future conflicts will come more rapidly, last longer, and take place on a much more technically challenging battlefield" (DoD, 2015, p. i).

Acknowledging that military success alone is insufficient, the US Army speaks of "leverage," "partners", and continues in the same document to endorse "soft power," and different kinds of intervention operating through international agencies—indeed, even the production of the manual itself was heralded as symbolic of this turn: "the first doctrine of any type to undergo a comprehensive joint, service, interagency, intergovernmental, and nongovernmental review" (Caldwell & Leonard, 2008, p. 6). Lieutenant General William B. Caldwell, the author of FM 3-07, co-authored an article with Lieutenant Colonel Steven M. Leonard, the head of the Combined Arms Center, in which they proclaimed the arrival of a "Brave New World" that would require different modes of operation:

"The forces of globalization and the emergence of regional economic and political powers are fundamentally reshaping the world we thought we understood. Future cultural and ethnocentric conflicts are likely to be exacerbated by increased global competition for shrinking natural resources, teeming urban populations with rising expectations, unrestrained technological diffusion, and rapidly accelerating climate change. The future is not one of major battles and engagements fought by armies on battlefields devoid of population; instead, the course of conflict will be decided by forces operating among the people of the world. Here, the margin of victory will be measured in far different terms than the wars of our past. The allegiance, trust, and confidence of populations will be the final arbiters of success". (Caldwell & Leonard, 2008, p. 6)

Here we see another articulation of the force multipliers idea: "Forces operating among the people of the world," whose "allegiance, trust, and confidence" are critical in the new battlefield of this brave new world brought on by globalization.

Given these prevailing winds, the US Army announced in 2014 that its doctrine would "change dramatically in the near future" as military leaders developed the operational concept of "Strategic Landpower". General Robert W. Cone, who commands the US Army Training and Doctrine Command (TRADOC), also announced that a new warfare function would be added, called "engagement": "the new warfighting function would involve skills used to influence foreign governments and militaries" (Sheftick, 2014/1/16). Along with "engagement," Gen. Cone emphasized the need for a "Human Domain" program which would take the place of the Human Terrain System (for more on HTS, see past volumes in this series). Keeping up the appearance of science, a recent military article on the "Human Domain" opens with a quote from a 19th-century economist: "Man, the molecule of society, is the subject of social science" (Henry Charles Carey quoted in Herbert, 2014, p. 81).

As with the concept of force multipliers, which Powell above identified as originating from US participation in the Central American counterinsurgencies and invasions of Grenada and Panama, so do Caldwell and Leonard find precedents for their planning not only in the US war against Vietnam but even further back when they link the colonial history of the US, the wars against Indians, Mexico, and the civil war with current formulations of counterterrorism and counterinsurgency. This is rare and frank historicization. What Caldwell and Leonard are advocating is a renewal of the Civil Operations and Revolutionary Development Support (CORDS) program, from the Vietnam war, as the basis for "whole-of-government" thinking in counterinsurgency, where stability equals pacification. As they state, "effective interagency integration—a true whole-of-government approach—offered the best solution to insurgency and best hope for lasting success" and is "fundamental to full-spectrum operations" (Caldwell & Leonard, 2008, pp. 8-9). FM 3-07 was thus explicitly intended to provide information that the branches of the armed forces, "interagency and intergovernmental partners, nongovernmental community, and even the private sector can refer to and put to use" (Caldwell & Leonard, 2008, p. 10). What they mask, however, is the extreme lethality of CORDS, and the fact that ultimately it failed to achieve US objectives. Suddenly, their attempt to historicize failed them. What is useful, on the other hand, is the fact that in the understanding of military strategists, force multipliers, whole-of-government, and full-spectrum, are always ultimately and intimately tied to violence. Indeed, once the US commits itself by seeking out force multipliers in other societies, it is committing itself to a slippery slope of increasingly direct intervention when those "multipliers" (local politicians, local armies, journalists, NGOs, etc.) fail to secure the desired gains, leaving the US with stark choices: more direct intervention (as in Libya) or humiliating defeat (the Bay of Pigs, Cuba).

Collaboration, partners, and coalitions underline the force multiplication sought by the US in avoiding what Obama calls overextension, and what historians similarly call overstretch, which is the

classic contradiction of imperialism as much as Obama may publicly gainsay this fact. The emphasis on coalitions, though not invented by Obama's predecessor, George W. Bush, was certainly
present in Bush's 2002 *National Security Strategy*, and then largely repeated by Obama. In 2002, Bush maintained that the US was
"guided by the conviction that no nation can build a safer, better
world alone," adding in significant language that, "alliances and
multilateral institutions can multiply the strength of freedom-loving
nations," listing the United Nations, the World Trade Organization, the Organization of American States, and NATO along with
"coalitions of the willing" as the preferred multipliers of US policy
(Bush, 2002, p. v).

While NATO is an obvious choice, the influence of the US in
the OAS has declined considerably. Some might not be prepared to
recognize the WTO and UN as arms of US policy, but this is due
to a significant amount of misdirection and misrecognition. The
WTO has been an excellent vehicle for the US to push its liberaliz-
ing trade agenda, which would see US corporations forced into sectors of national economies where they are currently barred or
impeded, while pressuring other societies to commodify education
and open local media to even greater US penetration, not to mention the privatization and deregulation of other public goods and
social services (see Germann, 2005; Scherrer, 2005). The UN,
popular misconceptions in the US notwithstanding, has become an
imposer and enforcer of liberal capitalist norms of governance (see
Cammack, 2006). "Good governance," as Parthasarathy (2005, p.
192) convincingly demonstrates, has become "one of the direct *instruments* of capitalist production," by imposing commodified Western law and ethics that open nations to foreign capital. In a grand
display of Western ethnocentrism, various UN agencies, particularly the UN Human Rights Council (UNHRC), have even gone as
far as equating the absence of multi-party elections with "human
rights abuse" (e.g. UNHRC, 2015). The UNHRC, and its supportive NGOs such as the US-staffed and Soros-funded Human
Rights Watch, impose a singular, Eurocentric definition of democracy whose implementation has not only blocked popular and direct forms of democracy, but also directly contributed to the
generation of inter-ethnic strife in many post-colonies of the periphery. Meanwhile, most US anthropologists have remained silent
on the issue of enforced impositions of Western-style democracy,
while some actively participate as consultants to the State Department, or involve themselves in various "pro-democracy" campaigns that aim at regime change.[1]

Having already identified "America" with the "cause of freedom," Bush added: "America will implement its strategies by organizing coalitions—as broad as practicable—of states able and willing to promote a balance of power that favors freedom" (Bush, 2002, p. 24). Obama then essentially repeated the same theme in his 2010 *National Security Strategy*:

> "The burdens of a young century cannot fall on American shoulders alone—indeed, our adversaries would like to see America sap our strength by overextending our power. In the past, we have had the foresight to act judiciously and to avoid acting alone. We were part of the most powerful wartime coalition in human history through World War II, and stitched together a community of free nations and institutions to endure a Cold War....we will be steadfast in strengthening those old alliances that have served us so well....As influence extends to more countries and capitals, we will build new and deeper partnerships in every region". (White House, 2010, p. ii)

The emphasis on coalitions finds its way into military doctrine. FM 3-07 discussed above lists the following goals:

> "Encouraging partner nations to assume lead roles in areas that represent the common interests of the United States and the host nation. Encouraging partner nations to increase their capability and willingness to participate in a coalition with U.S. forces. Facilitating cooperation with partner militaries and ministries of defense. Spurring the military transformation of allied partner nations by developing multinational command and control, training and education, concept development and experimentation, and security assessment framework". (US Army, 2008b, p. 1-12)

Former NATO commander, General Wesley Clark, maintained that "having allied support" makes a military power stronger, calling an alliance a "force multiplier" (Green, 2003, p. 38). Obama repeated this recently, using the "force multiplier" phrase with reference to Libya and NATO: "We're going to continue investing in our critical partnerships and alliances, including NATO, which has demonstrated time and again—most recently in Libya—that it's a force multiplier" (Obama, 2012). Also on Libya, former US Secretary of State Madeleine Albright said that, "building a multilateral coalition to deal with foreign conflicts actually strengthens the hand of the United States. The support of the United Nations Security Council and the Arab League for the NATO mission in Libya was a 'force multiplier'," and she advised using the "responsibility to protect" principles essentially for propaganda to build military coalitions, thus lessening US military and political expense (however nominally) (Landler, 2013/7/23).

Chapters in this volume speak directly to the alliance and coalition aspects of force multiplication, in military and economic terms. Thus chapter 1, "Protégé of an Empire: Influence and Exchange between US and Israeli Imperialism," by John Talbot, deals with the question of Israel as a force multiplier of US empire in the Middle East. Talbot's research sought to uncover how the relationship between the US and Israel impacts the foreign policy and global actions of both. Further his work seeks to understand what exactly is the "special" relationship between the US and Israel. His chapter explores two prominent answers to these questions and posits its own. One answer is that there is a significant and powerful pro-Israel lobby in the US which has a grappling hold on the US Congress, media, and within universities—suggesting that these are Israel's own "force multipliers". The Israel lobby's actions create ardent support for Israel's actions and pro-Israel foreign policy even when this goes against US interests. The second position argues that the US is not being manipulated; rather it is acting according to its own imperial interests. The argument assumes Israel was, and is, in a strategic position which works to protect the US' imperial and economic interests. Both the vast reserves of oil in the Middle East and the spread of cultural imperialism are of interest to the US empire. The chapter ends with a position that the relationship is neither one-sided nor symbiotic. The US is supporting a protégé in the realms of nationalism, colonialism, imperialism, exceptionalism, state violence, heavy militarization, the creation of a state of emergency, and empire. Israel is acting as the US itself does while relying on its support. Understanding this relationship alongside the other standpoints can help make sense of otherwise irrational actions in which each actor may engage on the global stage. Talbot's work has added significance in that it was produced just as the Concordia Students' Union (CSU) officially supported the international boycott, divestment and sanctions (BDS) campaign against Israeli occupation, a decision that was the product of a historic vote by a majority of Concordia undergraduate student voters, reinforcing the decisions by graduate students and other campus bodies.

In chapter 2, "The New Alliance: Gaining Ground in Africa," Mandela Coupal Dalgleish focuses on the New Alliance for Food Security and Nutrition which claims that it will bring 50 million people out of poverty in sub-Saharan Africa. He examines the origins of the New Alliance as well as the narrative that fuels New Alliance strategies. The chapter also considers how the value chains, growth corridors and public-private partnerships are furthering the interests of corporations while causing the further impoverishment of smallholder farmers in sub-Saharan Africa. The relaxation and reduction of regulations and laws related to trade and ownership, which are required for African countries to participate in the New Alliance, are enabling occurrences of land grabbing, contract farming and the loss of diversity and resilience in African farming systems. This chapter is also very much related to discussions (see the following sections) of "connected capitalism," the existence of the corporate oligarchic state at the centre of imperial power, and of course by invoking "alliance" the chapter's contents relate to force multiplication. In this instance, force multiplication has to do with gaining productive territory and projecting power by remaking food security into something controlled by Western transnational corporations and subject to Western oversight.

In chapter 3, "Cocaine Blues: The Cost of Democratization under Plan Colombia," Robert Majewski asks: Is the "war on drugs" in Colombia really about drugs? Majewski finds that the situation is more complex than simply a war on drugs. Instead he shows that rather than limiting actions to controlling and eradicating drug production, the US is on a imperialist quest of forging Colombia into a country able to uphold US ideals of democracy, capitalism and the free market. Through the highly militarized Plan Colombia that came to light in 2000, the US has utilized a number of mechanisms to restructure the country to its own liking. The ways in which US imperial aims are being attained are both through ideological and more direct means. Ideologically, the rule of law acts as a legal basis for the implementation of Americanized democracy. In a more direct manner, the US is training the Colombian army and employing private military security companies to carry out its objectives. As Majewski argues, the final aim is to create a secure environment for foreign capital to flourish, an environment that is even today seen as under threat by insurgent groups such as the Colombian Revolutionary Armed Forces (known by their Spanish acronym, FARC). As we will see in the following sections, the US' cultivation of ties to the Colombian military is an excellent example of what Special Forces and US Army documents describe when speaking of force multipliers and "foreign internal defense," allowing the US a presence by proxy inside the Colombian polity.

Chapter 4, "Bulgarian Membership in NATO and the Price of Democracy," by Lea Marinova, examines Bulgaria's membership in NATO—where Bulgaria now serves as one of the newer force multipliers of a force multiplying alliance that works to project US dominance. Some of the central questions raised by this chapter in examining the nature of Bulagria's NATO membership are: What are the main arguments on the side of NATO which favour Bulgarian participation in the Alliance, and to what ends? How is Bulgaria advantaged from this allegiance? Through the examination of the Bulgarian government's "Vision 2020" project and the participation of Bulgaria in NATO missions, it is argued that NATO is an instrumentalization of US imperialism. Through the exposition of specific socio-historical predispositions which led to that association, the link between the interests of the US in having Bulgaria as an ally by its side in the "global war on terrorism" is demonstrated. Marinova argues that it is important to produce critical investigation of organizations such as NATO, which claim to promote "democracy, freedom and equality," because behind this discourse there is a reality of creating political and economic dependency, while public and political attention is removed from this reality as the country's internal problems continue to escalate.

Chapter 5, "Forced Migrations: An Echo of the Structural Violence of the New Imperialism," by Chloë Blaszkewycz, shows how borders too can be used as force multipliers, or feared as force diminishers—either way, Blaszkewycz brings to light the *territoriality* of the so-called new imperialism which is routinely theorized as being divorced from the territorial concerns of the old colonial form of imperialism. Her chapter explores migratory movement as being influenced by the structures supporting the new imperialism. Harsha Walia's concept of border imperialism is used as a starting point to understand the different level of oppression and forms of violence coming from the US new imperialism. Even though scholars are less likely to talk about the territorial forms of domination in the new imperialism, when analyzing migratory movement one is confronted with the fortification of borders, both material and psychological ones. Therefore, adding the concept of the border into imperialism is a paramount, Blaszkewycz argues. Border imperialism legitimizes structural, psychological, physical and social violence towards migrants through narratives of criminalization and apparati of control such as detention centres that are an extension of the prison system. In brief, in a paternalistic way the US is compelling the migration trajectory of Others and forces people to be in constant movement. Therefore this is also a significant contribution for bridging migration studies with studies of imperialism.

Chapter 6, "Humanitarian Relief vs. Humanitarian Belief," by Iléana Gutnick, continues themes that were heavily developed in the fourth of our volumes, *Good Intentions*. It plays an important role in this volume for highlighting how humanitarian doctrines, NGOs, and development, are forms of foreign intervention that also serve as force multipliers for the interests of powerful states. Moreover, Gutnick argues that humanitarian aid discourse is voluntarily misleading in that it shifts the public's focus of attention towards seemingly immediate yet irrelevant ways of coping with the world's problems. The pursuit of development has become the basis of action for foreign intervention in all sectors. This chapter tries to present the actual causes of "poverty" in an attempt to recontextualize it within its political framework to shed light on possible solutions, if there are any.

Chapter 7, "On Secrecy, Power, and the Imperial State: Perspectives from WikiLeaks and Anthropology," which has been written and somewhat redeveloped since 2010, focuses on the demand for secrecy that is occasioned by an imperial state relying heavily on covert operations and whose own forms of governance are increasingly beholden to the operations of a "shadow state". This chapter is thus related to discussions of "connected capitalism" and the corporate oligarchic state discussed below. I proceed by examining how WikiLeaks understands strategies of secrecy, the dissemination of information, and state power, and how anthropology has treated issues of secret knowledge and the social conventions that govern the dissemination of that knowledge. In part, I highlight a new method of doing research on the imperial state and its force multipliers, which rests heavily on the work of antisecrecy organizations, of which WikiLeaks is paramount.

Scientific Imperialism

"A fundamental law of Netwonian physics applies also to military maneuver: one can achieve overwhelming force by substituting velocity for mass". (Maj. Gen. Robert H. Scales, 2003)

"Are we to reserve the techniques and the right to manipulate peoples as the privilege of a few planning, goal-oriented and power-hungry individuals to whom the instrumentality of science makes a natural appeal? Now that we have techniques, are we in cold blood, going to treat people as things?" (Gregory Bateson quoted in Price, 2008, pp. 35-36)

Major General Robert Scales is a fan of scientific allusions. In one publication he classed world wars into a typology where World War I was "the chemists' war," World War II was "the physicists' war," World War III (the Cold War) was "the information researchers' war," and World War IV (the "war on terror") is "the social scientists' war," based on a typology produced by Alan Beyerchen, a historian at Ohio State University (Scales, 2006). Scales sees World War IV as dispersed, distributed and nonlinear, with an emphasis on human and biological "amplifiers". World War IV, he argues, "will cause a shift in classical centers of gravity from the will of governments and armies to the perceptions of populations" and success will depend on "effective surrogates" (Scales, 2006). "In war, speed kills," he wrote in a book as if producing an incontrovertible formula (Murray & Scales, 2003, p. 245). Scales is not a self-made man, nor a scientist; if his writings gained notoriety, and he gained prominence, it is due to institutions, cultural phenomena, and an ideology that precedes him, and that was appointed by political elites. The relationship between modern science and imperialism is a long recognized one, and here we will only glimpse select, contemporary, aspects relevant to the current period of the new imperialism.

Introducing the 2002 *National Security Strategy*, then US President George W. Bush announced that, "innovation within the armed forces will rest on experimentation with new approaches to warfare, strengthening joint operations, exploiting U.S. intelligence advantages, and taking full advantage of science and technology" (Bush, 2002, p. 30). From early on after September 11, 2001, the connections were drawn between selling warfare as scientifically sophisticated and calling for "joint operations" and "interoperability" with other militaries. Here I will focus on the "science" that is used to bolster the political and intellectual credentials of contemporary interventionism.

As others have observed, since World War II science and development have become two new reasons of state, added to that of national security and, "in the name of science and development one can today demand enormous sacrifices from, and inflict immense sufferings on, the ordinary citizen. That these are often willingly borne by the citizen is itself a part of the syndrome; for this willingness is an extension of the problem which national security has posed over the centuries" (Nandy, 2005, p. 21). Science, as Nandy notes, can inflict violence in the name of national security and development. Furthermore, science is becoming "a substitute for politics" in many societies (Nandy, 2005, p. 27). Nandy traces the idea of science as a reason of state to a speech made by President John F. Kennedy in 1962, in which Kennedy declared one of America's major national goals to be, "the scientific feat of putting a man on the moon....science was, for the first time, projected in Kennedy's speech as a goal of a state and, one might add, as a substitute for conventional politics" (Nandy, 2005, p. 22; see Kennedy, 1962). Kennedy showed that, "a wide enough political base had been built in a major developed society for the successful use of science as a goal of state and, perhaps, as a means of populist political mobilization" (Nandy, 2005, p. 23). The sign of science has acquired so much value, that it appears the political and military elites have decided that even just the sign rather than the substance of science will suffice—hence, "force multipliers" advanced as if a serious, scientific concept.

In other words, what we are dealing with here is more scientism than science—an image, veneer or allusion to science, in a rhetorical play that produces what we might call an aesthetic of science. This rests on the cultural work that has been done such that "scientificity" is socially accredited" and becomes an important objective because of the force of "belief which produces the appearance of truth" (Bourdieu, 1990, p. 28).

Scientism can also be used to quell intellectual insurgency, or at least to keep it at bay and thin its ranks. In terms of science in relation to politics, as Bourdieu (1990, p. 6) explained, "political ambition...is dissimulated by scientistic neutralism". Science acts as a social force that produces legitimacy:

> "In the struggle between different representations, the representation socially recognized as scientific, that is to say as true, contains its own social force, and, in the case of the social world, science gives those who hold it, or who appear to hold it, a monopoly of the legitimate viewpoint, of self-fulfilling prophecy". (Bourdieu, 1990, p. 28)

Appeals to science and reason work to "block off the paths leading (back) to power" (Bourdieu, 1990, p. xxv).

In light of what Nandy and Bourdieu explained, Scales makes sense: his Newtonian overtures cleanse the field of discussion of the massive amount of bloodshed and intimidation wrought by US intervention. Instead of frank political analysis, we are treated to the simplistic pseudo-physics of "force multipliers" that bounce against "demultipliers," a "spoiling factor" that results from "the enemy having and using a specific force multiplier," implying "a reciprocal type effect" (Powell, 1990, pp. 6, 7). Obviously, the idea being copied here and pasted onto complicated social and political realities is the idea that for every action there is an equal and opposite reaction (Newton's Third Law of Motion—this same idea returns to our discussion later in the guise of the "blowback" concept). Time is also treated in military analyses as something that reigns above social and cultural realities—reference is made to "the golden hour," or "that limited amount of time in which we enjoy the forbearance of the host nation populace" (Caldwell & Leonard, 2008, p. 11). Scientism in US intervention also facilitates the militarization of civilian diplomatic activities, in the name of "development": in 2011 it was announced that the US Agency for International Development (USAID) planned to establish a "Geographic Intelligence Center" utilizing Geographic Information Systems (GIS) to focus on "mapping a number of topics such as food security, development economics, cultural issues, social issues, political issues" (Rasmussen, 2011). Both the hardware and software to be used had been developed in multiple forms by the Defense Department, and the program itself closely mirrored that of the Human Terrain System. As a West Point blog stated in conclusion: "the ability to apply geospatial analysis and spatial thinking is a force multiplier in achieving mission objectives" (Rasmussen, 2011).

Yet, who are these "effective surrogates" that Scales mentioned above? For now they appear to form a lifeless category, without their own (conflicting) interests or competing local agendas. Recent history is filled with the US' numerous "ineffective" surrogates who would become targets of the US itself in some cases, from Ngo Dinh Diem, the president of South Vietnam overthrown in a US-backed coup on November 1, 1963, to Hamid Karzai, the president of Afghanistan, to those formerly on the CIA payroll such as General Manuel Noriega in Panama and Saddam Hussein in Iraq. In the same vein, the assumption is that "surrogates" will offer pure submission to US policy, and not pursue their own interests. Sometimes the results of such a flawed assumption become the basis for public revelations, such as the recent one concerning extensive fraud, waste, and mismanagement of US development funding in Afghanistan, that highlights the role of force multipliers in dispersing and limiting US efforts: "The reports by the special inspector general underscore the inherently chaotic nature of development that relies on private contractors and local agencies. Records disappear, agencies do not measure progress accurately and outright corruption drains government funds, especially in war zones" (Nixon, 2015/8/24).

Machinism

> "It was indeed as a machine that the colonialists themselves often envisaged the operations of colonial power". (Young, 1995, p. 166)

The force multiplier, as defined in physics, is precisely a machine. But then why would the machine be used to understand socio-cultural aspects of political power? As some historians have observed, in American thinking the "machine in all of its manifestations—as an object, a process, and ultimately a symbol—became the fundamental fact of modernism" (see Wilson, Pilgrim, & Tashjian, 1986, p. 23). That industrialization should inspire the mechanization of social life and the production of cultural meaning such that the machine is fetishized, is understandable. The choice of "force multiplier" as the mechanized means to explain power is thus not accidental. What the choice (however unconscious) reveals is the manner in which the strategists of "American leadership" think of the qualities of US power, and the qualities of other human beings. The omnipresence of the machine brings to mind the philosophical viewpoint of the Iranian revolutionary sociologist, Ali Shari'ati, and his work on *machinism*. As Shari'ati explained, "Machinism leads to the domination of the Machine over human life and substitution of the Machine for creative and determining man. Hence man becomes absent from himself" (quoted in Manoochehri, 2005, p. 296). A "man" who has become "absent from himself" then is the ideal "force multiplier" that serves as a spear-carrier for the US empire. Edward Said also pointed out the *machinist* conception of British imperial ideologues, such as Lord Cormer, who saw the British empire as consisting of a seat of power in the West and a "great embracing machine" in the East: "What the machine's branches feed into it in the East—human material, material wealth, knowledge, what have you—is preceded by the machine, then converted into more power" (Said, 1978, p. 44).

In this manner of conceptualization, US strategists reveal a stark inhumanity in their own power, while diminishing the human qualities of their "surrogates," who appear as divorced from their own cultures, as free-floating *actors* who will somehow lead others to "prosperity," which in light of these machinist understandings can only mean a barren path of imitative consumption. Put simply, the "force multiplier" idea betrays a deeply bleak conception of humanity—but even more troubling is that sometimes there seem to be agents willing to satisfy the conception's conditions.

The Imperial Mechanics of Control

Gen. Petraeus' notion that "cultural awareness" is a "force multiplier" was offered as part of a spread of supposed insights on how to achieve success in the military occupation of Iraq (see Petraeus, 2006, p. 3; see Figure I.1). Among these were related ideas of acting through the efforts of Iraqis: quoting from the counterinsurgents' favourite source of colonial inspiration, T. E. Laurence, Petraeus wrote, "do not try to do too much with your own hands". He stressed the need for rapid action: "every Army of liberation has a half-life". Petraeus added that, "increasing the number of stakeholders is critical to success" and that "ultimate success" (left undefined) depends on "local leaders". Others were to act as mechanisms of US control, in this alleged science of counterinsurgency. Both "community," "culture," and "gender" would also form part of the imperial mechanics of control as force multipliers.

Figure I.1: General Petraeus and His Force Multipliers

US Army General David H. Petraeus (centre), then commander of NATO's US-led International Security Assistance Force in Afghanistan, is shown on April 13, 2011, with the Governor of Helmand province, Gulab Mangol (right), and unspecified "other national leaders". They are being briefed by Abdul Karim Barahawi, the provincial governor of Nimroz, before attending a conference of "local authorities and tribal members" led by President Karzai in Zaranj, Nimroz province. (Photo: US Marine Corps, Sgt. Mallory VanderSchans)

Community has since then been redefined as an arm of the police state. "The community" was to be included in "law enforcement's battle against the threat of terrorism," an FBI intelligence analyst wrote, and the FBI should "train residents to become its eyes and ears because officers simply cannot do it alone," predictably adding as a conclusion: "building law enforcement-community partnerships can constitute the ultimate force multiplier" (Gaylord, 2008, p. 17). For its part, the US Department of Homeland Security identified "the community" as playing a central role in information collection and planning efforts. Homeland Security also concluded that this role "can be likened to the force multiplier effect—the community acting as the 'eyes and ears' of law enforcement" (Carter & Gore, 2013, p. 295). As for "culture," what Petraeus called "cultural awareness" became "cultural intelligence" in the works of others, who advertised it as "a force multiplier that is relatively inexpensive and, if properly harnessed, can furnish a return on investment far in excess of its cost"—then chillingly adding with the tone of someone training customer service representatives: "After all, conflict in general, and military operations specifically, are all about the people" (Spencer, 2009, n.p.). Gender, about which more will be discussed further on, would also be cast as a force multiplier of US military operations, as highlighted in the opening quotes of this chapter. This is deeply problematic, in part due to the following reason:

> "to become an object of knowledge is to become a potential target. So to introduce gender, or bodies, or human suffering into the system for producing knowledge about war automatically means that knowledge about gender, or bodies, or human suffering becomes part of the targeting machine". (Orford, 2010, p. 335)

Where matters become more confusing is when dealing with people as force multipliers of US interests, or as the eyes and ears of the US security apparatus. Are such people selfless? Why would they serve as force multipliers? Bringing to the fore their basic, instrumentalist assumptions, US military writers openly speak of buying support (Petraeus, 2006, p. 5; DeFrancisci, 2008, pp. 177, 179). Thus money becomes the force multiplier; however, where the confusion arises is about whom or what is the force multiplier in this equation. There seems to be little effort devoted to making any distinction in the military literature.

Force Multipliers and Secrecy: Categories without Contents?

In no US military or State Department document that is meant for public access will one find anything like a list of specific, named entities that constitute "force multipliers". The category is continually multiplied and expanded—everything from a strategically situated fuel depot to a NGO is a force multiplier—ranging from things, to persons, organizations, to social groups and cultural constructs, and even states of mind. This cannot be a science if it refuses to identify its units of analysis or its basic methodology. This pretend science lacks even the most rudimentary bases for developing an analytical frame, such as a typology, defined categories, and so on. This realization might lead some to raise questions of the real value of the scientific-sounding rhetoric deployed by officials—since it fails to adequately describe, let alone explain, then what does it serve? More to the point, what does it obscure, even as it reveals the basic instrumentalism at the root of US conceptions of the role the world's *others* in its plans? Perhaps the military and State Department have found a tactful, neutral-sounding trope for speaking

of what is in fact tacitly understood by them as servitude, deception, exploitation, and subordination—a successful trope it seems,
given the lack of any study in the English language that is critical of
the force multipliers trope.

On the other hand, as in the examples that follow, we know of
many actual instances of individuals, communities, and organizations that have collaborated with US imperial projects—including
journalists, "human rights activists," trade unions, entertainment
industries, churches, armed ethnic factions, government officials,
and so forth. The US may lack a science of force multipliers, but it
does not lack actual proxies that play that role. What lies unspoken
between the official, publicly accessible document on force multipliers (like the ones referenced in this chapter), and the eventual revelations of which persons and groups colluded with the US, is a
body of documentation that is secret. This is where WikiLeaks (see
chapter 7, this volume) serves as one of the entities that fills this
obvious gap, where we can learn of the named entities that act as
proxies, as agents, as indirect instruments of US power, as identified for example in the diplomatic cables published by WikiLeaks,
among other troves of data.

However, simply compiling a catalogue of such proxies, however interesting and illuminating, would be insufficient and potentially incomplete. The reason is that interpretation is still required—
it is not a mere matter of factual listing. "Force multipliers" may
risk equalizing and homogenizing considerable diversity, while pa-
pering over deep contradictions and potential reversals. Difficulties
are caused by differences in intentionality among the actors concerned, the duration of collaboration, the material extent of collaboration, and the diversity of actors' external relationships, to
name only four factors. Association may be confused with affilia-
tion, if two very different "force multipliers" are simultaneously
present in a US-centred network. As an example, X and Y are both
proxies of the US, but X and Y are otherwise opposed to each
other (on military, religious, ethnic, or broadly political grounds)—
they have a common association with the US, but are not affiliated
with one another. The fact that they are both allied to the US does
not entail that they are allies to each other. Then there can be proxies that may be serving different interests of competing state powers, that is, proxy X collaborates with states A, B, and C, where A,
B, and C are competing against each other.

Misrecognition among actors may occur as well: X believes
that the US is actually its proxy, not the other way around, a misrecognition that forgets the unequal distribution of power between

the two. Indeed, historical amnesia, combined with opportunism in the quest for short-term gain, and a political naïveté that allows X to believe it can pick and choose among facets of US power, and that it may choose when and for how long it can rely on US support, is at the base of misrecognition. A current example of this involves the People's Defense Units (or YPG), the militia of the Kurdish Democratic Union Party in Rojava, Syria. When it thought convenient, the YPG welcomed the US-led NATO bombardment of positions of the encroaching Islamic State (ISIS), helping to legitimize and validate US intervention among some Western leftists (anarchists in particular) who also assumed that NATO could be used like an *à la carte* item—a similar miscalculation made by some Libyan insurgents, in the very recent past. Divorced from any of the apparently dreaded "propaganda" about imperialism, NATO is misunderstood as another Western package to be imported and consumed, as if it could be somehow disaggregated from the agendas, interests, rationales and policies of the power-hungry state structures that make NATO possible. The reflex anti-anti-imperialism that meets with the approval of the US State Department meant that anti-imperialists were to be mocked, while those calling for US intervention invoked spurious analogies with the Spanish Civil War, and received applause. A few months later and it would now be the YPG who would be in NATO's sights, as Turkey (a NATO member) bombarded its positions with NATO's approval—and nobody mentioned "Spain" any more. Turkey refuses to make a distinction between the YPG and ISIS, especially since Turkey is fighting its own domestic war against armed elements of the Kurdish Workers Party (PKK) who are allied to the YPG. Apparently absent in all of this was any careful thinking about history, context, direction, and purpose of US power projection in Iraq and Syria, which certainly is not designed to serve the interests of the putatively socialist and strategically insignificant YPG. Ants cannot long afford to dream that they are elephants.

Diverging agendas and momentary role reversals also render the force multipliers' landscape problematic. One example would be that, at the same time as the US claims to be fighting a "war on terror," pitching itself in battle against "Islamic extremists," it has tacitly collaborated with such forces in Bosnia, Kosovo, pre-9/11 Afghanistan, Chechnya, Libya, and Syria, to name the better known examples. Momentary convergences—when enemies are shared in common, and opportunism is the deciding factor on both sides—may mean that a group such as Al Qaeda is a force multiplier in one moment, but not in the next. ISIS (whatever it may be) can be

the target of US bombardments, but at the same time it is the crea-
ture of funding, material support, and recruitment from Saudi Arabia and the Gulf states, that is, US allies. This is why one cannot
merely *list* "force multipliers," because the positioning as such is
often momentary, shifting, subject to reversal and even fighting
among "force multipliers" allied to the US. In addition, the lessons
of the old colonial principle of divide and rule have not been lost
on US strategists, even though they may be lost to the opportunists
who cry for air support.

The US may have found strength in its weakness—its diminishing resources requiring the supportive work of others, who thus
renew and extend US power. However, it may also be creating
many new weaknesses in this new strength, as symbolically represented by its own ambassador in Libya, along with CIA agents and
US military forces, being attacked and murdered in Benghazi, allegedly by those who benefited from US intervention in Libya.

Stealth Imperialism: Infiltration, Disruption, Destabilization

The force multiplier mechanism is not just something envisioned in
military writing, but is instead a cornerstone of US intervention,
both overt and covert. The CIA uses the term "disruption" when
referring to the covert support of allied agencies who aid the CIA
in the capture of so-called "terrorists"—collaborating security
forces in other countries then hide the fact of CIA involvement
(Johnson, 2004, pp. 15, 16). Regarding destabilization, in 1987 the
US created the Special Operations Command, based in Tampa,
Florida; its mission was to engage in "low-intensity conflict" by
covering units that worked closely with the CIA and Defense Intelligence Agency (DIA), while training units from target nations with
the aim of marshalling them towards destabilizing or overthrowing
their own governments (Johnson, 2004, pp. 71-72). As Chalmers
Johnson explained, in 1991 the US Congress, "inadvertently gave
the military's special forces a green light to penetrate virtually every
country on earth" (Johnson, 2004, p. 72). Congress did so by passing (Section 2011, Title 10) that authorized the Joint Combined
Exchange Training (JCET) program, allowing the Pentagon to send
Special Operations Forces on overseas exercises with military units
of other countries, "so long as the primary purpose of the mission
was stated to be the training of our soldiers, not theirs" (Johnson,
2004, p. 72). One consequence is that such forces can then engage
in espionage: "They return from such exercises loaded with information about and photographs of the country they have visited,

and with new knowledge of its military units, terrain, and potential adversaries" (Johnson, 2004, p. 72). This law also permitted US Special Forces to "train foreign military forces in numerous lethal skills, as well as to establish relationships with their officer corps aimed at bringing them on board as possible assets for future political operations" (Johnson, 2004, p. 72). By 1998 the Special Operations Command had established JCET missions in 110 countries (Johnson, 2004, p. 72). During 1998 alone, Special Forces operations "were carried out in each of the nineteen countries of Latin America and in nine Caribbean nations" (Johnson, 2004, p. 73).

In 1990 the US Army published *Doctrine for Special Forces Operations* (Field Manual No. 31-20) which described one of the principal activities of Special Forces on JCET missions as training foreign militaries in what the Army calls "Foreign Internal Defense" (FID). As Johnson noted, "most of the training exercises are meant to prepare foreign militaries for actions against their own populaces or rebel forces in their countries" (Johnson, 2004, p. 73) Brig. Gen. Robert W. Wagner of the US Southern Command in Miami told the *Washington Post* that FID is the "heart" of special operations, and an officer of the US Special Forces Command asserted that FID is "our bread and butter" (quoted in Johnson, 2004, p. 73). Stripped of the euphemisms, Johnson called FID little more than "instruction in state terrorism" (Johnson, 2004, p. 73).

Special Forces do not just train foreign militaries as part of FID missions, they also support insurgent groups trying to overthrow their governments:

> "SF can conduct a UW [Unconventional Warfare] mission to support an insurgent or other armed resistance organization. The United States may undertake long-term operations in support of selected resistance organizations that seek to oppose or overthrow foreign powers hostile to vital US interests. When directed, SF units advise, train, and assist indigenous resistance organizations. These units use the same TTP [tactics, techniques, and procedures] they employ to conduct a wartime UW mission. Direct US military involvement is rare and subject to legal and policy constraints. Indirect support from friendly territory will be the norm". (US Army, 1990, p. 1-17)

Using local actors, in fact even creating insurgent armies, with the explicit aim of overthrowing foreign governments is stated in very direct terms within the Army document, in an absolutely brazen violation of international law:

"The United States cannot afford to ignore the resistance
potential that exists in the territories of its potential enemies. In
a conflict situation or during war, SF can develop this potential
into an organized resistance movement capable of significantly
advancing US interests….the objectives may range from
interdicting foreign intervention in another country, to opposing
the consolidation of a new hostile regime, to actually
overthrowing such a regime". (US Army, 1990, p. 9-5)

What the US Army deceptively terms "resistance" organizations,
are intended as force multipliers, "that enhance US national interests" (US Army, 1990, p. 9-5).

Even as Indonesia was conducting genocide in East Timor, US
JCET missions in Indonesia were expanded in the 1990s, despite
the US Congress cutting off military aid (Johnson, 2004, p. 78). It is
interesting to note the individual force multipliers at work, and
their web of interests: beneficiaries of the JCET missions were US
partners in Indonesia, such as Lt. General Prabowo, a business
partner of President Suharto; Prabowo's wife was Suharto's daugh-
ter and she owned a sizeable share of Merrill Lynch Indonesia;
Prabowo was himself "a graduate of elite military training courses
at Fort Benning, Georgia, and Fort Bragg, North Carolina" and
had spent "ten years fighting guerrillas in East Timor, where he
earned a reputation for cruelty and ruthlessness"—his units participated in 24 of the 41 US military exercises (Johnson, 2004, p. 78).
Indonesian commandos under Prabowo were also trained by the
US in "military operations in urban terrain" following the outbreak
of the Indonesian economic crisis (Johnson, 2004, p. 78). US
President Bill Clinton's Secretary of Defense, William Cohen, visited Indonesia at the height of the economic crisis, meeting for
hours with Prabowo, with the visit taken as a green light "to use
force to maintain the political status quo in the face of protests
against the International Monetary Fund's hyperausterity measures"
(Johnson, 2004, p. 79).

The introduction of US "military advisors" into a "host nation" requires the government of that host nation (HN) to serve as
a force multiplier by paving the way for a US military presence:
"before advisors enter a country, the HN government carefully explains their introduction and clearly emphasizes the benefits of
their presence to the citizens" (US Army, 2003, p. I-5). The US
Army and its Special Forces also instruct the host government to,
"provide a credible justification to minimize the obvious propaganda benefits the insurgents could derive from this action"—
which serves to underline the esteem in which propaganda is held

by the US military, and their worry about their status and presence being named for what it is: "the country's dissenting elements label our actions, no matter how well-intended, an 'imperialistic intervention'" (US Army, 2003, p. I-5). Again, how the US and its client state are judged, is a matter of utmost strategic importance for the US in a counterinsurgency situation, as it indicates under the heading of "populace and resources control": "if the insurgents win popular support among the majority of the populace, the HN government's military successes are irrelevant" (US Army, 2003, p. 3-22). Given the degree to which public opinion can impact on the US military, it is no wonder then that it undertakes major operations in Hollywood, in Silicon Valley, and reacts as harshly as it has done against WikiLeaks (see chapter 7 in this volume).

When US leaders speak of "engagement" they are summing up the full range of activities described above. As retired US Army Colonel Andrew Bacevich explains about engagement,

"this anodyne term encompasses a panoply of activities that, since 2001, have included recurring training missions, exercises, and war games; routine visits [abroad]...by senior military officers and Defense Department civilians; and generous 'security assistance' subsidies to train and equip local military forces. The purpose of engagement is to increase U.S. influence, especially over regional security establishments, facilitating access to the region by U.S. forces and thereby laying the groundwork for future interventions". (Bacevich, 2008, p. 47)

As he also explains, US requests for over-flight rights and permission to use local military facilities are also a part of "engagement" and a form of intervention that can permit escalation when desired.

"Stealth imperialism" was a term used by Chalmers Johnson to describe the Pentagon's JCET operations, as well as the US' public and private arms sales abroad. He noted that the US is the world's largest exporter of weapons, the source of 49% of global arms exports, selling to over 140 countries (Johnson, 2004, p. 88). The sale of weapons could be construed as having an intended "force multiplier" effect—as Johnson explains, according to the White House under Bill Clinton, "the United States' arms export policies are intended to deter aggression," and to "increase 'interoperability' of the equipment of American and allied armies" (Johnson, 2004, p. 88). Arms sales also provide justification for contacts with foreign military officers: "as a means to get to know [foreign military] leaders personally and to develop long-term relationships of trust" (Johnson, 2004, p. 91).

However, Johnson's understanding of imperialism, like that of his other libertarian colleagues in academia, was almost exclusively focused on the "big government" dimensions of imperialism, such as military expansion with the growth in the number of bases abroad, heightened military expenditures, the militarization of foreign policy, and so forth. In addition, they usually prefer to speak of "empire" rather than imperialism, and their narratives often retain that margin of US patriotism that sees occasional "good intentions" behind US "miscalculations". What they also tend to diminish even when speaking of "US interests," given their generally anti-Marxist stance, is in-depth discussion dealing with capital investments, debt, natural resources, labour, trade or aid. Johnson and other scholars in his circle, notably his contemporary, Andrew Bacevich, had ties to US military or intelligence agencies at some point in their careers, and their scholarly work tends to be in the areas of political science and history, which possibly explains their focus, but not their bias perhaps. Had they expanded their understanding of imperialism to include something more than the power of states over other states, and bemoaning the failure of "citizens" to stand up to the national security state, they might have developed the idea of "stealth imperialism" further to better match actual practice, and to better grasp the large range of what military, political, and corporate leaders mean when they speak of "force multipliers".

A more comprehensive analysis of "stealth imperialism" must include the workings of US-dominated financial institutions such as the International Monetary Fund and the World Bank, and Western-dominated multilateral institutions such as the World Trade Organization, each of which has done far more to remake societies around the world than what the US military usually achieves. The IMF, World Bank, and WTO have served to extend the power of US-based transnational corporations over global production, exchange, and finance, while other non-US but still Western corporations have benefited as well (Ash, 2003, p. 239). Even in the view of such a mainstream, establishment economist as Jeffrey Sachs, "the IMF is essentially a covert arm of the U.S. Treasury," adding,

> "Not unlike the days when the British Empire placed senior officials directly into the Egyptian and Ottoman financial ministries, the IMF is insinuated into the inner sanctums of nearly 75 developing country governments around the world—countries with a combined population of some 1.4 billion".
> (Jeffrey Sachs quoted in Johnson, 2004, p. 210)

Even though Johnson quotes Sachs, his understanding of imperialism remained nonetheless restricted to familiar political and military themes. Instead, as we shall see further on, the conceptualization and employment of "force multipliers" today is largely dominated by the biggest US corporations, in "partnership" with the state and "civil society". What is described in terms of "connected capitalism" below is not separate from or added to "stealth imperialism," it is firmly a part of it. (Had we not sought to multiply terms beyond Kwame Nkrumah's "neo-colonialism," we might have been better off.)

Precedents: Practicing with Cuba

Dissatisfied with an excessive reliance on nuclear weapons as a strategy for countering Soviet influence during the early years of the Cold War, General Maxwell D. Taylor, US Army Chief of Staff (1955-1959) during the Eisenhower years, emphasized *flexible response* which in turn introduced the idea of what are now called "full spectrum operations": effective security meant the US would need to acquire the means "to react across the entire spectrum of possible challenge"; this would involve a greater range of capabilities that would allow the US "to respond anywhere, any time, with weapons and forces appropriate to the situation" (Taylor quoted in Bacevich, 2010, p. 61). Under President John F. Kennedy, non-nuclear "options" would gain greater weight as part of a "flexible response" to the spread of socialism in the periphery (Bacevich, 2010, p. 65). An impetus to expand this range of options came in the wake of the disastrous defeat for the US-sponsored invasion at the Bay of Pigs, Cuba. General Taylor reappeared as Kennedy's chair of the Cuba Study Group, after the failure of Operation Zapata (the Bay of Pigs invasion). That group included CIA director Allen Dulles and Robert Kennedy. The group urged the president to persist in attempting to overthrow the government of Cuba, recommending that "new guidance be provided for political, military, economic and propaganda action against Castro" (Bacevich, 2010, p. 75).

Allegedly "wary of action that smacked of naked imperialism" (Bacevich, 2010, pp. 76-77) the White House welcomed the Cuba Study Group's recommendations which took the shape of "Operation Mongoose". This Operation was headed by Attorney General Robert Kennedy and involved, "an aggressive program of covert action that aimed to get rid of Castro and subvert his revolution" — Robert Kennedy declared his intention to "'stir things up on

[the] island with espionage, sabotage, [and] general disorder',"
working with Cuban exiles, and with direct military intervention as
a last resort (Kennedy quoted in Bacevich, 2010, p. 77). All government agencies in the US would coordinate their efforts to overthrow the Cuban government. Robert Kennedy's "Special Group
(Augmented)" secretly colluded "with the Mafia in plots to assassinate Castro, fantastical schemes aimed at inciting popular insurrec-
tion, and a program of sabotage directed at Cuba's food supply,
power plants, oil refineries, and other economic assets" (Bacevich,
2010, p. 78). Thirty-two specific tasks were involved in Attorney
General Kennedy's plan, ranging from "'inducing failures in food
crops' and mounting sabotage attacks to recruiting defectors and
devising 'songs, symbols, [and] propaganda themes' to boost the
morale of an all but nonexistent indigenous resistance" (Bacevich,
2010, p. 78). Rather than negating "paranoid conspiracy theory,"
US plans fully embraced conspiracy, relying on the use of non-US
government operatives to do some of the dirty work of US imperialism. In addition—and this is relevant to one of the opening theses of this chapter—the failure of covert options always entailed
"upping the ante" to more overt, direct responses. The failure of
US force multipliers can often commit the US to more direct use
of force.

The "Science" of Global Domination

While it is an odd mix of physics, biology, and geometry that has
captured the communications strategy of military planners, the
messages themselves are very telling about how such planners go
about envisioning US global domination, and the parts to be played
by others in assuring that dominance. Some thus speak about the
"center of gravity" in "hybrid wars"—writing in *Military Review*,
Colonel John J. McCuen declared:

> "We in the West are facing a seemingly new form of war—
> hybrid war. Although conventional in form, the decisive battles
> in today's hybrid wars are fought not on conventional
> battlegrounds, but on asymmetric battlegrounds within the
> conflict zone population, the home front population, and the
> international community population". (McCuen, 2008, p. 107)

As Orford suggested above, and as borne out here, everyone is a
target population. How do you combat resistance to such a monu-
mental ambition to dominate all of us? By using us against ourselves—here is another rendition of the force multiplier theme:

"counter-organization necessitates recruiting and training cadres from the local population and then organizing, paying, equipping, and instilling them with values adequate to their task" (McCuen, 2008, p. 111). However, if we are so amenable to US command and manipulation, so easy to bend because we come empty, then from where does resistance stem for which "counter-organization" is needed? Thinking beyond the more challenging questions of logic, McCuen proceeds to tell us that the way to think about success in "hybrid wars" is to adopt Clausewitz's notion of the "center of gravity": "the 'hub of all power and movement, on which every-thing depends...the point at which all our energies should be di-rected'" (McCuen, 2008, p. 111). All our energies, in other military documents, means every branch of the US federal state: "A whole of government approach is an approach that integrates the collabo-rative efforts of the departments and agencies of the United States Government to achieve unity of effort toward a shared goal" (US Army, 2008b, p. 1-4).

The US Army speaks explicitly in terms of "the science of con-trol" in its *Operations* Field Manual 3-0 (US Army, 2008a, p. 6-1). Achieving "control" involves what the Army calls "full spectrum operations" (a concept that as we saw originated in the US desire to conquer Cuba during the Cold War). Such operations require,

> "continuous, simultaneous combinations of offensive, defensive, and stability or civil support tasks. In all operations, commanders seek to seize, retain, and exploit the initiative while synchronizing their actions to achieve the best effects possible. Operations conducted outside the United States and its territories simultaneously combine three elements—offense, defense, and stability". (US Army, 2008a, p. 3-1)

Added to these concepts, former US Secretary of Defense, Robert Gates, outlined the idea of "asymmetric warfare" which clearly rests on changing others outside of the US, in terms of their culture and behaviour, so that they embody the new territory in which "US interests" are planted:

> "We can expect that asymmetric warfare will be the mainstay of the contemporary battlefield for some time. These conflicts will be fundamentally political in nature, and require the application of all elements of national power. success will be less a matter of imposing one's will and more a function of shaping behavior— of friends, adversaries, and most importantly, the people in between". (Gates, 2008, p. 6)

In line with this concept of asymmetric warfare, Robert Gates explained his view of the subordinate role of others in US plans, labeled as "force multipliers" by some:

> "arguably the most important military component in the War on terror is not the fighting we do ourselves, but how well we enable and empower our partners to defend and govern themselves. The standing up and mentoring of indigenous army and police—once the province of special Forces—is now a key mission for the military as a whole". (Gates, 2008, p. 6)

What Gates' views rest on is a vision of the globalization of US counterinsurgency doctrine. War as the blunt use of force was now deemed to be ineffective, in large part due to an unspoken acknowledgment of the successful use of force by the Iraqi and Afghan resistance. Instead, counterinsurgency doctrine mandated, "a collaborative undertaking involving not simply military forces but a wide range of other government agencies, along with private contractors, international entities like the United Nations, and nongovernmental organizations that may or may not even share U.S. policy objectives" (Bacevich, 2010, p. 200). In this context Gates praised the role of anthropologists in the military, Texas A&M agriculture faculty on the ground in Afghanistan, and Kansas State University for its work in Afghanistan, by way of explaining that force multipliers are as much domestic as foreign:

> "we also need new thinking about how to integrate...government capabilities with those in the private sector, in universities, in other non-governmental organizations, with the capabilities of our allies and friends—and with the nascent capabilities of those we are trying to help". (Gates, 2008, pp. 7-8)

Needless to say at this point, US diplomats are not exempt from executing their role in in-depth social and cultural intervention. Thus, speaking of "community diplomacy" (DoS, 2010, pp. 63-64), the US State Department introduced the concept of the "circuit rider":

> "Where building new physical platforms of engagement outside of capitals is not cost effective, embassy circuit riders offer a promising alternative. Circuit riders will be subject-matter experts based at an embassy who systematically travel to key areas of a country to allow embassy access to targeted communities and groups. These roving diplomats, properly supported, can significantly expand our embassies' ability to engage on specific issues, with a broader cross section of a

country's people, or in areas of a country that have particular foreign policy relevance to the United States". (DoS, 2010, p. 51)

The language of US diplomacy does not shy away from speaking of "target peoples". A country can have an "area" within it (likely either a reference to valuable natural resources, or a bastion of political opposition to the national government) that is of "foreign policy relevance" to the US, which inevitably empties another nation of its sovereignty. The US has already stated that it has every intention of using such "circuit riders" in Cuba as embassies are reestablished.

Imperial Half-Lives:
Theoretical Assumptions of Force Multiplication

While Gen. Scales mentions mass and velocity, military scientism turned to *time* in Gen. Petraeus' conception of the right doctrine of warfare. It is a conception without a tested formula, but it does sound "smart" to target audiences. However, the question of the time dimension is nonetheless significant because it calls into play the need for "force multipliers"—even though this too is laden with untested theoretical assumptions.

Speaking of time, some officers have written about "the 'golden hour'" which is "that limited amount of time in which we enjoy the forbearance of the host nation populace" (Caldwell & Leonard, 2008, p. 11). Gen. Petraeus thus urged that, in a situation like Iraq,

> "the liberating force must *act quickly, because every Army of liberation has a half-life* beyond which it turns into an Army of occupation. The length of this half-life is tied to the perceptions of the populace about the impact of the liberating force's activities. From the moment a force enters a country, its leaders must keep this in mind, striving to meet the expectations of the liberated in what becomes a race against the clock….we were keenly aware that sooner or later, the people would begin to view us as an Army of occupation. Over time, the local citizenry would feel that we were not doing enough or were not moving as quickly as desired, would see us damage property and hurt innocent civilians in the course of operations, and would resent the inconveniences and intrusion of checkpoints, low helicopter flights, and other military activities. The accumulation of these perceptions, coupled with the natural pride of Iraqis and resentment that their country, so blessed in natural resources,

had to rely on outsiders, would eventually result in us being seen less as liberators and more as occupiers. That has, of course, been the case to varying degrees in much of Iraq". (Petraeus, 2006, p. 4)

Bacevich also observed that "the post-Vietnam military have come to regard time as the principal limit in limited wars" (quoted in Bacevich, 2010, p. 195). Petraeus offers his conclusion above, however, even as he publicly calls for the elimination of "exit timelines"—clearly disregarding his own "science" of time (see Halper, 2010/8/13 and Petraeus & O'Hanlon, 2015/7/7). Indeed, when engaged in politics to support US military occupations, Petraeus has consistently argued for *more* time, without any reference to "half-lives," which would in case make little sense in a context of permanent war where careers and profits are made to depend on war. Thus, on the one hand, Petraeus "the scholar" and "guru of counterinsurgents" has to sound "smart" about limits to occupation while, on the other hand, Petraeus the politician-entrepreneur has to sound limitless about US investments in occupation. When the alleged scientists fail to take their own science seriously, then it is incumbent on the public to be severely skeptical about what is being peddled.

Though not stated directly, the assumption is that limited time increases reliance on local force multipliers. That almost constitutes the beginning of a formula. However, the problem is that the force multiplier concept itself—ever growing as it is—is riddled with inconsistency, ambiguity, and untested assumptions. Even military insiders, among the few to examine the concept of force multipliers to any degree, have found a *failure* to "develop the concept with regard to the exact nature and utility of force multipliers as operational planning factors" along with "a void" in the doctrinal literature in terms of the development of the concept (Powell, 1990, pp. 2, 9). Even in studies which via "a cross-national time-series dataset of post-civil-conflict and post-natural-disaster states" purport to produce empirical answers to the question of whether international non-governmental organizations engaged in humanitarian work can be a "force multiplier" for military action in achieving "human security outcomes," the "force multiplier" concept is itself left undefined and its assumptions are thus not tested (see for example, Bell et al., 2013). More recently, the term seems to have been dropped altogether, showing that at the very least there is uncertain and unsteady reliance on this concept. In fact, even calling "force multipliers" a *concept* may be asking too much for it to be respected as "scientific".[2] Instead, its real value is as a political statement about the multiple forms and directions of US intervention. When the neutralizing scientistic euphemisms are filtered out, the force multiplier agenda bespeaks an ideological ambition of US global intervention, occupation, and domination, which rests firmly on the support of non-US actors, and non-US state actors.

Imperial Mechanisms:
Destabilization and the Physics of Domination

Using unmistakably imperial language, US Secretary of State Hillary Clinton in 2010 outlined ways of "protecting our interests and projecting our leadership in the 21st century" (DoS, 2010, p. iv), euphemizing global domination in terms of "American global leadership" which she saw as resting on "our global military advantage," while needing to "lead through civilian power" (DoS, 2010, p. 8). On the one hand, Clinton indicated the government's commitment to "shaping the international order to advance American interests" (DoS, 2010, p. 9). On the other hand, she conflated this with "supporting the spread of universal values" (DoS, 2010, p. 9), which are *clearly not universal* if they need to be spread in the first place, and by a self-seeking US ironically. Like her military counterparts, Clinton renewed the justification for US intervention and destabilization, using a happy gloss. The US would support those who support its "values" (meaning, the US would support itself), and this implies the idea of force multipliers: "We will support democratic institutions within fragile societies, raise human rights issues in our dialogues with all countries, and provide assistance to human rights defenders and champions" (DoS, 2010, p. 10). The force multiplier idea is further implied by Clinton when she spoke of pursuing "new ways of doing business that help us bring together like-minded people and nations," in what she branded as, "21st century statecraft" that would "extend the reach of our diplomacy beyond the halls of government office buildings" (DoS, 2010, p. v). Clinton's primary target population, the pool that offered the best force multipliers for US foreign policy, consisted of youths: "In the Middle East and North Africa, for example, large youth populations are altering countries' internal politics, economic prospects, and international relations. The United States must reach out to youth populations to promote growth and stable democratic government" (DoS, 2010, p. 13). A year later, Clinton would violently stomp out Libyan socialism and Pan-African leadership in the name of the "Arab Spring" and a supposed "popular

uprising", by youths of course, leaving alone the fact that the leaders were evidently mostly elderly men.

Clinton's sermons mostly consisted of rewording what George
W. Bush had outlined nearly a decade before in his national security strategy. In 2002 Bush committed the US to encouraging "the
advancement of democracy and economic openness" in China and
Russia, while more broadly using the post-9/11 "moment of opportunity," in his words, "to extend the benefits of freedom across
the globe" and thus to "actively work to bring the hope of democracy, development, free markets, and free trade to every corner of
the world" (Bush, 2002, p. iv). In a sweeping statement of intent to
remake the face of the world so it would look back at the US with
an American smile, Bush declared: "We will extend the peace by
encouraging free and open societies on every continent" (Bush,
2002, p. iii). This could be seen as the "large load" in the force multiplier equation at the start of this chapter. Bush's successor would
identify the instruments to be used in making for a "small effort"
on the part of the US:

> "The United States Government will make a sustained effort to
> engage civil society and citizens and facilitate increased
> connections among the American people and peoples around
> the world—through efforts ranging from public service and
> educational exchanges, to increased commerce and private sector
> partnerships". (White House, 2010, p. 12)

In an unexpectedly astute observation, a prominent neoconservative identified the US idea of "multilateralism" as involving the
geopolitical objective of "remaking the international system in the
image of domestic civil society" (Krauthammer, 2002-2003).

Imperialism by Invitation or by Imitation?
Empire's "Mimic Men"

US efforts in remaking the international system according to an
image reflecting the US are not usually in complete vain, since a
path has already been laid for them. To continue with the analogy,
the discussion above is about widening and then paving the track
so that it becomes a permanent highway. None of the military or
diplomatic documents consulted (not even those with the highest
of scientific pretense) ever bothers to go into any detail about the
origins, development, and constitutions of the actual people who
are constructed as force multipliers. On the other hand, Harvard

historian Charles S. Maier addressed these ideas under the lemma of "empire by invitation" or "consensual empire" (Maier, 2002). While US leaders speak in terms of "partners," "alliances," and "coalitions," Maier is not convinced that any of these adequately describe the nature of the US as "a major actor" (in his minimalist terms) in the international system. Instead, it is more accurate to speak of "the subordination of diverse national elites who—whether under compulsion or from shared convictions—accept the values of those who govern the dominant center or metropole," Maier maintains. What distinguishes an empire from an alliance is the inequality in terms of power, resources, and influence between leaders at the centre of empire and the national subordinates who are, at most, their nominal counterparts. Political, economic, and cultural leaders in the periphery "hobnob with their imperial rulers". Even those who organize resistance, Maier argues, "have often assimilated their colonizers' culture and even values". Maier endorses the Cultural Imperialism thesis in explaining these deep ties between the US core and what V.S. Naipaul (1967) called "the mimic men" of the periphery:

> "Empires function by virtue of the prestige they radiate as well as by might, and indeed collapse if they rely on force alone. Artistic styles, the language of the rulers, and consumer preferences flow outward along with power and investment capital—sometimes diffused consciously by cultural diplomacy and student exchanges, sometimes just by popular taste for the intriguing products of the metropole, whether Coca Cola or Big Mac". (Maier, 2002, p. 28)

As for Naipaul's "mimic men," these tend to be members of the new national elites in "formerly" colonized territories, who have acquired the tastes and prejudices of the colonial master, who aspire to the culture and identity of the colonizer, while cringing from the culture of the colonized. Mimic men ultimately find themselves displaced, disenchanted, and alienated, not able to fully join the ranks of the master class in the colonial mother country, but divorced from the culture into which they were born and which causes them shame. It is also important to note that Naipaul's protagonist, Ralph Singh, is a politician, and was educated in the UK.

Elsewhere I wrote in similar terms to Maier's about the relationships between the domestic and international versions of the US (Forte, 2014c). As I outlined there, one can discern what we might call a National United States of America (NUSA) and a

Globalized United States of America (GUSA). NUSA is a simple reference to the current political geography of the US, filled in by places that can be specified with geographic coordinates, inhabited by people in relatively dense relations with one another. Most of the inhabitants of NUSA refer to themselves as "Americans," or are "Americans in waiting" (immigrants awaiting eventual citizenship). GUSA is not so neatly geographic, but it can still be found and seen, concretely. GUSA's existence can be observed (in no particular order of importance) in the adoption of US consumption patterns and standards by local elites around the world, who may also be dual US citizens. The existence of a transnational capitalist class, a large part of which is US-educated, also manifests this globalization of US power. Military leaderships formed by funding and training by the US military, must also be included, as should the tens of thousands fighting in US uniforms with the promise of getting Green Cards. Political parties funded by the US and often led by people who spent some time living and studying in the US, and who adopt the US as a model, form a part of GUSA. GUSA includes upper-class neighbourhoods, districts, and gated communities, and those whose life patterns, choices, and personal orientations have been seriously influenced or remade by US cultural imperialism, in a process commonly referred to as "Americanization". One of my working hypotheses is that it is GUSA which is now largely responsible for sustaining and extending the imperial reach of NUSA. Leaving the critique of scientism behind, we should now move from this overview of the instrumentality of imperialist logic to consider some of the practices, tools and devices used to multiply, mirror, and extend US power globally.

That the so-called force multipliers of US dominance can comprise, to a significant extent, dependent and mimetic bourgeoisies in former colonies is something deeply problematic for scholars and critics such as Ali Shari'ati. As he argued, these elites consist of what has long been known and referred to as the "comprador bourgeoisie," the functionaries who benefit from the distribution of Western imports and the export of local resources, but also those who are among the most assimilated and who encourage a "modernization" of local tastes in order to expand the market for foreign imported goods (Manoochehri, 2005, p. 297). In Shari'ati's terms, assimilation applies to,

> "the conduct of the one who, intentionally or unintentionally, starts imitating the manners of someone else. Obsessively, and with no reservations he denies himself in order to transform his identity. Hoping to attain the goals and the grandeur, which he

sees in another, the assimilated attempts to rid himself of perceived shameful associations with his original society and culture". (Shari'ati quoted in Manoochehri, 2005, p. 297)

The issue of dependency is also useful in another sense, one related to the broader, critical literature on the political economy of under-development. Since the force multiplier idea is inherently an ex-pression of the *cost* function of foreign action, it is appropriate to understand it in the terms of political economy as an *extractive* proc-ess. Extraction, and the accumulation of capital (understood in all senses) at the core, is an essential outcome of any formula that pos-its the use of the most strategic resources at the least expense.

Speaking of the Bulgarian case (see chapter 4), as just one ex-ample, the force multiplication of increased "Americanization" in the early 1990s, could be viewed as taking on another facet, this one being a specialty of anthropologists who studied cargo cults. As explained better by Eleanor Smollett, an anthropologist with twenty years of research experience in Bulgaria,

> "The thought that keeps coming to me is *cargo*. A mechanical analogy to cargo cults is meaningless of course. There is no cargo cult in Bulgaria. There is no charismatic leader. We are not seeing a revitalization movement (though some monarchists have appeared) or a millenarian religious movement. But still, in this secular, highly educated, industrial society, there are echoes that say 'cargo'. The wealth that is coveted exists somewhere else, in an external society. The structure of that external society and the manner in which the wealth is produced are poorly understood. The young people who covet what they imagine is the universal wealth of the West were not suffering from unemployment, poverty or absolute deprivation under socialism (although, in the present situation, they are beginning to experience all of these). They were and are, however, experiencing relative deprivation, as compared with their external model. It is this relative deprivation that moves them, as David Aberle made clear long ago in discussion of cargo cults. And as Eric Hobsbawm pointed out in contrasting these movements with revolutions, the leadership of such movements has no clear programme or plan of implementation for a new social system. The expected improvement to society is based on faith. If we strip away the old institutions, then the foreign aid, the investment, the development, the cargo will come". (Smollett, 1993, p. 12)

The Mexican philosopher of liberation, Enrique Dussel, like Shari'ati, wrote on the fabrication of culture in the image of imperial culture that is represented by the new national elites, those he sees as historically the most assimilated. Dussel notes that imperial culture is,

> "particularly refracted in the oligarchic culture of dominant groups within dependent nations of the periphery. It is the culture that they admire and imitate, fascinated by the artistic, scientific, and technological program of the centre....On the masks of these local elites the face of the centre is duplicated. They ignore their national culture, they despise their skin color, they pretend to be white...and live as if they were in the centre". (quoted in Manoochehri, 2005, p. 294)

Dussel, however, does not see this culture as being confined to the oligarchic minority alone. Instead, a "pop" version is produced, "the kitsch vulgarization of imperialist culture," one that is encouraged, reproduced and distributed by the elites who thus help to expand the imperialist economy by supplying a willing market for its goods—which resonates in the research of Smollett in Bulgaria. The process then is one where the imperial culture is "refracted by oligarchical culture and passed on for consumption. It is by means of the culture of the masses that ideology propagates imperialist enterprise and produces a market for its product" (Dussel as quoted in Manoochehri, 2005, p. 294).

Shari'ati described the culmination of assimilation as being the creation of monoculture. However, we can add that matters do not stop there, since there is also the growth of something resembling a "monoeconomy" under neoliberal tutelage, and a "monopolitics" that absorbs the nation-states of the global periphery as the new wards and even outright protectorates under UN, EU, and NATO auspices. Thus are US strategists able to speak of growing "alliances" and the spread of "universal values"—monoculture is the smoothest path to acquiring the most efficient machines: the force multiplier.

On the other hand, in US military and diplomatic papers there is no exegesis, no treatment, description or interpretation of the nature of those reduced in their roles to functional force multipliers. One wonders who US writers think these *people* are, what image of these human beings exists in their minds. It would appear, from the unspoken assumptions, that the average force multiplying person is conceived as being idealistic, one who associates the US with his/her highest ideals, and thus one who suspends judgment, and defers questioning. Above all, the force multiplier, being on the front line, is willing to sacrifice. These are to be sensed then as the perfect Christian Soldiers, in the Church of American Divinity, and the reader's job is to have *faith* in these force multipliers.

There is also an "ecological fallacy" at work in US writings about "civil society" and "youth" or other social collectivities as force multipliers. The ecological fallacy is, "a confusion of the forest and the trees or, more accurately, the observing of one and the drawing of inferences about the other" (Stevenson, 1983, p. 263). One result of this fallacy is drawing conclusions about individuals, on the basis of their membership in social groups. Specifically, this fallacy emerges as such in State Department documents that automatically cast "civil society" worldwide as opposed to the state, as pro-US democracy, and as a natural ally of the US.

The Instruments of Imperial Practice

Both the US Departments of State and Defense have created multiple programs for "targeting" foreign audiences and "winning hearts and minds"—a subject that is far broader than what is presented below (or even in previous volumes in this series). Hillary Clinton's "21st century statecraft" was mentioned earlier. The approach involved using communications technologies "to connect to new audiences, particularly civil society" as part of an "engagement" strategy (DoS, 2010, p. 65). As parts of its "public diplomacy," the State Department created "Regional Media Hubs" in Miami, London, Brussels, Pretoria, Dubai, and Tokyo, in order to "increase official U.S. voices and faces on foreign television, radio, and other media, so that we are visible, active, and effective advocates of our own policies, priorities, and actions with foreign audiences...serving as a resource and tool for amplifying the regional dimension of our message" (DoS, 2010, pp. 60-61). In addition, the State Department created the "Virtual Student Foreign Service," enlisting the aid of US university students to support US diplomatic missions (DoS, 2010, p. 66). Also dealing with students, the State Department expanded the "ACCESS Micro-scholarships" program so that, "teenagers, particularly in the Muslim world," could be funded "to attend English classes and learn about America" (DoS, 2010, p. 61), thus utilizing conventional techniques of cultural imperialism, targeting Muslim youths and enforcing the dominance of the English language. While some would say that these programs are "peaceful," the State Department also announced it was partnering with the Pentagon, in particular by using USAID in support of the Pentagon's regional Combatant Commands (DoS, 2010, p. 54).

One of the more central and consistent tools used to deepen US intervention has arisen from the exploitation of gender issues to win "hearts and minds" as part of the US' globalization of its counterinsurgency practices (see Byrd & Decker, 2008, p. 96; Pas, 2013; King, 2014). The State Department itself officially announced that the "protection and empowerment of women and girls is key to the foreign policy and security of the United States....women are at the center of our diplomacy and development efforts—not simply as beneficiaries, but also as agents of peace, reconciliation, development, growth, and stability" (DoS, 2010, p. 23). As "women are increasingly playing critical roles as agents of change in their societies," the US would, "harness efforts and support their roles by focusing programs to engage with women and expand their opportunities for entrepreneurship, access to technology, and leadership" (DoS, 2010, p. 58). Also, as Pas points out under the heading of "security feminism," the fetishizing of oppressed women is used as an opportune asset to ideologically advance the cause of imperialist intervention: "the war becomes about her. In this process the host country is also feminized and the American heterosexual pursuit becomes about gallantly 'saving' the Muslim woman from Islam. While America strives to save the Muslim woman from her alleged theological oppression she is effectively put on the front lines" (Pas, 2013, p. 56).

The CIA has also instrumentalized gender issues as part of a covert campaign to bolster international support for US wars. In 2010, after the Dutch government fell in part because of the issue of its participation in the war in Afghanistan, the CIA began to worry about a possible electoral backlash in the upcoming elections in France and Germany, both of which suffered mounting casualties among their forces in Afghanistan. According to a confidential CIA memorandum made public by WikiLeaks,

> "Some NATO states, notably France and Germany, have counted on public apathy about Afghanistan to increase their contributions to the mission, but indifference might turn into active hostility if spring and summer fighting results in an upsurge in military or Afghan civilian casualties and if a Dutch-style debate spills over into other states contributing troops". (CIA, 2010, p. 1)

A CIA "expert on strategic communication" along with public opinion analysts at the State Department's Bureau of Intelligence and Research (INR) came together to "consider information approaches that might better link the Afghan mission to the priorities of French, German, and other Western European publics" (CIA, 2010, p. 1). This was critical to the US since Germany and France respectively commanded the third and fourth largest troop contingents in Afghanistan, and any withdrawal would have been a significant blow not just to military operations but especially to the public image of the US-led occupation effort, leading to a crumbling in the credibility of the US-led NATO alliance and its "International Security Assistance Force" in Afghanistan. The CIA was already aware that, though not a top election issue, the majority of public opinion in Germany and France was against participation in the Afghan war (CIA, 2010, p. 1). The CIA's strategic information exercise in Europe was based on the following logic,

> "Western European publics might be better prepared to tolerate a spring and summer of greater military and civilian casualties if they perceive clear connections between outcomes in Afghanistan and their own priorities. A consistent and iterative strategic communication program across NATO troop contributors that taps into the key concerns of specific Western European audiences could provide a buffer if today's apathy becomes tomorrow's opposition to ISAF, giving politicians greater scope to support deployments to Afghanistan". (CIA, 2010, p. 2)

The question of *girls* in Afghanistan was thus brought to the fore: "The prospect of the Taliban rolling back hard-won progress on girls' education could provoke French indignation, become a rallying point for France's largely secular public, and give voters a reason to support a good and necessary cause despite casualties" (CIA, 2010, p. 2). The CIA proposed that,

> "Afghan women could serve as ideal messengers in humanizing the ISAF role in combating the Taliban because of women's ability to speak personally and credibly about their experiences under the Taliban, their aspirations for the future, and their fears of a Taliban victory. Outreach initiatives that create media opportunities for Afghan women to share their stories with French, German, and other European women could help to overcome pervasive skepticism among women in Western Europe toward the ISAF mission". (CIA, 2010, p. 4)

The CIA thus advanced the idea that, "media events that feature testimonials by Afghan women would probably be most effective if broadcast on programs that have large and disproportionately female audiences" (CIA, 2010, p. 4).

While there is no chain of leaked documents to show that this CIA-organized strategy session led to the formulation and then implementation of a specific propaganda effort that followed these guidelines, we do know that Western media, as well as the messages widely and prominently circulated by Western human rights NGOs such as Amnesty International and Human Rights Watch, have over the years tended to heavily capitalize on the image of Afghan women and girls allegedly suffering from "Taliban oppression" as a major impulse toward supporting at least some US aims in Afghanistan. Even the otherwise anti-war US activist organization, Code Pink, sent a delegation to Afghanistan that spoke out about what could happen to Afghan women and girls if the US-led NATO occupation should come to an abrupt end: "We would leave with the same parameters of an exit strategy but we might perhaps be more flexible about a timeline," said Medea Benjamin to the *Christian Science Monitor*, adding: "That's where we have opened ourselves, being here, to some other possibilities. We have been feeling a sense of fear of the people of the return of the Taliban. So many people are saying that, 'If the US troops left the country, would collapse. We'd go into civil war.' A palpable sense of fear that is making us start to reconsider that" (Mojumdar, 2009/10/6; for more, see Code Pink, 2009/10/7a, 2009/10/7b, and Horton, 2009).

The goal of instrumentalizing Afghan women for pro-war public relations reappeared in another of the documents released to WikiLeaks, published by the Media Operations Centre of the Press and Media Service of NATO headquarters in Brussels. The document titled, "NATO in Afghanistan: Master Narrative as at 6 October 2008," laid out a series of propaganda talking points oriented toward the domestic mass media in troop contributing nations, which NATO spokespersons were to follow. NATO's "master narrative" concerning Afghan women was to tell the public that, "Presidential, Parliamentary and Provincial elections have taken place and women are now sitting in the Afghan Parliament. 28% of the MPs of the Lower House are female. Legitimate and representative government is now in place" (NATO, 2008). What is standard about these approaches is their superficiality, stressing numbers over qualitative realities, or in some cases inventing numbers outright, hence the recent admission that a large number of "ghost schools" exist in Afghanistan, that were either never constructed (but were paid for), or that were but have no teachers of pupils.

As with gender, the rights of lesbian, gay, bisexual, and transgender persons, has become another vehicle for the US to sell itself politically, or to create another wedge device for intervention and for practicing divide and rule. Thus in 2011, the State Department launched, "the Global Equality Fund to protect and advance the human rights of LGBT persons by supporting civil society organizations to protect human rights defenders, challenge discriminatory legislation, undertake advocacy campaigns, and document human rights violations that target the LGBT community". Consequently, "over $7.5 million was allocated to civil rights organizations in over 50 countries; more than 150 human rights defenders have been assisted" (DoS, 2014b, p. 24). There is very little in the realm of "human rights," LGBT and women's activism, NGOs and "civil society" that is not touched by the US in nations that it is targeting—as the State Department itself proclaims, "advancing human rights and democracy is a key priority that reflects American values and promotes our security" (DoS, 2010, p. 42). The concept of "human security" has also been effectively reworked as part of a militarized, absolute security agenda (see McLoughlin & Forte, 2013).

In its search for more "force multipliers," the State Department, particularly under the Obama administration, has established a series of programs to attract and enlist US and foreign students, corporate executives, and new media users. A program titled "100,000 Strong in the Americas"[3] was launched by Obama in order to increase the number of US students studying throughout the Americas to 100,000, and likewise to increase the number of students from the Americas studying in the US to 100,000, by 2020. There is no explanation as to why 100,000 is the magic number—unless it is in fact founded on numerological mysticism. To fund the program, the State Department was joined by Partners of the Americas (see below) and NAFSA: Association of International Educators (NAFSA, 2013). US universities, without any known exception, are participants. The "Innovation Fund" that supports the program is hailed as a "public-private partnership," in line with the growing corporatization, privatization, and outsourcing that now dominates ostensibly public institutions in North America. Obama's program promises a propaganda boost to private corporations: "Highlight your corporate efforts to create jobs and international education for young people through media placement and recognition".[4] This connection between government, private business, and universities, brings to the foreground the widening idea of force multiplication employed by the US.

As just mentioned, Partners of the Americas is part of the above program. Partners of the Americas was first formed as part of the Alliance for Progress in 1964,[5] during an earlier phase of US-led hemispheric counterinsurgency, marked by a developmentalist and militarized drive against "communism" as the US sought shore up its dominance by countering the example of revolutionary Cuba. Partners of the Americas involves itself in elections in Latin America, and in mobilizing people to impact on the selection of candidates for positions in justice systems such as Bolivia's, until Partners' partner, USAID, was expelled from the country. Partners boasts of funding hundreds of unnamed "civil society organizations" in 24 countries in the Americas.[6]

Among similar initiatives launched by the Obama administration, again by turning over part of US foreign policy to gigantic corporate entities, is the so-called "Alliance for Affordable Internet" (A4AI), which includes Google and the Omidyar Network. The program has clear political, strategic, and neoliberal aims. One of its top aims is to "reduce regulatory barriers and encourage policies to offer affordable access to both mobile and fixed-lined internet, particularly among women in developing countries".[7] A4AI is active in an unspecified number of countries in Africa, Asia and Latin America, the only ones mentioned thus far being Ghana, Nigeria, Mozambique, and the Dominican Republic. Understanding that limitations to Internet access persist, the US government is directly involved in expanding the potential market of those listening to its messages, watching its corporate advertisements, and consuming US exports, both material and ideological.

A program that specifically targets Africa and what could be its future leaders, is the Young African Leaders Initiative (YALI) which has launched the "Mandela Washington Fellowship" (MWF) program. The State Department partnered with RocketHub on a crowdfunding campaign to support projects created by graduates of the MWF. The first class of 500 Mandela Washington Fellows arrived in June 2014, "to study business and entrepreneurship, civic leadership, and public management at U.S. campuses, followed by a Presidential Summit in Washington".[8] The target audiences, as expected are women, youths, and "civil society". So far 22 MWF projects have been funded. In undertaking this initiative, the US is reinforcing classic patterns of cultural imperialism.

It should become clearer how the employment of "force multipliers" can be seen as threat to target states, when it comes to Western reactions to penetration of their own states. For example, when speaking of China's force multipliers—or "agents of influence"— Western agencies such as the UK's Ministry of Defence (MoD) speak in no uncertain terms of their presence as a threat, constructed in terms of espionage, specifically naming "the mass of ordinary students, businessmen and locally employed staff" who work on behalf of China's state intelligence gathering apparatus (MoD, 2001, p. 21F-2; see also WikiLeaks, 2009). What may be presented as innocuous ties of friendship, partnership, and aid when it comes to Western use of force multipliers, is instead dramatically inverted when speaking of Chinese influence, using a markedly more sinister tone:

> "The process of being cultivated as a 'friend of China' (ie. an 'agent') is subtle and long-term. The Chinese are adept at exploiting a visitor's interest in, and appreciation of, Chinese history and culture. They are expert flatterers and are well aware of the 'softening' effect of food and alcohol. Under cover of consultation or lecturing, a visitor may be given favours, advantageous economic conditions or commercial opportunities. In return they will be expected to give information or access to material. Or, at the very least, to speak out on China's behalf (becoming an 'agent of influence')". (MoD, 2001, p. 21F-2)

Connected Capitalism and Connected Militarism

> "The hidden hand of the market will never work without a hidden fist—McDonald's cannot flourish without McDonnell Douglas, the builder of the F-15. And the hidden fist that keeps the world safe for Silicon Valley's technologies is called the United States Army, Air Force, Navy and Marine Corps". (Friedman, 1999/3/28)

With keenly supportive interest from the State Department and Pentagon, Neville Isdell, former chairman and CEO of the Coca-Cola Co., has articulated what he calls "connected capitalism," mixing profit with at best nominal social responsibility, out of an acknowledgment of growing global revulsion toward the dominance of capitalists (see Trubey, 2010/4/27). Isdell held a conference in South Africa, which we should note was organized by *CNN* and *Fortune* magazine, where he was joined by Federal Reserve Bank of Atlanta president and CEO Dennis Lockhart, GE Technology Infrastructure CEO John Rice, and executives from companies such as Coke, United Parcel Service Inc., SunTrust Banks Inc., and agencies such as USAID and CARE. "People are now questioning the capitalist model that we have," Isdell remarked, but then added that capitalism, "is the best way to take people out of poverty and to grow the world economy". He urged on his fellow corporate leaders:

> "A corporation can't lose sight of turning a profit, but it must also use the weight of its brand and the power of its people, as well as its intellectual and actual capital, to help be a change agent in hard-to-solve global issues. For instance, with Coke, water is the company's No. 1 social priority, and it is the world's largest beverage maker's most-used commodity". (Quoted in Trubey, 2010/4/27)

Of course Coca-Cola is interested in water, without a doubt—but it is interested in it as a commodity, not as a basic and inalienable right. Isdell worries that, "capitalism is in danger of being torn asunder by forces outraged by abuses on Wall Street, bailouts of banks and automakers," and his notion of "connected capitalism," while finally admitting current social irresponsibility by those in his class of world rulers, does little to change that. Indeed, there is an excess of irony to Isdell's remarks, given Coca-Cola's deplorable history of human rights violations in its operations in Colombia (see Foster, 2010).

In what would could easily be described as a program of cultural imperialism, the US State Department, in partnership with the Coca-Cola Company and Indiana University, sponsors roughly 100 students annually from the Middle East and North Africa, to attend a month-long summer entrepreneurship program at Indiana University's Kelley School of Business, with students undertaking an "immersion scholarship program" (Opportunity Desk, 2015/2/18; see also Indiana University, 2013, 2014; see Figure I.2). Thus the website for the US Embassy in Amman, Jordan, features the "Coca-Cola Scholarship Program" and points out the targets of the scholarship: "preference will be given to candidates who have limited or no experience of travel to the United States," which could be understood to mean those who may not have been as Americanized as others and thus stand out as a valuable asset for conversion (US Embassy-Amman [USEA], 2015). Nada Berrada, a Moroccan business student, said she wanted to become "a Coca-Cola Ambassador" because "Coca-Cola is not only about happiness, but it's also about inspiration" (Priselac, 2013/7/19). Coca-Cola chairman and CEO Muhtar Kent told the visiting students, "this is your start-up phase—your chance to be a great agent for positive change," adding, "you can and will make a real difference, so stay in touch with each other...and with Coca-Cola"—and in his parting "words of wisdom," as a company writer put it, he advised students to, "develop an abiding respect for cash. Keep some on you at all times. Touch it and feel it and know it's real. Never let money become an abstraction" (Priselac, 2013/7/19). Interestingly, as far as "positive agents for change" can go, the program in 2012, on how to "Make Tomorrow Better," did not include any Libyan students. Yet Libyan students had been praised only a year earlier by corporate and public media in North America, during the US-led destruction of the nation's state structures that opened the way to ongoing civil war. Contrary to the White House's "failed states" admission mentioned earlier, even with the use of local "force mul-tipliers" the extreme collapse of a nation-state can and has hap-pened, and will do so again.

Figure I.2: The US State Department's Connected Coca-Cola Capital-ists from the Middle East and North Africa

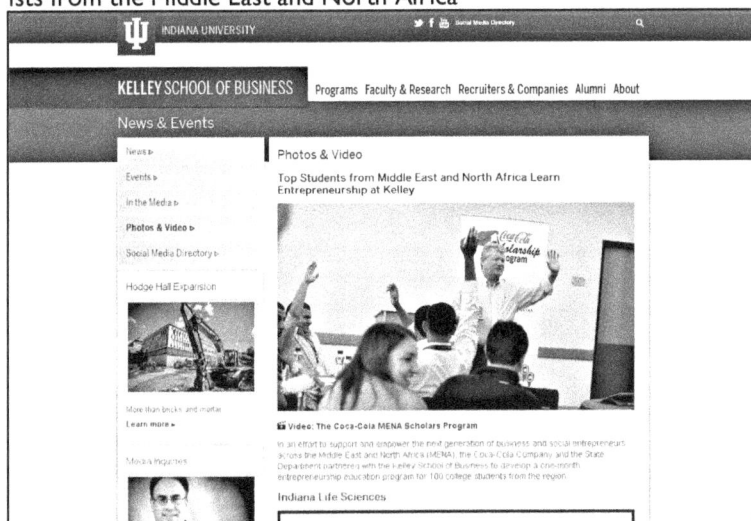

This is a still from the website of the Kelley School of Business at Indiana Univer-sity, showing a session held with students from the Middle East and North Africa as part of the US State Department's program in partnership with Coca-Cola. As if Indiana University's mission has been reduced to uncritically producing corpo-rate propaganda, the university's "news room" website speaks of Coca-Cola "re-freshing consumers" who "enjoy" its drinks, as "the world's most valuable brand," claiming that the company's initiatives "support active, healthy living". Then, the university asks readers to follow Coca-Cola in Twitter (Indiana University, 2013).

The Coca-Cola CEO's "connected capitalism" also attracted the attention of key speakers within the US military, in a growing display of what anthropologist Bruce Kapferer (2005) described as the corporate-oligarchic state at the base of contemporary imperialism. Admiral James Stavridis was the Supreme Allied Commander Europe (SACEUR) and Commander of the US European Command (EUCOM); Evelyn N. Farkas was his Senior Advisor for "Public-Private Partnership". The two reminded their readers that the most recent National Security Strategy at the time, "calls on the executive branch to work with the private sector, repeatedly referring to public-private partnerships" (Stavridis & Farkas, 2012, p. 7). It was under that banner of "public-private partnerships"—for which they single out Coca-Cola and Isdell's "connected capitalism—that they explained collaboration as a "force multiplier". It is a force multiplier, they maintain, because it permits the state to share "the resource burden". From "whole-of-government" they move to "whole-of-society": binding the state, corporations, universities, and NGOs, which "can save the government money" (Stavridis & Farkas, 2012, pp. 8-9). Rather than just an idea, they note the rise of what we can call "connected militarism" as a complement to "connected capitalism":

> "the U.S. Southern Command, U.S. European Command, U.S. Northern Command, U.S. Pacific Command, U.S. Special Operations Command, and U.S. Africa Command all have full-time personnel dedicated to garnering efficiencies and fostering effectiveness for DOD by collaborating with the private sector—businesses, academic institutions, and non-profits". (Stavridis & Farkas, 2012, p. 9)

Members of an organization calling itself Business Executives for National Security (BENS) have worked with the US Southern Command in countering drug cartels and have also worked with NATO forces in Afghanistan and in the Baltic states (Stavridis & Farkas, 2012, p. 10). The Enduring Security Framework (ESF), also exists as a public-private collaboration between the Pentagon, the Department of Homeland Security, and the Director of National Intelligence, and "representative information technology and defense industrial firms" (Stavridis & Farkas, 2012, p. 16).

What is not raised for discussion in the self-interested, corporate sales piece by Stavridis and Farkas, is the nature of direct benefits for private corporations, beyond being able to tell the public how good they feel about being partners. Private corporations have been "partnering" with the Pentagon for decades. Increased corporatization of governance has accelerated the process. As journalist Ken Silverstein observed, "with little public knowledge or debate, the government has been dispatching private companies—most of them with tight links to the Pentagon and staffed by retired armed forces personnel—to provide military and police training to America's foreign allies" (quoted in Johnson, 2004, p. 85). While Stavridis and Farkas do point out that, "for corporate or non-profit entities, collaboration with the government may offer access to information and sometimes intelligence, as well as legitimacy" (2012, p. 13), they refuse to comment on what that means. However, others have commented: "One reason privatization appeals to the Pentagon is that whatever these companies do becomes 'proprietary information'. The Pentagon does not even have to classify it; and as private property, information on the activities of such companies is exempt from the Freedom of Information Act" (Johnson, 2004, p. 85). Likewise, private corporations are able to secure such information and own it, taking away from the public what originally belonged to the public, at least in principle.

Security for US Capitalists: The State Department and its Global Partners

Very much in line in with the idea of "connected capitalism," the US State Department created the office of advisor for global partnerships, a Senate-confirmed position (Stavridis & Farkas, 2012, p. 17; see also DoS, 2015, 2015/3/12). The Secretary of State's Office of Global Partnerships, instituted in 2009, is officially described as, "the entry point for collaboration between the U.S. Department of State, the public and private sectors, and civil society" (DoS, 2015). Its programs cover the Americas, scholarships for the Middle East, the training of "young African leaders," and spreading the US-dominated Internet to "poor communities" (DoS, 2015/3/12). The State Department says its Global Partnership Initiative has spent $650 Million in public and private resources on "diplomacy and development," reaching 1,100 "partners" from 2009 through 2012, and cultivating 6,500 private sector contacts.[9] In its official propaganda, GPI boasts that its method involves starting with one country, 10 cities, 100 investors, 1,000 partnerships—which as much as these are figures too neat to be anything but invented for glossy brochures and happy-looking websites, at least this 1-10-100-1000 progression graphically shows how deeply entrenched the "force multiplier" idea has become in official circles, military and civilian.[10]

The "partners" listed for the State Department's GPI include philanthropic foundations, universities, airlines, weapons manufacturers, software companies, Google, Yahoo, soft drink manufacturers, retail giants, entertainment, banks, and oil companies (DoS, 2014b, pp. 30-31), the core corporate sectors of the contemporary US economy. Among the US universities working under GPI are, as listed in 2014: University of Kansas, University of Massachusetts Boston, University of Washington, Northwestern University, and the University of California system (DoS, 2014b, p. 31).

Since the creation of the Overseas Security Advisory Council (OSAC) in 1985 under the Reagan administration, the State Department has been involved in "security cooperation" with US "private sector interests worldwide". Since 1985, universities, churches, and NGOs have been added to the State Department's list of security partners. This arrangement is directly the result of demands placed on the state by US corporations: "The increase in terrorism over the last 30 years and the continuing threat against U.S. interests overseas has forced many American companies to seek advice and assistance from the U.S. Government, particularly the State Department".[11] This has been the case since OSAC's conception: "In 1985, a handful of chief executive officers from prominent American companies met with then Secretary of State George P. Shultz to promote cooperation between the American private sector worldwide and the U.S. Government on security issues".[12] More than 3,500 US corporations, educational institutions, "faith-based institutions," and NGOs are OSAC "constituents".[13] Current members include Northwestern University, the University of California system, McGraw Hill, and a range of the most familiar names in US entertainment, software, weapons manufacturing, financial industries, from Monsanto to Raytheon, Boeing, Microsoft, Walt Disney, Wal-Mart, Target, VISA, joined also by the Pentagon, FBI, and the Department of Homeland Security.[14]

Similarly, USAID, which established its "Global Development Alliance" in 2001 (see USAID, 2007), has worked with various corporations such as Coca-Cola (on water projects in 13 countries) and with Wal-Mart in Brazil. By 2005, USAID claimed to have established more than 400 such alliances, using $1.4 billion of its own funds with a further $4.6 billion from its partners (Stavridis & Farkas, 2012, p. 11).

The US Military's Connected Capitalists: Mass Media's "Military Analysts"

Several years ago, a series of exposés demonstrated US corporate mass media's use of "military analysts" and "experts" who are retired senior military officers, serving in the private sector and with continued access to the Pentagon with the proviso that they repeat the Pentagon's talking points on war (Barstow, 2008/4/20, 2009/11/28, 2011/12/24). This program, which bridged the Department of Defense, mass media, and corporations with military contracts, was described by Barstow (2008/4/20):

> "The effort... has sought to exploit ideological and military allegiances, and also a powerful financial dynamic: Most of the analysts have ties to military contractors vested in the very war policies they are asked to assess on air....Records and interviews show how the Bush administration has used its control over access and information in an effort to transform the analysts into a kind of media Trojan horse—an instrument intended to shape terrorism coverage from inside the major TV and radio networks".

A military retiree turned analyst-lobbyist military would gain access to current inside information in the Pentagon, which would be useful for the private weapons contractors they served, and in return they would sell the administration's talking points to the public. This is "connected" in the same way a totalitarian system is connected. Information presented to the public was often fabricated, exaggerated or otherwise distorted, to boost public support for the war in Iraq. "A few" of these so-called analysts "expressed regret for participating in what they regarded as an effort to dupe the American public with propaganda dressed as independent military analysis" (Barstow, 2008/4/20). Thousands of records that were made public revealed "a symbiotic relationship where the usual dividing lines between government and journalism have been obliterated"—because the mass media had themselves been enlisted as "force multipliers": "Internal Pentagon documents repeatedly refer to the military analysts as 'message force multipliers' or 'surrogates' who could be counted on to deliver administration 'themes and messages' to millions of Americans 'in the form of their own opinions'" (Barstow, 2008/4/20).

NGOs as US Force Multipliers

The US military has been very interested in utilizing nongovernmental organizations. In 2005 then President George W. Bush signed National Security Presidential Directive 44 (NSPD-44), instructing US forces to "coordinate USG [US government] stability operations with foreign governments, international and regional organizations, nongovernmental organizations, and private sector entities" (US Army, 2008b, pp. 1-13-1-14). Referring to NGOs in particular, the US Army noted with interest, "their extensive involvement, local contacts, and experience," which make "NGOs valuable sources of information about local and regional governments and civilian attitudes toward an operation" (US Army, 2008b, p. A-10). The same document then added, however: "military forces do not describe NGHAs [non-governmental humanitarian aid groups] as 'force multipliers' or 'partners' of the military, or in any fashion that could compromise their independence or their goal to be perceived by the population as independent" (US Army, 2008b, p. E-2). The reason for this little-noticed political move was to minimize the apparent damage done by US Secretary of State Colin Powell, when he declared to leaders of NGOs at a foreign policy conference in 2001, "I am serious about making sure we have the best relationship with the NGOs who are such a force multiplier for us, such an important part of our combat team" (Powell, 2001). Regardless of the minimal corrective offered by the US Army, seven years after Powell spoke, the fact remains that in its actions the US military has consistently worked in tandem with NGOs, particularly in Iraq and Afghanistan. Indeed, some in the military even publicly boast of such partnerships:

> "*NGOs are increasingly working in tandem with the military* on mutually agreed projects and objectives across the globe. Arzu, a Chicago-based NGO that is a significant foreign employer of Afghan women, and the non-profit Spirit of America have teamed up to sell 'peace cords,' bracelets that *symbolically and literally support U.S. and NATO operations in Afghanistan.* Employment in Afghanistan generated by the sales of the cords creates an environment conducive to the success of those operations". (Stavridis & Farkas, 2012, p. 10, emphases added)

"Non-state actors offer significant opportunities to expand the reach and effectiveness of U.S. foreign policy," the US State Department asserted in its First Quadrennial Diplomacy and Development Review. The State Department added:

> "The potential of civil society organizations around the world to advance common interests with us is unprecedented....Civil society, universities, and humanitarian organizations can often act in areas or in a manner that a government simply cannot: as neutrals or aid providers in conflict zones; as thought-leaders; and as intermediaries between states or between states and peoples. They are indispensable partners, force multipliers, and agents of positive change". (DoS, 2010, p. 14)

Force multipliers, partners, intermediaries, agents of change—all of these are contained in the State Department's language, as it perfectly echoes the terms in favour in the military. The State Department makes it plainly clear that it intends to use NGOs abroad as tools of US foreign policy, frequently using "civil society" as a rhetorically pretentious cover:

> "We will reach beyond governments to offer a place at the table to groups and citizens willing to shoulder a fair share of the burden. Our efforts to engage beyond the state begin with outreach to civil society—the activists, organizations, congregations, and journalists who work through peaceful means to make their countries better. While civil society is varied, many groups share common goals with the United States, and working with civil society can be an effective and efficient path to advance our foreign policy". (DoS, 2010, pp. 21-22)

In those straightforward terms, the US declares its intention of using its diplomatic stations to undermine the sovereignty of all other states, particularly those which it has targeted for "improvement". "Civil society groups"—largely undemocratic, unaccountable and elitist—will "shoulder a fair share of the burden" for the sake of US interests. In addition, this is an "efficient" path for the US, as it spreads costs to others, furthering the idea that such groups are instrumentalized as force multipliers, of the type we see defined in physics texts more than in social science.

Since the US makes some investment in the use of its force multipliers among the citizens of other nations, it is of course anxious about their having as much room to manoeuvre as possible. Thus the State Department declared, "we will oppose efforts to restrict the space for civil society and create opportunities for civil society to thrive within nations and to forge connections among them". Not just barring restrictions on the space for "civil society"—a term used by US officials as if they were referring to a subcontractor of their own government—but it also important to diminish the realm of a sovereign state by eroding its boundaries, thus: "we will promote open governments around the world that are accountable and participatory" (DoS, 2010, p. 22). The State Department speaks of "engaging beyond the state," which in very plain terms is understood to mean bypassing other states: "engagement must go far beyond government-to-government interactions. Non-state actors, ranging from non-governmental organizations to business, religious groups to community organizations, are playing an ever greater role, both locally and globally.

And in this information age, public opinion takes on added importance" (DoS, 2010, p. 59). US diplomats are to function as the "circuit riders" mentioned previously: "it is increasingly important for American diplomats to meet not only with their foreign ministry counterparts, but also with tribal elders or local authorities. Our diplomats must build partnerships and networks, implement programs, and engage with citizens, groups, and organizations" (DoS, 2010, p. 59). In 2011, US Secretary of State Hillary Clinton opened what she called a "strategic dialogue with civil society," and the choice of the term "strategic" clearly cannot be taken lightly. In addition she created the position of Senior Advisor for Civil Society and Emerging Democracies (DoS, 2010, p. 59), intending to further institutionalize this deeper form of US intervention, where something akin to occupation and indirect role becomes the standard operating procedure.

If the State Department thinks it can use NGOs as its tools, it is due in part to the fact that some NGOs have been more than willing to serve as such. In some noteworthy cases, such as the first war against Iraq, "NGOs supplied the necessary legitimacy for the U.S. 'police interventions,' a legitimacy expressed in terms of human rights and respect for law" (Ash, 2003, p. 239). NGOs, funded by US philanthropic foundations, help to maintain the illusion of an international social contract, as if speaking for a nonexistent world electorate. As Ash explained, with the US government professing a "commitment to human rights, democracy, and rule of law," this "promised hope and gave the system respectability, even among its critics," with the result that revelations of war crimes, atrocities, and negation of human rights are treated as "flaws," or "mistakes," and "far from undermining the system, they generated calls for improving it" (Ash, 2003, p. 239).

In *Good Intentions* (Forte, 2014), space was devoted to the role of NGOs in supporting US imperial ventures, as part of successive US governments' "diplomacy, development, defence" programs. The US prefers to work through non-state actors because it grants US intervention cover, a veneer of popularity and legitimacy when uncovered, and it serves the basic capitalist aim of undermining the power of states not sufficiently "open" and "responsive" to US capital. Horace Campbell (2014) further explained how NGOs served as "force multipliers" for the US:

> "During the nineties military [j]ournals such as *Parameters* honed the discussion of the planning for the increased engagement of international NGO's and by the end of the 20th century the big international NGO's Care, Catholic Relief Services , Save The

Children, World Vision, and Medicins Sans Frontieres (MSF) were acting like major international corporations doing subcontracting work for the US military. At the time when the book *The Road to Hell: the Ravaging Effects of Foreign Aid and International Charity* was written by Michael Maren to expose the role of humanitarian agencies in Somalia, there was already enough information to expose the militarization of humanitarian work".

The US government has formally institutionalized its partnership with NGOs through the State Department's Office of Civilian-Military Cooperation (CMC).

The role of NGOs as "a Trojan Horse for world imperialism" was also demonstrated in the propaganda leading up to the planned US armed attacks against Syria in August-September (2012):

> "Among the most strident voices was that of Bernard Kouchner, the co-founder of Médecins Sans Frontières (Doctors Without Borders—MSF) and former foreign minister in the right-wing government of President Nicolas Sarkozy. He impatiently asked in late July, 'The famous American drones, where are they?' imploring the imperialist powers to take military action in the name of humanitarianism. The MSF, recipient of the 1999 Nobel Peace Prize, was the first to report the August 21 attack in Ghouta, Syria, which the US hoped to use as a direct pretext for a military assault. As the organization admitted, the MSF's decision to issue an international press release on the incident— which had not taken place in an MSF hospital, but in its 'silent partner' facilities in rebel-controlled areas—was highly political" (Hanover, 2013/12/30).

Indeed, MSF doctors were not even present in the area of the alleged government attack. A month after the fact, Hanover noted, the New York Times "belatedly mentioned that doctors are often 'notoriously wrong' when assessing chemical weapons injuries". Since then, Seymour Hersh has shown that the US President Barack Obama and his officials were "knowingly lying when they claimed that the Syrian government had carried out the sarin gas attack last August" (Hanover, 2013/12/30).

Academic Multipliers

> "I had no hint that, as a student of Asia, I would become as much a spear-carrier for empire as I had been in the navy" (Johnson, 2004, p. xxvi)

A great many books have been, and continue to be written about the collaboration and complicities between universities and their scholars and the US imperial state, from before the Cold War, during, and after. This topic largely exceeds the confines of this chapter, but as we saw in the case of OSAC above, it is important to remember that US universities and numerous academics, including very prominent ones, have played roles supportive of specific and broad US foreign policy goals. The scientization of discourse is itself one result of the Cold War repression of academic dissent in the US. The elites have enlisted "science" as a means of "containing the future by controlling the present politics of knowledge" (Nandy, 2005, p. 28)

In the period since September 11, 2001, there has been a major push in parts of Europe and North America to re-enlist academics as "force multipliers," ranging from various research streams funded by military and intelligence agencies, to outright incorporation into military units active in war zones. In what is a representative point of view considering the nature of attendees at the annual Halifax International Security Forum, a participant from the Hoover Institution in the US told his audience that, "ideas the best force-multipliers. They incite and intoxicate, making men fight to the death and fueling boundless cruelty" (Joffe, 2014). However, Joffe bitterly bemoaned the fact that "the West" has lost the "fervor" that drove "global conquest," and he condemned "postmodernism" as a "force diminisher" for being an ideology that abjures racism, imperialism, oppression—as if these are virtuous stances that need further reinforcement. Joffe then denounced intellectuals as a "force inhibitor: "Once the spearhead of nationalism, the West's intelligentsia is now its fiercest critic. The West's warrior culture is disappearing outside the US, Israel, Britain, and France" (Joffe, 2014). The elite is clearly getting desperate when such fullthroated and crude diatribes, that represent the worst, most reactionary orthodoxy, are offered proudly to the public as important contributions.

The Desire to Annex Cuba from the Inside Out

In the context of the recent resumption of diplomatic relations between Cuba and the US, it is important to note and understand in light of the above sections that the term "engagement" reappears in the US narrative on Cuba: "I believe that we can do more to support the Cuban people and promote our values through engagement" (Obama, 2014b). Announcing the new phase of Cuba-US relations, Obama stated, "I am convinced that through a policy of engagement, we can more effectively stand up for our values". Obama insists that, "the United States has supported democracy and human rights in Cuba through these five decades," as he attempts to sell his policy as a continuation of that theme, in order to allay the fears of domestic expatriates and more reactionary elements of Cuban-American opinion. Obama's policy is clearly in line with everything he has said in the passages quoted throughout this chapter: he intends to rely on force multipliers. His call for lifting travel restrictions on US citizens, is thus justified as follows: "Cuban Americans have been reunited with their families, and are the best possible ambassadors for our values". Repeatedly throughout his announcement, Obama speaks of "engagement," "openness," US citizens traveling to Cuba and serving as "ambassadors" who take part in "people-to-people engagement". Obama also committed the US to supporting "humanitarian projects," the growth of a Cuban private sector, and to open the floodgates to US telecommunications access to Cuba. In other words, if we have learned anything, then we would understand that there is nothing at all innocent about Obama's remarks. This does not mean that Cuba will not or cannot resist; it means it must continue to do so, only with even greater vigilance.

In the years and months leading up to the December 17, 2014, announcement of renewed diplomatic ties, a series of reports revealed several programs of covert US intervention in Cuba, which Obama would hope to institutionalize as "normal bilateral relations". For example, in 2009 Alan Gross, a USAID contractor, was imprisoned in Cuba for crimes against the state: "Gross was sent to Cuba to secretly distribute Internet equipment to Jewish community groups, part of a congressionally mandated program to encourage Cuban democracy" (DeYoung, 2014/12/17). More recently, in a series of detailed revelations published by the Associated Press, USAID, "infiltrated Cuba's hip-hop scene, recruiting unwitting rappers to spark a youth movement against the government", having developed a four-year program that compromised critics of the government. We also learned that the hip-hop operation ran simultaneously with two other USAID programs: "the launch of a secret 'Cuban Twitter' [ZunZuneo] and a program that sent Latin American youth to provoke dissent—and also involved elaborate subterfuge, including a front organization and an exotic financial scheme to mask American involvement". At the centre of the plot was Creative Associates International, "a company with a multimillion-dollar contract from USAID," whose goal was stated as follows: "commandeer the island's hip-hop scene 'to help Cuban youth break the information blockade' and build 'youth networks for social change'" (Butler et al., 2014/12/11). Soon after the reports were published, USAID director Raj Shah resigned (Kumar, 2014/12/17). The Cuban American "youth group," Roots of Hope, which was involved with the covert USAID program to create ZunZuneo, is currently partnering with Google as the latter seeks to essentially build Cuba's Internet. A US academic, Ted Henken, "a Baruch College professor who has studied Cuba's Internet issues," told a newspaper that, "it is less likely that Web connection and services coming from the United States, such as Google's, will be seen as a Trojan horse now that the Obama administration has explicitly rejected a regime change policy and moved toward engagement" (quoted in Torres, 2015/7/3). While Henken may understand certain Internet issues, he botched the analysis of what the US government means by "engagement," given what we have learned in previous sections here, from US government documents themselves.

What has been covert—and denied until it was exposed—can become more or less overt now, if one takes Obama's announced intentions at face value, and if one believes the Cuban authorities and the revolutionary system that has benefited the majority will simply be passive unlike ever before. Obama is first of all interested in spearheading the development of the Cuban private sector: "Our travel and remittance policies are helping Cubans by providing alternative sources of information and opportunities for self-employment and private property ownership, and by strengthening independent civil society". Several announced policy changes are intended to make it easier for US citizens "to provide business training for private Cuban businesses and small farmers and provide other support for the growth of Cuba's nascent private sector". Secondly, the US hopes to expand "Internet penetration" in Cuba; allowing for the commercial export of US telecommunications goods and services, "will contribute to the ability of the Cuban people to communicate with people in the United States". Thirdly, in order to provide political protection for these US intrusions, "a critical focus of our increased engagement will include continued strong support by the United States for improved human rights conditions and democratic reforms in Cuba," and in very bold language the White House adds: "Our efforts are aimed at promoting the independence of the Cuban people so they do not need to rely on the Cuban state". The intention to diminish the power of the Cuban state, to sideline it, and to thus lower the sovereign protection of Cuba, is stated plainly in commonplace neoliberal terms. The US Congress is already funding "democracy programming" in Cuba—ironic, given Cuba's already extensive system of participatory democracy and mass mobilization (White House, 2014).

In language that reminds one of the meaning of "circuit rider," Obama stated the following in his July 1, 2015, announcement of the upcoming opening of embassies:

> "With this change, we will be able to substantially increase our contacts with the Cuban people. We'll have more personnel at our embassy. And our diplomats will have the ability to engage more broadly across the island. That will include the Cuban government, civil society, and ordinary Cubans who are reaching for a better life." (White House, 2015b)

However, since US diplomats will be required to inform the Cuban authorities of their travel in the island, and since they will be watched regardless, it's not certain that the US will be doing anything other than placing a few Cuban individuals on the front-line of US policy. The "normalization" of relations is nowhere explained by Cuban authorities as a desire to surrender or to change the socio-economic system to become more like the US. Instead, it is cast as a victory for Cuba, since it was obtained without having given the US any of its long-sought concessions and since it involved a more than tacit admission by the US that decades of seeking regime change amounted to a complete failure.

The Physics of Blowback and Overstretch

Another sort of physics emerged, right from within the same establishment of military and political institutions that produced "force multipliers". If this other physics has attained the prominence that it has, such that it now has a foothold in academia and is a firm part of popular discourse in the US primarily, it is due at least in part to the social prominence and respectability of the false physics that it counters. By this other physics I mean the concepts of "blowback" and "overstretch" which, like "force multipliers," are useful for descriptively pointing to certain "real-world" phenomena, but are impoverished half-attempts at theory. I return to the question of theory, and theorization, in the concluding paragraphs of this chapter.

Blowback: In Its Restricted and Extended Senses

Blowback is a *reaction to force*: a reaction to "hard power," and particularly a reaction to covert operations. The term originates from "a classified government document in the CIA's post-action report on the secret overthrow of the Iranian government in 1953" (Johnson, 2004, p. xii). As Chalmers Johnson explained further, "blowback" was invented by the CIA "to describe the likelihood that our covert operations in other people's countries would result in retaliations against Americans, civilian and military, at home and abroad" (Johnson, 2004, p. ix). As a former CIA analyst, Johnson would have been familiar with CIA terminology, and he did a great deal to popularize the term. From the CIA, it became the centrepiece of academic analysis with Johnson. In its "most rigorous definition," blowback does not mean "mere reactions to historical events but rather to clandestine operations carried out by the U.S. government that are aimed at overthrowing foreign regimes, or seeking the execution of people the United States wanted eliminated by 'friendly' foreign armies, or helping launch state terrorist operations against overseas target populations" (Johnson, 2004, p. xi). Thus a reaction against force multipliers is also implied by blowback. "As a concept," Johnson adds, "blowback is obviously most easily grasped in its straightforward manifestations. The unintended consequences of American policies and acts in country X lead to a bomb at an American embassy in country Y or a dead American in country Z" (2004, p. xi). In a broader sense, "blowback is another way of saying that a nation reaps what it sows" (Johnson, 2004, p. xi). Thus far the concept appears simple enough, blending very basic action-reaction with common moral approaches to human affairs, rooted in biblical proverbs.

The idea of blowback hinges on the motivation to retaliate. As Johnson puts it, "American policy is seeding resentments that are bound to breed attempts at revenge" (2004, p. 65). Without resentment there is no compulsion to seek revenge; without an effort made to exact revenge, there can be no blowback. "The most direct and obvious form of blowback" has tended to occur "when the victims fight back after a secret American bombing, or a U.S.-sponsored campaign of state terrorism, or a CIA-engineered overthrow of a foreign political leader" (Johnson, 2004, p. 9). Blowback involves the creation of force multipliers in reverse. The Defense Science Board (1997, p. 15) resists identifying US intervention as a cause for retaliation, but nonetheless stated the following highly suggestive conclusion based on the data it accumulated:

"Historical data show a strong correlation between US involvement in international situations and an increase in terrorist attacks against the United States. In addition, the military asymmetry that denies nation states the ability to engage in overt attacks against the United States drives the use of transnational actors".

Blowback is also understood in an "extended" sense by Johnson, one that departs from what he calls straightforward examples. Blowback in this broader sense "includes the decline of key American industries because of the export-led economic policies of our satellites, the militarism and arrogance of power that inevitably conflict with our democratic structure of government, and the distortions to our culture and basic values as we are increasingly required to try to justify our imperialism" (Johnson, 2004, pp. xi-xii). This can be a more productive approach to blowback, one that can link to a series of related theses describing the wider fallout of US interventionism, and not just the covert kind. In words that echo those of former President Dwight Eisenhower and Senator J. William Fulbright, Johnson laments the extravagant growth of a self-seeking military establishment nearly beyond civilian control, and an increasingly impoverished citizenry forced to pay for perpetual wars and bailouts (Johnson, 2004, pp. 218, 221, 222). Andrew Bacevich makes similar points, tying blowback into overstretch:

"as events have made plain, the United States is ill-prepared to wage a global war of no exits and no deadlines. The sole superpower lacks the resources—economic, political, and military—to support a large-scale, protracted conflict without, at the very least, inflicting severe economic and political damage on itself. American power has limits and is inadequate to the ambitions to which hubris and sanctimony have given rise". (Bacevich, 2008, p. 11)

One of Johnson's primary conclusions was that "more imperialist projects simply generate more blowback" (2004, p. 223)—simple, and even inevitable, he thus maintained: "efforts to maintain imperial hegemony inevitably generate multiple forms of blowback" (2004, p. 229). Inevitability is scaled down to "in all likelihood," when Johnson argued that world politics in the twenty-first century will be driven primarily by blowback from the second half of the twentieth century, "that is, from the unintended consequences of the Cold War and the crucial American decision to maintain a Cold War posture in a post-Cold War world" (2004, p.

229). In words that foresaw the current US and NATO conflict with Russia, Johnson offered some wise words:

> "The American empire has become skilled at developing self-fulfilling—and self-serving—prophecies in order to justify its policies. It expands the NATO alliance eastward in part in order to sell arms to the former Soviet bloc countries, whose armies are being integrated into the NATO command structure, with the certain knowledge that doing so will threaten Russia and elicit a hostile Russian reaction. This Russian reaction then becomes the excuse for the expansion". (Johnson, 2004, p. 92)

As previewed above, Johnson like Bacevich also carried over the implications of blowback into his arguments about what he calls overstretch (more about that in the next section). Since the US is reaching the limits in what it can afford in terms of its ongoing military deployment and interventions, it has begun to extract "ever growing amounts of 'host-nation support' from its clients, or even direct subsidies from its 'allies'. Japan, one of many allied nations that helped finance the massive American military effort in the Gulf War, paid up to the tune of $13 billion. (The U.S. government even claimed in the end to have made a profit on the venture.)" (Johnson, 2004, p. 221). Here we see a formulation that derives from the "science" that has been proffered by military and intelligence elites: because "overstretch" results from "blowback" (in the broad sense), the US needs to lean more heavily on "force multipliers".

If we take blowback in its restricted sense, it appears to be a useful concept—when actual blowback happens. It is a simple, arguably simplistic, concept that derives its credibility from Newtonian physics. Isaac Newton's "third law of motion," as most readers can recite already, is that "for every action, there is an equal and opposite reaction". But is there? Since the attacks of "9/11" are seen by writers following Johnson as "blowback"—then there should have a very long line of culprits if the concept really worked. Everyone from Chileans to Argentinians, Uruguayans, Bolivians, Colombians, Nicaraguans, Vietnamese, Cambodians, Filipinos, Japanese, Germans, Italians, Russians, Serbians, Libyans, Congolese, etc., etc., should have been plotting multiple attacks for decades. In fact, given the wide array of grievances and resentments, spread near and far, if there is one conclusion that can be safely derived is that, understood in its restricted sense, *blowback almost never happens*. When such blowback does happen, then of course it is a relatively easy thing to call it a "self-fulfilling proph-

ecy" and to appear convincing. We should be cautious about assuming blowback to be either simple, or simply inevitable (as Johnson tends to do), since it offers another falsely scientific,
mechanical formulation that does not stand even the most basic
empirical testing.

It is far more useful to broaden blowback, but to do so in a
manner that goes beyond Johnson's attempt. When blowback is
understood in cyclical, socio-economic and cultural terms, alternat-
ing between external and internal events that sometimes operate in
tandem, in a nation-state where blowback was already to be found
before any given external actions, where new domestic effects are
generated by the importation of the techniques of war and domination, with mounting political and economic costs, then we have the
foundation not for a productive concept, but a theory. For example, the security spectacle produced in US airports, the militarization of the police, the increased number of riots in African-
American inner cities, the bankruptcy of whole cities, the excessive
production of violent movies and games, and many other phenomena, can all be taken as constituting blowback.

Otherwise, what embarrasses the simple concepts of blowback
and force multipliers, is the apparent reality of some of the US'
own force multipliers becoming the vectors of blowback, such as
Saudi Arabia, Al Qaeda, and numerous "Islamist militias" in Libya.
Blowback, in Johnson's formulations, also rests on the common
assumption of "unintended consequences". It is increasingly difficult to find US security and international relations writers mention-
ing consequences without qualifying them as "unintended". Why
must they always be assumed to be unintended, even in cases
where a battery of officials have testified before Congress about the
likely outcomes of US military intervention in cases such as Libya?
While neither the idea of an omniscient, ubiquitous and all-
powerful US, nor a perfectly innocent and ignorant US, is convincing, we must allow some room for cases where chaos, disorder, and
fragmentation were the unspoken aims of US interventions abroad.
Chaos can be very profitable, especially for those who have turned
permanent war into a lucrative industry. Even understood in Johnson's broad sense, blowback can be profitable. Bacevich (2008, p.
173) argues that some wish to maintain US dependence on imported oil, imported goods, and foreign credit:

> "The centers of authority within Washington—above all, the
> White House and the upper echelons of the national security
> state—actually benefit from this dependency: It provides the
> source of status, power, and prerogatives. Imagine the impact

just on the Pentagon were this country actually to achieve anything approaching energy independence. U.S. Central Command would go out of business. Dozens of bases in and around the Middle East would close. The navy's Fifth Fleet would stand down. Weapons contracts worth tens of billions of dollars would risk being canceled".

Overstretch: The Unnatural Limits of Imperialism

Overstretch, like blowback, forms part of a publicly acceptable American way of speaking of the "dilemmas" of "global leadership," and has been the case at least since the 1966 publication of *The Arrogance of Power* by then US Senator J. William Fulbright. Fulbright, referring to the history of "great nations," noted that they have always set out upon missions to police the world, "and they have wrought havoc, bringing misery to their intended beneficiaries and destruction upon themselves" (Fulbright, 1966, p. 138). There is an implicit idea of blowback, in the broad sense. What is now called overstretch, Fulbright called overextension:

> "America is showing some signs of that fatal presumption, that overextension of power and mission, which has brought ruin to great nations in the past. The process has hardly begun, but the war which we are now fighting [in Vietnam] can only accelerate it. If the war goes on and expands, if that fatal process continues to accelerate until America becomes what she is not now and never has been, a seeker after unlimited power and empire, the leader of a global counter-revolution, then Vietnam will have had a mighty and tragic fallout indeed". (Fulbright, 1966, p. 138)

Overextension stemmed from "our excessive involvement in the affairs of other countries," excessive in part because US empire was now "living off our assets and denying our own people the proper enjoyment of their resources" (Fulbright, 1966, p. 21). The "excessive preoccupation with foreign relations over a long period of time" is a "drain on the power that gave rise to it, because it diverts a nation from the sources of its strength, which are in its domestic life" and Fulbright warned that, "a nation immersed in foreign affairs is expending its capital, human as well as material" and faced the prospect of ruin by expending its "energies in foreign adventures while allowing...domestic bases to deteriorate" (Fulbright, 1966, pp. 20-21). Repeatedly in his book Fulbright argued against a foreign policy that involved the US "in the affairs of most of the nations of the world while its own domestic needs are neglected or postponed" (Fulbright, 1966, p. 134), emphasizing his warning that "an ambitious foreign policy built on a deteriorating domestic base is possible only for a limited time" (Fulbright, 1966, p. 217).

The concept of imperial "overstretch" is now regularly associated with the work of the historian Paul Kennedy (1989), which describes a situation that arises when a state's engagements and presence beyond its borders result in mounting costs, while the ability to meet such costs begins to diminish. This concept of empire living beyond its means has also become popularized, largely as a form of safe critique: imperialism is to be rejected, when it becomes too costly to the imperialists. Overstretch seems to stand out, after the fact. However, there is clearly a concern among political and military elites in Washington that overstretch is a distinct possibility, either right now or in the near future, hence the growing proliferation in usage of the force multiplier idea, of spreading costs, and "sharing the burden" as Hillary Clinton put it. Johnson also links overstretch to blowback: "the duties of 'lone superpower' produced military overstretch; globalization led to economic overstretch; and both are contributing to an endemic crisis of blowback" (2004, p. 215). Some root the problem of overstretch in policies that began to take shape from the start of the 1960s, with an increased US emphasis on maintaining a "forward presence," to be "forward deployed," and thus ultimately able to project power anywhere on earth (Bacevich, 2010, pp. 22, 150, 162). The "American credo of global leadership" commits the US to what is in effect "a condition of permanent national security crisis," or constant "semiwar" (Bacevich, 2010, p. 27). This placement of US "interests" everywhere on earth, an effective territorialization that parallels older forms of colonialism, is best expressed in the words of then CIA Director Allen Dulles in 1963:

> "The whole world is the arena of our conflict....our vital interests are subject to attack in almost every quarter of the globe at any time...[it is essential] to maintain a constant watch in every part of the world, no matter what may at the moment be occupying the main attention of diplomats and military men". (Quoted in Bacevich, 2010, p. 40)

Bacevich also anchors the dynamics of overstretch in an extended critique of the perceived moral qualities of all Americans, in terms of their hubris, sanctimony, convinced of their own exceptional qualities and as destined to lead the world, their overconfidence and arrogance, and so forth. His analysis relies heavily on the works of a theological scholar, Reinhold Niebuhr. There is very little in the way of a materialist analysis, of discussion of capital and labour, trade and investment, production and consumption, or even inequality as Bacevich speaks of "Americans" as a largely undifferentiated and unitary entity, with shared moral qualities (or defects) and shared understandings. Rather than the rigorously imitative scientism of his former colleagues in the US military, Bacevich indulges in theology and morality. Empire exists in his work largely as a quality of the mind, and secondarily as expressed by military action. It is an argument that resonates with the Christian, anti-big government crowd of libertarian Republicans (Bacevich professes to be Republican)—and thus what is largely excluded is any discussion of the role of "big business," which is shielded from his critique.

This is not to say that there is little to learn from Bacevich's works, as much as they tend to repeat each other, and that one should ignore the ideological and cultural dimensions of imperialism, such as the civilizing mission, universalism, and assimilation. His critique can also be useful as a corrective to the mainstream propaganda—here he is quoting Niebuhr:

> "One of the most pathetic aspects of human history is that every civilization expresses itself most pretentiously, compounds its partial and universal values most convincingly, and claims immortality for its finite existence at the very moment when the decay which leads to death has already begun". (Bacevich, 2008, p. 12)

While his critique is more political-military than economic, Bacevich as a senior officer and insider offers much that is valuable concerning the state's practice of global interventionism and the reigning ideology.

Going back to Fulbright, one may also detect an assumption that US imperialism was meant to be profitable to all US citizens, like an investment that promised returns, only these returns are now failing to materialize. Moreover, the resources needed to sustain this global overextension are dwindling (Fulbright does not object to *extension* as such, only to an undefined *excess* of it). This is a view that differs sharply with understandings of imperialism found in the works of Marxists, or in anthropological writings such as Kapferer (2005). Thus Fulbright does not admit that imperialism need be profitable only to a select few (Kapferer's corporate oligarchy), that exploitation and inequality at home is fully consistent with imperial extension, and that the resources to sustain empire may be dwindling at home, but expanding abroad.

Imperialism as a Syndrome

Diverse theories of imperialism and their research methodologies tend to focus attention on a select aspect of the phenomenon (the economic, political, military, or moral as we just saw), rather than taking a holistic approach that would approach imperialism as a grouping of phenomena, processes, and practices. "Imperialism as a syndrome" might be what we call this holistic approach, one that understands and explains imperialism as ideology, narratives, values, beliefs, ways of living, social relationships, and ways of producing, consuming and exchanging.

While imperialism is safely spotted in a projection outwards from the state at the heart of an empire, imperialism also involves domesticated replication of patterns of foreign domination, an internalization of imperialism, down to everyday social relations and cultural meanings. Home is a laboratory for conceiving and devising practices of domination, just as occupied territories abroad furnish laboratories for the further refinement and reworking of the techniques of oppression which are then imported back into the home state of empire. In other words, the US did not invent its imperialism only after its first foreign intervention. Instead we see a continuum between the dominant vilification of "savagism" in the eighteenth and nineteenth centuries, and "terrorism" in the twenty-first century. There is also a continuum between the internal colonial wars against Indigenous Peoples, the formation of reservations and residential schools, and the counterinsurgency and school building programs undertaken by the US in Afghanistan, and the growth of the prison-industrial complex at home, the militarization of policing, and mass surveillance of citizens. The mistake commonly made in public discourse is to treat these as individual and separate phenomena, when we know and experience the fact that they do not occur as individual or separate: one is preceded by the other which enables, justifies, permits or requires the next phenomenon in the chain. War overseas, for example, is inevitably tied to monitoring and suppressing anti-war dissent at home—not, in other words, separate phenomena to be treated apart from each other.

Imperialism may be seen as a social relationship, not just an "international" one between states. As a social relationship it is shaped by and produces a belief system, self-conceptions, identities, and practices that are driven by goals of accumulation-via-domination—by principles of a life that is lived at the expense of the lives of others. Interpersonal encounters are militarized by the technologies of warfare and security. Bodies are pathologized (e.g. the black teenager in a "hoodie" assumed to be a threat). Classes are exploited as if those born into them had a natural duty to serve the wealthy and make the wealthy even richer. Imperialism is not just something that states do to other states—it might even be easier to extirpate if that is all it was.

As a way of life, imperialism thrives on the domination of the non-human world, laying waste to it if necessary, through excess consumption that boasts of massive accumulation, and the social respectability and political clout that is won by the demonstrated ability of the few to consume massively. Indeed, even the creation of categories such as "human" and "non-human" is the ideological infrastructure set up to prepare for an assault on our environment and all of its other inhabitants. Moreover, destructive exploitation of the environment under capitalism is mirrored socially, through the unequal differential allocation of the "benefits" of this exploitation. Historically, it is under capitalism that imperialism reaches the most extreme limits of this sort of thinking and practice, of consumption through destruction, of production through annihilation, and exchange via dispossession, with the concomitant scaling of rewards according to class and race. Furthermore, this sort of imperialism has itself reached an extreme under US dominance. This is merely offered as the barest and most rudimentary of synopses.

To his credit, of the writers consulted for this chapter, Bacevich has glimpsed the dual inner-outer dynamic of imperialism when he argues that "the impulses that have landed us in a war of no exits and no deadlines come from within" (Bacevich, 2008, p. 5). He explains his argument by adding that, "foreign policy has, for decades, provided an outward manifestation of American domestic ambitions, urges, and fears," with foreign policy increasingly becoming an expression of "domestic dysfunction—an attempt to manage or defer coming to terms with contradictions besetting the American way of life" (Bacevich, 2008, p. 5). He takes this approach even further when he theorizes that, "Washington is less a geographic expression than a set of interlocking institutions," and it extends from the executive, judicial and legislative branches to beyond, including law enforcement more generally, plus think tanks and interests groups, lawyers and lobbyists, big banks and other financial institutions, and universities (Bacevich, 2010, p. 15). Washington is a place in name only, otherwise it travels across places as it transcends, forming a system as only an imperial capital could. I would add that Washington is also not just "American," but includes at least the dominant classes of what I earlier called the

Global USA, that vast network of elites and their dependents, whose ambitions comprise acting, thinking, eating, drinking, dressing, and even talking like "Americans". My thesis is also that without this GUSA, the US imperialist project would collapse with dramatic rapidity, hence the importance of our discussion focusing on "force multipliers".

Conclusions, Questions, Orientations

If the present provides a hint of what it is to come, the nastiest, ugliest, and bloodiest wars to be fought this century will be between states opposed to continued US dominance, and the force multipliers of US dominance. We see the outline of sovereign self-defense programs that take diverse forms, from the banning of foreign funding for NGOs operating in a state's territory, controlling the mass media, arresting protesters, shutting down CIA-funded political parties, curtailing foreign student exchanges, denying visas to foreign academic researchers, terminating USAID operations, to expelling US ambassadors, and so forth. In extreme cases, this includes open warfare between governments and armed rebels backed by the US, or more indirectly (as the force multiplier principle mandates) backed by US allies. US intervention will provoke and heighten paranoia, stoking repression, and create the illusion of a self-fulfilling prophecy that US interventionists can further manipulate, using logic of this kind: they are serial human rights abusers; we therefore need to intervene in the name of humanity. There will be no discussion, let alone admission, that US covert intervention helped to provoke repression, and that the US knowingly placed its "force multipliers" on the front line. "Force multipliers" also requires us to understand the full depth and scope of US imperialism comprising, among other things: entertainment, food, drink, software, agriculture, arms sales, media, and so on.

Yet, in the end, we are still left with a basic question: *What is a force multiplier?* There are even more answers to this question than there are persons answering it. Beyond the most basic definition in physics, we see a proliferation of examples of force multipliers, reflecting a weak pseudo-science that reifies actual policies, offering mixed results in practice. Given the scientistic and positivist approach that achieved hegemony during the Cold War in US universities and the military, the conceptualization of force multipliers reveals familiar problems arising from the naturalization of social phenomena, of "man" as "molecule" of society. As an impoverished form of political science, one that is formulaic, mechanical, utilitarian, and ideologically-driven, the force multiplier idea nonetheless poses difficult anthropological questions about the agency of others. My hope was that military writers did not choose to write "force multipliers," because candidly calling them "quislings," "shills," "dupes," "pawns" or "suckers" would have been too "politically incorrect," or would have validated older, Cold War-era accusations of the US supporting "stooges," "lackeys," "cronies," "henchmen," "running dogs," or "lap dogs". In other words, my hope was that this was not yet another imperial euphemism. Regardless of the intentions behind the terminology, whether conscious or not, the basic idea of using humans as a form of *drone*, one that is less expensive yet more precise and in less need of constant guidance, seems to be the persisting feature of the force multiplier concept.

If the concept is not a mere euphemism, then there is still an absence of sound theorization of force multipliers on the part of the Pentagon, and by that I mean that while an inchoate lexical infrastructure exists consisting of nested synonyms derived from the natural sciences, there is little more than crude utilitarianism and functionalism to hold the terms together. Some may wish to retort, "then *that* is the theory" by noting the presence of functionalist assumptions and premises derived from rational-choice theories. However, the presence of theory should also involve the process of theorization, which entails questioning, revising, and exposing one's assumptions to a dialogue with other theories and with facts that appear to challenge the validity of the theory. There may be a lot of real-world destruction by the US military and intelligence apparatus, but there is no winning as such—the absence of theorization is killing the imperial political and security structures, but their exposure to critical theories will only hasten their defeat. No wonder then that so many right-wing "pro-military" columnists in the US routinely scoff at and dismiss "post-colonialism"—theirs is a hegemony in trouble, turned narcissistic: unable to find their mirror image in many sectors of the social sciences and humanities, they resort to angry triumphalism and cyclical repetition of the same failed "solutions," repeated over and over again. On the other hand, they can find their mirror-image in academia, and particularly anthropology, in other ways: many US anthropologists' convoluted (meta)theoretical fumblings, obfuscated by pretentious language whose deliberate lack of clarity masks deep confusion and bewilderment, stands out particularly in the cases of topics which are "new," such as democracy or globalization. In this sense, both the

US military and US anthropology in some quarters share in common a proliferation of theoretical-sounding rhetoric and a lack of scientific theory. Not coincidentally, both also share an apparent aversion to even saying the word "imperialism". One might detect a certain decadence in imperial intellectual life, of which the force multiplier theoretical pretense is but one small example.

Clearly there are numerous examples of agents serving as "force multipliers," and almost as clear is the absence of theorization, let alone reason for imperial elites to feel confident about success when the political, economic, and cultural projects they represent are domestically bankrupt and alienating. Counterinsurgency in Afghanistan and Iraq, and "winning hearts and minds," certainly did happen in some places and to some extent, which gives partial weight to the "force multiplier" idea at the core of these processes. However, on the whole, counterinsurgency programs have been defeated in Afghanistan just as in Vietnam before.

Notes

1   The involvement of US anthropologists in initiatives that support US foreign policy is still a very much neglected subject, apart from the narrower focus on militarization which has tended to obscure and defer discussion of this relationship. The focus on militarization, shorn of any concept of imperialism, also allows for some US academics to disingenuously shift the critique of militarization to nations that are trying to defend themselves against imperial aggression. Some of the few anthropologists who claim to study "empire," only do so with regard to topics and histories that either bolster US foreign policy (by focusing on China and Tibet, for example), and/or stay silent about the US (by writing about other empires, usually in the past). Whether serving as consultants to the State Department on the Central African Republic, writing journal articles on Ukraine that tend to back anti-Russian narratives, or supporting sanctions against Eritrea, the support of US academics for liberal imperialist projects of "democracy-promotion," "empowering civil society," "LGBT rights," or "stabilization," represents their joining an earlier wave of anthropologists who consulted on Western "development" projects funded by the World Bank and USAID, and an earlier wave that enthusiastically engaged in efforts to support warfare in WWI and WWII. Indeed, the American Anthropological Association has recently gone as far as officially celebrating the memory of President Obama's mother, an anthropologist who worked for USAID, an agency correctly interpreted as an arm of US intervention and destabilization around the world.

2   There is a much broader question here of North American socializa-
    tion patterns that grant "science" (natural science, positivism, ex-
    perimentation, numbers) an iconic value, even reflected in some
    children's games where they mimic caricatures of scientists. This is
    largely beyond the scope of this chapter, except to say that the prac-
    tice of military technocrats to sound as "scientific" as possible will
    have some unconscious resonance with sectors of the population.
    More importantly, science becomes associated with acceptance of,
    and obedience to the status quo, while criticism of the status quo will
    be automatically dubbed as "ideological".
3   The website for "100,000 Strong for the Americas" can be found at
    http://www.100kstrongamericas.org/100000-strong-explained
4   http://www.100kstrongamericas.org/get-involved-opportunities
5   Partners of the Americas presents a brief history of the organization
    at http://www.partners.net/partners/History.asp
6   http://www.partners.net/partners/Overview12.asp
7   Alliance for Affordable Internet:
    http://www.state.gov/s/partnerships/releases/reports/2015/238828
    .htm#A4AI
8   Details on YALI and the MWF were presented at:
    http://www.state.gov/s/partnerships/releases/reports/2015/238828
    .htm#YALI
9   http://www.state.gov/s/partnerships/achievements/202394.htm
10 http://www.state.gov/s/partnerships/achievements/202394.htm
11 https://www.osac.gov/Pages/AboutUs.aspx
12 https://www.osac.gov/Pages/AboutUs.aspx
13 https://www.osac.gov/Pages/AboutUs.aspx
14 https://www.osac.gov/Pages/AboutUs.aspx

References

Al Jazeera. (2014/3/14). Letter to John Kerry on Venezuela: Forty-six
    Experts Call on Secretary of State to Respect Legitimacy of Maduro
    Government. *Al Jazeera America*, Match 14.
    http://america.aljazeera.com/opinions/2014/3/letter-to-john-kerryonvenezuela.html

Ash, G. (2003). The Empire's Coming Crisis. In Andrew J. Bacevich
    (Ed.), *The Imperial Tense: Prospects and Problems of American Empire* (pp.
    238–244). Chicago: Ivan R. Dee.

Avison, J. (1989). *The World of Physics (2nd ed.)*. Cheltenham, UK: Thomas
    Nelson and Sons Ltd.

Bacevich, A.J. (2008). *The Limits of Power: The End of American
    Exceptionalism.* New York: Metropolitan Books, Henry Holt and
    Company.

———— . (2010). *Washington Rules: America's Path to Permanent War*.
    New York: Metropolitan Books, Henry Holt and Company.

Balluck, K. (2014/4/27). Obama Writes that He's 'Working Behind the Scenes' on Venezuela. *The Hill*, April 27.
http://thehill.com/policy/international/204495-obama-working-behind-the-scenes-on-venezuela

Barstow, D. (2008/4/20). Message Machine: Behind TV Analysts, Pentagon's Hidden Hand. *The New York Times*, April 20, A1.

——————. (2008/11/29). One Man's Military-Industrial-Media Complex. *The New York Times*, November 29, A1.

——————. (2011/12/24). Pentagon Finds No Fault in Ties to TV Analysts. *The New York Times*, December 24, A20.

Bell, S.R.; Murdie, A.; Blocksome, P.; & Brown, K. (2013). "Force Multipliers": Conditional Effectiveness of Military and INGO Human Security Interventions. *Journal of Human Rights*, 12(4), 397–422.

Bourdieu, P. (1990). *Homo Academicus*. Stanford, CA: Stanford University Press.

Bryan, J. (2010). Force Multipliers: Geography, Militarism, and the Bowman Expeditions. *Political Geography*, 30, 1–3.

Bush, G.W. (2002). The National Security Strategy of the United States of America. Washington, DC: The White House.

Busby, S. (2014). U.S. Concern about Venezuelan Government's Response to Ongoing Protests. Washington, DC: US Department of State.
http://www.state.gov/j/drl/rls/rm/2014/223425.htm

Butler, D.; Weissenstein, M.; Wides-Munoz, L.; & Rodriguez, A. (2014/12/11). US Co-opted Cuba's Hip-Hop Scene to Spark Change. *Salon.com/Associated Press*, December 11.
http://www.salon.com/2014/12/11/us_co_opted_cubas_hip_hop_scene_to_spark_change/

Byrd, M.W., & Decker, G. (2008). Why the U.S. Should Gender Its Counterterrorism Strategy. *Military Review*, July-August, 96–101.

Caldwell, W.B., & Leonard, S.M. (2008). Field Manual 3–07, Stability Operations: Upshifting the Engine of Change. *Military Review*, July-August, 6–13.

Cammack, P. (2006). U.N. Imperialism: Unleashing Entrepreneurship in the Developing World. In Colin Mooers (Ed.), *The New Imperialists: Ideologies of Empire* (pp. 229–260). Oxford: Oneworld.

Campbell, H. C. (2014). Understanding the US Policy of Diplomacy, Development, and Defense: The Office of Transition Initiatives and the Subversion of Societies. *CounterPunch*, May 2–4.
http://www.counterpunch.org/2014/05/02/the-office-of-transition-initiatives-and-the-subversion-of-societies/

Capote, R. (2014/3/25). Interview with Ex-CIA Collaborator: "The CIA's Plans in Venezuela Are Far Advanced". *Chavez Vive Magazine*, March 25.

http://venezuelanalysis.com/analysis/10533

Carasik, L. (2014/4/8). Obama Continues Bush's Policies in Venezuela. *Al Jazeera America*, April 8.

http://america.aljazeera.com/opinions/2014/4/nicolas-maduro-onobamaandbushspoliciesinvenezuela.html

Carter, J.G., & Gore, M.L. (2013). Conservation Officers: A Force Multiplier for Homeland Security. *Journal of Applied Security Research*, 8(3), 285–307.

CIA. (2010). CIA Red Cell Special Memorandum, March 11. Langley, VA: US Central Intelligence Agency.

https://file.wikileaks.org/file/cia-afghanistan.pdf

Clinton, H.R. (2009). Remarks at the Global Philanthropy Forum Conference, April 22. Washington, DC: US Department of State.

http://m.state.gov/md122066.htm

Code Pink. (2009/10/7a). Afghan Women Speak Out: Dr. Roshnak Wardak. *Code Pink*, October 7.

http://web.archive.org/web/20101012084530/http://codepink.org/blog/2009/10/afghan-women-speak-out-dr-roshnak-wardak/

———— . (2009/10/7b). Afghanistan: Will Obama Listen to the Women? *Code Pink*, October 7.

http://web.archive.org/web/20101012092038/http://codepink.org/blog/2009/10/afghanistan-will-obama-listen-to-the-women/

Defense Science Board. (1997). *The Defense Science Board 1997 Summer Study Task Force on DoD Responses to Transnational Threats.* Volume 1, Final Report, October. Washington, DC: US Department of Defense.

DeFrancisci, L.J. (2008). Money as a Force Multiplier in COIN. *Military Review*, May–June, 177–184.

DeYoung, K. (2014/12/17). Obama Moves to Normalize Relations with Cuba as American is Released by Havana. *The Washington Post*, December 17.

Forte, M.C. (2014a). Imperial Abduction Lore and Humanitarian Seduction. In Maximilian C. Forte (Ed.), *Good Intentions: Norms and Practices of Imperial Humanitarianism* (pp. 1–34). Montreal: Alert Press.

———— . (2014b). A Flickr of Militarization: Photographic Regulation, Symbolic Consecration, and the Strategic Communication of "Good Intentions". In Maximilian C. Forte (Ed.), *Good Intentions: Norms and Practices of Imperial Humanitarianism* (pp. 185–279). Montreal: Alert Press.

———— . (2014c). Surveillance, Dissent, and Imperialism. *Zero Anthropology*, March 1.

http://zeroanthropology.net/2014/03/01/surveillance-dissent-and-imperialism/

Foster, L. (2010). Soft Drink: Hard Power. In Maximilian C. Forte (Ed.), *Militarism, Humanism, and Occupation* (pp. 181–192). Montreal: Alert Press.

Friedman, T.L. (1999/3/28). A Manifesto for the Fast World. *The New York Times Magazine*, March 28.

https://www.nytimes.com/books/99/04/25/reviews/friedman-mag.html

Fulbright, J.W. (1966). *The Arrogance of Power*. New York: Random House.

Gates, R.M. (2008). Beyond Guns and Steel: Reviving the Nonmilitary Instruments of American Power. *Military Review*, January-February, 2–9.

Gaylord, A.A. (2008). Community Involvement: The Ultimate Force Multiplier. *FBI Law Enforcement Bulletin*, 77(4), 16–17.

Germann, C. (2005). Content Industries and Cultural Diversity: The Case of Motion Pictures. In Bernd Hamm & Russell Smandych (Eds.), *Cultural Imperialism: Essays on the Political Economy of Cultural Domination* (pp. 93–113). Toronto: University of Toronto Press.

Green, J. (2003). Force Multiplier. *The Atlantic Monthly*, 292(3), 38-40.

Halper, D. (2010/8/13). Gen. Petraeus Wants More Time in Afghanistan. *The Weekly Standard*, August 13.

http://www.weeklystandard.com/blogs/gen-petraeus-wants-more-time-afghanistan

Hanover, N. (2013/12/30). The Humanitarian Industry: A "Force Multiplier" for Imperialism. *World Socialist Web Site*, December 30.

https://www.wsws.org/en/articles/2013/12/30/huma-d30.html

Heiss, B.M. (2014). Russian Federation Anti-Gay Laws: An Analysis & Deconstruction.

https://archive.org/details/RussianFederationAnti-gayLawsAnAnalysisDeconstruction

Herbert, M. (2014). The Human Domain: The Army's Necessary Push Toward Squishiness. *Military Review*, September-October, 81–87.

Hickel, J., & Kirk, M. (2014/11/20). The Death of International Development. *Al Jazeera English*, November 20.

http://www.aljazeera.com/indepth/opinion/2014/11/death-international-developmen-2014111991426652285.html

Horton, S. (2009). Is Medea Benjamin Naive or Just Confused? Code Pink Rethinks Afghan Withdrawal. *AntiWar.com*, October 8.

http://original.antiwar.com/scott/2009/10/07/is-medea-benjamin-confused/

Hurley, W.J. (2005). A Clarification of the Concepts of Force Multiplier and Returns to Force Scale. *Defence & Peace Economics*, 16(6), 463–465.

Indiana University. (2013). IU Hosts 100 Students from Middle East, Near Asia and North Africa in Coca-Cola, State Department Program. *IU News Room*, June 4.

http://newsinfo.iu.edu/news/page/normal/24280.html

———. (2014). Top Students from Middle East and North Africa Learn Entrepreneurship at Kelley. *Kelley School of Business (Indiana University), Photos and Video*.

http://kelley.iu.edu/News/Video/photoVideo.html

Joffe, J. (2014). The New Propagandists: The Battle for the Narrative. *Halifax International Security Forum*.

http://halifaxtheforum.org/the-new-propagandists-the-battle-for-the-narrative%E2%80%A8

Johnson, C. (2004). *Blowback: The Costs and Consequences of American Empire.* New York: Holt Paperbacks.

Johnston, J. (2014/2/21). What the Wikileaks Cables Say about Leopoldo López. *Center for Economic and Policy Research: The Americas Blog,* February 21.
http://www.cepr.net/blogs/the-americas-blog/what-the-wikileaks-cables-say-about-leopoldo-lopez

Kapferer, B. (2005). New Formations of Power, the Oligarchic-Corporate State, and Anthropological Ideological Discourse. *Anthropological Theory,* 5(3), 285–299.

Kennedy, J.F.K. (1962). Address at Rice University on the Nation's Space Effort. Boston: The John F. Kennedy Presidential Library and Museum.
http://www.jfklibrary.org/Asset-Viewer/MkATdOcdU06X5uNHbmqm1Q.aspx

Kennedy, P. (1989). *The Rise and Fall of the Great Powers.* New York: Vintage Books.

King, H. (2014). Queers of War: Normalizing Lesbians and Gays in the US War Machine. In Maximilian C. Forte (Ed.), *Good Intentions: Norms and Practices of Imperial Humanitarianism* (pp. 89–101). Montreal: Alert Press.

Krauthammer, C. (2002-2003). The Unipolar Moment Revisited. *The National Interest,* Winter.
http://nationalinterest.org/print/article/the-unipolar-moment-revisited-391

Kumar, A. (2014/12/17). USAID Administrator Shah Resigns. *McClatchyDC,* December 17.
http://www.mcclatchydc.com/2014/12/17/250315/usaid-administrator-shah-resigns.html

Landler, M. (2013/7/23). U.S. Urged to Adopt Policy Justifying Intervention. *The New York Times,* July 23.
http://www.nytimes.com/2013/07/24/us/politics/us-urged-to-adopt-policy-justifying-intervention.html?_r=0

Lischer, S.K. (2007). Military Intervention and the Humanitarian "Force Multiplier". *Global Governance,* 13(1), 99–118.

Maier, C.S. (2002). An American Empire? The Problems of Frontiers and Peace in Twenty-First-Century World Politics. *Harvard Magazine,* November-December, 28–31.

Manoochehri, A. (2005). Enrique Dussel and Ali Shari'ati on Cultural Imperialism. In Bernd Hamm & Russell Smandych (Eds.), *Cultural Imperialism: Essays on the Political Economy of Cultural Domination* (pp. 290–300). Toronto: University of Toronto Press.

McCuen, J.J. (2008). Hybrid Wars. *Military Review,* March–April, 107–113.

McLoughlin, K., & Forte, M.C. (2013). Emergency as Security: The Liberal Empire at Home and Abroad. In Kyle McLoughlin & Maximilian C. Forte (Eds.), *Emergency as Security: Liberal Empire at Home and Abroad* (pp. 1–19). Montreal: Alert Press.

Ministry of Defence (MoD). (2001). The Defence Manual of Security

(Volumes 1, 2 and 3, Issue 2). London: Ministry of Defence.

Mojumdar, A. (2009/10/6). "Code Pink" Rethinks Its Call for Afghanistan Pullout. *Christian Science Monitor*, October 6.
http://www.csmonitor.com/World/Asia-South-Central/2009/1006/p06s10-wosc.html

Murray, W., & Scales, R.H. (2003). *The Iraq War: An Elusive Victory.* Cambridge, MA: Harvard University Press.

NAFSA. (2013). Strategic Plan 2014–2016. Washington, DC: NAFSA, Association of International Educators.

Naipaul, V.S. (1967). *The Mimic Men.* New York: Vintage International.

Nandy, A. (2005). Science as a Reason of State. In Ackbar Abbas & John Nguyet Erni (Eds.), *Internationalizing Cultural Studies: An Anthology* (pp. 21–29). Oxford: Blackwell Publishing Ltd.

NATO. (2008). NATO in Afghanistan: Master Narrative as at 6 October 2008. Brussels: Media Operations Centre, Press and Media Service, NATO HQ.
https://file.wikileaks.org/file/nato-master-narrative-2008.pdf

Nixon, R. (2015/8/24). Critiquing U.S. Spending in Afghanistan, to Dramatic Effect. *The New York Times*, August 24.
http://www.nytimes.com/2015/08/25/us/politics/critiquing-us-spending-in-afghanistan-to-dramatic-effect.html

Obama, B. (2012). Remarks by the President on the Defense Strategic Review, January 5. Washington, DC: Office of the Press Secretary, The White House.

——— . (2014a). Statement by the President on ISIL, September 10. Washington, DC: Office of the Press Secretary, The White House.

——— . (2014b). Statement by the President on Cuba Policy Changes, December 17. Washington, DC: Office of the Press Secretary, The White House.

——— . (2015). Executive Order – Blocking Property and Suspending Entry of Certain Persons Contributing to the Situation in Venezuela, March 9. Washington, DC: Office of the Press Secretary, The White House

O'Connor, P. (2014/2/7). US Regime-Change Operation in Ukraine Exposed in Leaked Diplomatic Phone Call. *World Socialist Web Site*, February 7.
https://www.wsws.org/en/articles/2014/02/07/ukra-f07.html

Opportunity Desk. (2015/2/18). 2015 Coca-Cola MENA Scholarship Program for 100 Students to Travel to the United States. *Opportunity Desk*, February 18.
http://opportunitydesk.org/2015/02/18/2015-coca-cola-mena-scholarship-program/

Orford, A. (2010). The Passions of Protection: Sovereign Authority and Humanitarian War. In Didier Fassin & Mariella Pandolfi (Eds.), *Contemporary States of Emergency: The Politics of Military and Humanitarian Interventions* (pp. 335–356). New York: Zone Books.

Ossowski, Y. (2013/10/22). Russia's "Anti-Gay" Law Reveals US Media Misinformation and Hyperbole: Pundits Embarrass Themselves as Exponents of Godwin's Law. *PanAmPost*, October 22. http://panampost.com/yael-ossowski/2013/10/22/russias-anti-gay-law-reveals-us-media-misinformation-and-hyperbole/

Parthasarathy, D. (2005). From White Man's Burden to Good Governance: Economic Liberalization and the Commodification of Law and Ethics. In Bernd Hamm & Russell Smandych (Eds.), *Cultural Imperialism: Essays on the Political Economy of Cultural Domination* (pp. 191–210). Toronto: University of Toronto Press.

Pas, N. (2013). The Masculine Empire: A Gendered Analysis of Modern American Imperialism. In Kyle McLoughlin & Maximilian C. Forte (Eds.), *Emergency as Security: Liberal Empire at Home and Abroad* (pp. 47–71). Montreal: Alert Press.

Petraeus, D. H. (2006). Learning Counterinsurgency: Observations from Soldiering in Iraq. *Military Review*, January-February, 2–12.

Petraeus, D., & O'Hanlon, M. (2015/7/7). The U.S. Needs to Keep Troops in Afghanistan. *The Washington Post*, July 7. http://www.washingtonpost.com/opinions/afghanistan-after-obama/2015/07/07/63dd6dc2-1e8e-11e5-aeb9-a411a84c9d55_story.html

Powell, C. (2001). Remarks to the National Foreign Policy Conference for Leaders of Nongovernmental Organizations, October 26. Washington, DC: US Department of State. http://web.archive.org/web/20040701145046/http://www.state.gov/secretary/rm/2001/5762pf.htm

———. (2006). A Leadership Primer. Slides from a presentation at the 2006 International Petrochemical Conference, San Antonio, Texas, March 26. http://www.slideshare.net/guesta3e206/colin-powells-leadership-presentation?qid=4a917f51-96fc-45ce-9102-faf76d702d61&v=qf1&b=&from_search=1

Powell, D.S. (1990). *Understanding Force Multipliers: The Key to Optimizing Force Capabilities in Peacetime Contingency Operations.* Fort Leavenworth: School of Advanced Military Studies, United States Army Command and General Staff College.

Price, D.H. (2008). *Anthropological Intelligence: The Deployment and Neglect of American Anthropology in the Second World War.* Durham, NC: Duke University Press.

Priselac, M. (2013/7/19). Making Tomorrow Better: Coke Inspires Young Entrepreneurs from the Middle East and North Africa. *Coca-Cola*, July 19. http://www.coca-colacompany.com/stories/making-tomorrow-better-coke-inspires-young-entrepreneurs-from-the-middle-east-and-north-africa

Rasmussen , R. (2011). New USAID GeoCenter Can Benefit From Existing Defense Programs and Projects. *The Central Node (Network Science Center at West Point)*, August 4.

http://blog.netsciwestpoint.org/2011/08/04/new-usaid-geocenter-can-benefit-from-existing-defense-programs-and-projects

Said, E.W. (1978). *Orientalism*. New York: Vintage Books.

Scales, R.H., Jr. (2003). Statement by Major General (Ret) Robert H. Scales, Jr. Before the House Armed Services Committee, United States House of Representatives, October 21.

http://www.au.af.mil/au/awc/awcgate/congress/03-10-21scales.htm

————— . (2006). Clausewitz and World War IV. *Armed Forces Journal*, July 1.

http://www.armedforcesjournal.com/clausewitz-and-world-war-iv/

Sheftick, G. (2014/1/16). TRADOC: Strategic Landpower Concept to Change Doctrine. *Army.mil: Official Homepage of the United States Army*, January 16.

http://www.army.mil/article/118432/TRADOC__Strategic_Landpower_concept_to_change_doctrine/

Scherrer, C. (2005). The Role of GATS in the Commodification of Education. In Bernd Hamm & Russell Smandych (Eds.), *Cultural Imperialism: Essays on the Political Economy of Cultural Domination* (pp. 167–190). Toronto: University of Toronto Press.

Smollett, E. (1993). America the Beautiful: Made in Bulgaria. *Anthropology Today*, 9(2), 9–13.

Spencer, E. (2009). It's All About the People: Cultural Intelligence (CQ) as a Force Multiplier in the Contemporary Operating Environment. *Journal of Conflict Studies*, 29. [HTML document, no page numbers]

Stavridis, J., & Farkas, E.N. (2012). The 21st Century Force Multiplier: Public–Private Collaboration. *The Washington Quarterly*, 35(2), 7–20.

Stevenson, R.L. (1983). A Critical Look at Critical Analysis. *Journal of Communication*, 33(3), 262–269.

Thompson, M. (2014/6/26). How the U.S. Air Force Uses Twitter as a "Force Multiplier". *TIME*, June 26.

http://time.com/2927994/how-the-u-s-air-force-uses-twitter-as-a-force-multiplier/

Torres, N.G. (2015/7/3). Cuba Has Doubts as Google Pitches Expanded Internet. *Toronto Star*, July 3.

http://www.thestar.com/news/world/2015/07/03/cuba-has-doubts-as-google-pitches-expanded-internet.html

Trubey, J.S. (2010/4/27). Connecting With Capitalism. *Upstart Business Journal*, April 27.

http://upstart.bizjournals.com/companies-executives/2010/04/27/neville-isdell-taking-connected-capitalism-global.html?page=all

UNHRC. (2015). Human Rights Council Discusses the Situation of Human Rights in Belarus and Eritrea, June 23. Geneva: Office of the High Commissioner for Human Rights, United Nations.

http://www.ohchr.org/EN/NewsEvents/Pages/DisplayNews.aspx?NewsID=16134&LangID=E

USAID. (2007). Global Development Alliance. Washington, DC: US Agency for International Development.

US Army. (1990). Doctrine for Special Forces Operations (Field Manual No. 31–20). Washington, DC: Department of the Army.

——————— . (2003). FM 31-20-3, Foreign Internal Defense Tactics, Techniques, and Procedures for Special Forces. Washington, DC: Headquarters, Department of the Army.

——————— . (2008a). FM 3-0, Operations. Washington, DC: Headquarters, Department of the Army.

——————— . (2008b). FM 3-07, Stability Operations. Washington, DC: Headquarters, Department of the Army.

US Department of Defense (DoD). (2007). Joint Special Operations Task Force Operations. Joint Publication 3-05.1. April 26. Washington, DC: Joint Chiefs of Staff, US Department of Defense.

——————— . (2015). The National Military Strategy of the United States of America. Washington, DC: Joint Chiefs of Staff, US Department of Defense.

US Department of State (DoS). (2010). Leading Through Civilian Power: The First Quadrennial Diplomacy and Development Review. Washington, DC: US Department of State.

——————— . (2014a). Congressional Budget Justification, Volume 2: Foreign Operations. Washington, DC: US Department of State.

——————— . (2014b). State of Global Partnerships Report. Washington, DC: The Secretary's Office of Global Partnerships, US Department of State.

——————— . (2015). The Secretary's Office of Global Partnerships. Washington, DC: US Department of State.
http://www.state.gov/s/partnerships/

——————— . (2015/3/12). Department of State Releases 2015 State of Global Partnerships Report—Media Note, March 12. Washington, DC: Office of the Spokesperson, US Department of State.
http://www.state.gov/r/pa/prs/ps/2015/03/238833.htm

US Embassy-Amman (USEA). (2015). 2015 Coca-Cola Scholarship Program. Amman, Jordan: US Embassy.
http://jordan.usembassy.gov/ann_2015_coca_cola_030415.html

US Embassy-Caracas (USEC). (2006/11/9). USAID/OTI Programmatic Support for Country Team 5 Point Strategy. US Embassy, Caracas, Venezuela, November 9, Cable ID 06CARACAS3356_a.
https://wikileaks.org/plusd/cables/06CARACAS3356_a.html

Weisbrot, M. (2014/2/18). US Support for Regime Change in Venezuela is a Mistake. The Guardian (UK), February 18.
http://www.theguardian.com/commentisfree/2014/feb/18/venezuela-protests-us-support-regime-change-mistake

White House. (2010). National Security Strategy. Washington, DC: The White House.

——————— . (2014). Fact Sheet: Charting a New Course on Cuba, December 17. Washington, DC: Office of the Press Secretary, The

White House.

———— . (2015a). Fact Sheet: Venezuela Executive Order, March 9. Washington, DC: Office of the Press Secretary, The White House.

———— . (2015b). Statement by the President on the Re-Establishment of Diplomatic Relations with Cuba, July 1. Washington, DC: Office of the Press Secretary, The White House.

WikiLeaks. (2009). UK MoD Manual of Security Volumes 1, 2 and 3 Issue 2, JSP-440, RESTRICTED, 2389 pages, 2001. *WikiLeaks*, October 4. https://wikileaks.org/wiki/UK_MoD_Manual_of_Security_Volumes_1%2C_2_and_3_Issue_2%2C_JSP-440%2C_RESTRICTED%2C_2389_pages%2C_2001

Wilson, R.G.; Pilgrim, D.H.; & Tashjian, D. (1986). The Machine Age in America, 1918–1941. New York: Brooklyn Museum.

Young, R.J.C. (1995). Colonial Desire: Hybridity in Theory, Culture and Race. London: Routledge.

Chapter 1

Protégé of an Empire: Influence and Exchange between US and Israeli Imperialism

John Talbot

The relationship between the foreign policies of Israel and the US is one which is entrenched in the international political system, and has been for quite some time. This relationship is significant in terms of public policy development, as an alliance on the global stage, and it exercises a significant presence in media and public forums. However, it is not simply the relationship that creates action and international policies—there are more than just US intentions at work regarding this connection. Within the US there exists a significant interest group promoting ardent support for Israel and its actions. This interest group is much more than one all-encompassing body and contains many different components. While I specifically studied organizations such as the American Israel Public Affairs Committee (AIPAC; see Figure 1.1), I will make a slight generalization in referring to the overarching pro-Israel body as "the lobby". The influence, and generally grandiose presence, of the Israel lobby is remarkable in comparison to the actual population of Jewish individuals in the US. However, it is important not to overestimate the influence and power of lobbying groups or to assume that all Jewish individuals necessarily support them. Nevertheless, the effectiveness of the lobby is substantial concerning the type of knowledge communicated regarding Israel, the public pressure to support Israel's actions, and the lobby's overall influence on policy making. The point of this is to use the work of the lobby as a point of entry into a larger discussion of the nature of the US-Israeli relationship around the questions of power differentials between the two, and the extent of the two nations' degree of mutual interdependence.

Figure 1.1: John Kerry Meets with AIPAC

U.S. Secretary of State John Kerry meets with leaders of the American Israel Public Affairs Committee (AIPAC) Conference at the Washington Convention Center in Washington, D.C., on March 3, 2014. (Photo: US Department of State)

Israel, like the US, is heavily militarized and seeks to expand its influence over other territories. Outlining the influence of Israel on the US, and the influence on and strategic interest of the US in Israel, is critical to understanding the US-Israeli relationship. I will also outline the significance of the Israel lobby today and how its influence has changed over time. In particular, this chapter will critically explore the question of what the US-Israeli relationship means for empire-building. Rather than either a mere pawn of the US, or a powerful force determining US foreign policy, I argue that Israel should be seen as an imperial protégé. As the reader already knows, a protégé is one who is protected by another, that is, under the supervisory care and patronage of another. While it admits an overarching power differential between patron and protégé, it does not necessarily imply servitude on the part of the protégé, and obviously not a commanding influence.

Questions of Interest

If the US is defined as an imperialist nation, and one engaged in empire building, then we must consider what exactly the US gains from its support for Israel. When studying empire and imperialism from an anthropological perspective, it becomes important to highlight not only the explicit understandings of what is going on, but also the tacit happenstances which shape and influence the scenario at hand. An explicit example of imperial practice is the amount of military aid Israel receives each year from the US. Israel, according to a report from the Congressional Research Service, is "the largest cumulative recipient of US foreign assistance since World War II," and to date the US has provided Israel with $124.3 billion in bilateral assistance (in current, non-inflation-adjusted dollars) (Sharpe, 2015, p. 2; also, see Figure 1.2). In 2007, the US and the Israeli government agreed to a $30 billion military aid package covering the years of 2009 to 2018 (Sharpe, 2015, p. 4). This military aid could be seen as the outstretched hand of US empire holding onto a strategic position in the Middle East; the desire for US funding could also lead to an increase in US political influence over Israel. Here the "special" aspect of the relationship is highlighted as "Israel is the only recipient [of foreign military aid] that does not have to account for how the aid is spent, an exemption that makes it virtually impossible to prevent the money from being used for purposes the United States opposes" (Mearsheimer & Walt, 2006, p. 2). Does the US actually have a relationship of political control over Israel? If not, why would the US set aside its own interests and preferences in order to advance and financially support the interests of another state, as Mearsheimer and Walt argue (2006, p. 1)? Attempts to answer these questions often lead towards explanations of shared strategic interests or compelling moral imperatives, however, as this chapter argues, there is a deeper explanation that is not readily visible.

Figure 1.2: A US-Israeli Air Force

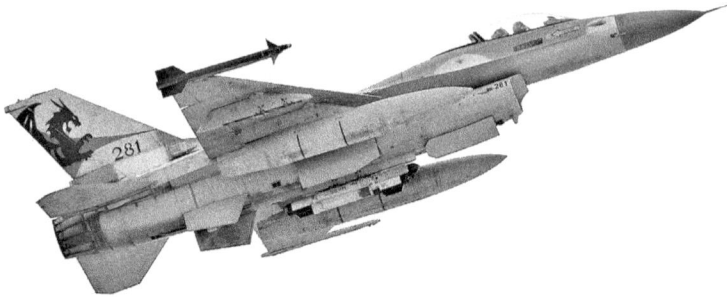

A US-made F-15E Strike Eagle, part of the Israeli Air Force's Squadron 115, takes part in "Blue Flag 2013," a multinational aerial combat exercise with participation of the air forces of the US, Israel, Italy, and Greece, held at the Ovda air base in southern Israel. US Ambassador Dan Shapiro was the guest of the Israeli Air Force, and he met the US personnel who are charged with operating and maintaining the airplanes. At the military exercise he commented, "It's a powerful symbol of the partnership between the United States and Israel when our pilots and Israeli pilots are flying together". (Photo: US Embassy, Tel Aviv)

In supporting Israel, the US is essentially supporting a state which sometimes directly defies it. Israel spies on the US, engages in racist and imperialist practices towards the states around it (sometimes in stark contrast with publicly stated principles of the US), and furthermore Israel does not adhere to the US ideal of a liberal democracy—a democracy where all people are purported to have equal rights (Mearsheimer & Walt, 2006, p. 9). These issues challenge the notion that the US-Israeli relationship is simply an imperialist or strategically-motivated one. The "force multiplier" concept discussed in the Introduction to this volume is put to the test by the US relationship with Israel. There is the question of how the US aiding Israel in warfare and occupation benefits the US, aside from providing a market for US military corporations. Another question concerns the assumption that the Israel lobby is completely steering things such as US intervention in Iraq. An additional question involves the potential of overestimating the influence of the lobby, while obscuring the fact that the US could be acting of its own accord to serve its own interests. "American Exceptionalism" and the supposed "moral duty" of the US to bring "rights" to the world is something the lobby can capitalize on, not something that it created. Further, "in late 2013 and early 2014,

AIPAC suffered a series of high-profile defeats that led some observers to question whether the group would retain its influence in coming years" (Right Web, 2014).

In this chapter I thus explore the potential that the US is not simply engaging in an imperial practice with Israel but instead financing a protégé—whether it is active on the US' behalf or not. Israel is a protégé in the practice of colonization, militarization, nationalism, and acts of imperialism. I also explore the metaphor of Israel being a "little brother" figure to the US—by this I mean it is mimicking and acting as the US itself does.

It is important to recognize that being critical of the Israel lobby and the Israeli government neither directly nor indirectly entails anti-Jewish sentiments. To be anti-Israel or anti-Zionist is not the same thing as being anti-Semitic. The public body of Israel and Jewish individuals are not always a reflection of the political elites representing them on the global stage. While an argument could be made that Israel, the Israeli lobby in the US, and the US' interests are the same, this argument would need to be further qualified: the institutionalized leadership of the lobby has driven pro-Israel politics to a point where they have become antithetical to what is good for both Israel and the US (Meerman, 2007). This is not a discussion about Jewish individuals, but rather it concerns the corporate, governmental, and institutional actors steering the US-Israeli relationship.

The Tail Wagging the Dog?

"Why has the United States been willing to set aside its own security in order to advance the interests of another state" (Mearsheimer & Walt, 2006, p. 1)? Why would US foreign policy shape itself to benefit another state over the interests of average US citizens? Answers to these basic questions are often generalized and rhetoricized with arguments of shared strategic interests and/or compelling moral imperatives. However, this is not an answer; here we are examining the significant influence of the Israel lobby as one manifestation of the US-Israeli relationship.

The US has made it completely clear that it is an ardent supporter of Israel on the global stage and this stance has arguably been more problematic than beneficial. Since the US is a permanent member of the UN, it has the power to veto resolutions which go against Israel's interests—resolutions that might have otherwise passed with a majority (Meerman, 2007). The US exists as a diplomatic ally which will use its power on the international stage to put an end to anything that may challenge Israel's actions. However, the lobby recognizes that influence comes from more than just the policy-makers and thus they, with their allies, also influence and station allies in the media and universities. Pastor John Hagee from Christians United for Israel in *The Israel Lobby* documentary states, "we have millions of people in the infrastructure...we have the major radio, television ministries in America supporting what we're doing" (Meerman, 2007). When faced with unfavourable reporting on Israel the "Lobby organizes letter writing campaigns, demonstrations, and boycotts against news outlets" (Mearsheimer & Walt, 2006, p. 21). There are people on university campuses in the US (and Canada) who are stationed to protect the interests of Israel (Meerman, 2007). At Concordia University in Montreal, organizations such as the Committee for Accuracy in Middle East Reporting in America (CAMERA), Hillel, and Israel on Campus are clearly in line with the lobby's vision. Indeed, the only ethnic community to be represented on Concordia's Board of Governors (which is supposed to be "representative of the wider community"), appears in the form of the Executive Director of Hillel Montreal.[1] The lobby uses this presence to shut down opponents and to completely halt discussion. Those who do speak out are met with such force that it creates a deterrent, stopping other people from criticizing anything pro-Israel (Meerman, 2007). If the goal is to "prevent critical commentary about Israel from getting a fair hearing in the political arena," then it is arguably true that they have achieved this in some sense (Mearsheimer & Walt, 2006, p. 16). The lobby's influence over the media and academia allows for a monopolization of the discourse surrounding Israel's actions.

> "The mission of AIPAC is to strengthen, protect and promote the U.S.-Israel relationship in ways that enhance the security of Israel and the United States" (AIPAC, 2014), clearly the rhetoric of security is not something used only for US motives. The lobby capitalizes on this discourse, assuming US support for Israel is a given. With the "War on Terror" after 9/11, US support for Israel has used as justification the claim that "both states are threatened by terrorist groups originating in the Arab or Muslim world". (Mearsheimer & Walt, 2006, p. 4)

The idea of stopping "rogue states" is one of the notorious publicly-stated aims of US neoconservatives (Mearsheimer & Walt, 2006, p. 4). Such rhetoric not only more easily generated support for Israel's actions, but it also prompted the US itself to act. US leaders constantly support Israel's repression of the Palestinians while taking aim at Israel's so-called primary enemies—Iran, Iraq, and Syria (Mearsheimer & Walt, 2006, p. 26). The recent Iraq war was justified in the media as integral to the US' security. However, an underlying fact was that there was no credible threat against the US from Iraq, but there arguably could have been one against Israel which in the past had been targeted by Iraqi missiles (Mearsheimer & Walt, 2006, p. 30; see Figures 1.3, 1.4, and 1.5).

When it is not the rhetoric of security it is the "victim of history" discourse which is completely used to the lobby's advantage. "Israel is a country born of victimhood," consisting of people who have constantly been driven from their homes, who had to deal with the devastating effects of the holocaust, and face anti-Semitism that still exists today (Meerman, 2007). While this is important to recognize, it is turning this narrative into public policy which becomes problematic, especially when it sanctions the displacement and abuse of others for the cause of one group's primacy.

Figure 1.3: US Patriots in Israel

In this photo, US-made and US-installed Patriot missiles are being launched to intercept an Iraqi Scud missile over the city of Tel Aviv on February 12, 1991. (Photo: Government Press Office, Israel)

Figure 1.4: US-directed "Interoperability" with Israel

A US Soldier with the 5th Battalion, 7th Air Defense Artillery Regiment checks cable connections before testing Patriot missile communications as part of "Austere Challenge 2012" in Beit Ezra, Israel, on October 24, 2012. Austere Challenge is a three-week bilateral exercise designed to increase air defense "interoperability" between the US and Israel. (Photo: US Department of Defense, Staff Sgt. Tyler Placie)

Figure 1.5: Defending Israel

Israel Air Defense Command's MIM-104D Patriot surface-to-air missile battery in 2014. (Photo: US Department of Defense, Erin A. Kirk-Cuomo)

Israel as a Force Multiplier for the US?

In response to what Mearsheimer and Walt present as a seemingly subservient US Congress, Noam Chomsky argues this standpoint may actually have appeal for the US: "it leaves the US government untouched on its high pinnacle of nobility...merely in the grip of an all-powerful force that it cannot escape" (Chomsky, 2006). Further he argues that,

> "Jewish influence over politics and opinion seriously underestimates the scope of the so called 'support for Israel'....the argument much overestimates the pluralism of American politics and ideology. No pressure group will dominate access to public opinion or maintain consistent influence over policy-making unless its aims are close to those of elite elements with real power". (Chomsky, 1999, p. 17)

There are times when the US Congress has gone directly against, and even humiliated the Israel lobby, in the name of its own "national interest" (Chomsky, 2006). With this in mind it is clear that configurations of domestic politics are complex and multilayered. Isolating certain areas of influence such as the lobby ignores the existence of US imperial interests at play, or the power of other lobbies, such as that of the oil companies. What has to be taken into consideration when evaluating the US-Israeli relationship is not just US interests in Israel, but rather its interests in the Middle East as a whole.

Control of oil is a decisive instrument of global policy and the Middle East is host to a vast amount of oil reserves. "A quick glance at a map of the Middle East places Israel in the vicinity of Iraq, Iran and Saudi Arabia," a hot bed of oil geo-politics over the last century (Urie, 2013). "Since World War II, it has been virtually an axiom of US foreign policy that these energy reserves should remain under U.S. control" (Chomsky, 1999, p. 17), and thus interest in Israel's position has been a necessary one to ensure US oil interests in the region were maintained. Israel became strategic in maintaining US influence in the region during the Cold War era as well, continuing to serve as a barrier against indigenous radical nationalist threats (Chomsky, 1999, p. 20). Justifying the beginnings and continuation of economic support thus became a rational action. Israel managed to provide camouflage for the US presence in the Middle East. The US does not have military bases or other launch pads in Israel, rather it is the defence contracts, development strategies, and the overarching economic support which encourages Israel to act according to the US' own strategic interests. Despite the lack of a direct military presence, Israel is surely regarded as a part of "the elaborate base and backup system for the Rapid Deployment Force ringing the Middle East oil producing regions" (Chomsky, 1999, p. 22). Israel was not only historically strategic for the US:

> "The War on Terrorism is the New World Order unleashed and unbound. It replays the Cold War dynamic, aims to reproduce its oppressive structure, and continues to satisfy longstanding U.S. interests in the Middle East: control of oil and rejection of Arab radicalism, which have led to support for colonial Israel". (Bashir, 2007)

The continuous development of neoliberal capitalism is advanced through the US relationship with Israel. US arms manufacturers and US-based multinational oil companies have gained significantly from Israeli aggression (Urie, 2014). The intense militarization of Israel and its persistent colonial engagements work in tandem with US imperial interests. The Zionist imperative of "Jewish supremacy in Palestine—as much land as possible, as few Palestinians as possible" was used to support US interests and resulted in a heavily militarized and fundamentalist Israel (Bashir, 2007).

For Israelis it is clear that at least in some ways they are subordinate to US aims. "Israel has had to subordinate itself to US imperial imperatives" due to its dependence on economic support; this, at times, "generates the occasional Israeli public resentment at the extent of U.S. control" (Bashir, 2007). "Israel has indeed understood that there is no occupation, no expansion, and no rejection of Palestinian national rights," without US support (Bashir, 2007).

Since the early entrenchment of the relationship during the Cold War, the US has been promoting its political ideology as well as its products within Israel. Foreign consumerism and dependency on US products are an important method of promoting US universalism and empire. It also acts to fundamentally serve US economic interests. Israel's perennial quest for US funding and support on the global stage has arguably bonded it to US values and influence. For Israel it is through both consent—the want of US support—and coercion—the fear of losing support—that Israel becomes a piece of US empire. Israel is unique as it is financed by imperialism but it is not economically exploited by it (Bashir, 2007). The promotion of a mentality of "sameness" links Israel and the US. Further, compliance without coercion rationalizes the US belief in its own exceptionalism as a necessary and progressive force of global modernization (Mirrlees, 2006, p. 204). Israel as a piece of US empire serves the integration of the world with the social relations and cultural values of US neoliberal capitalism: "the frontier, exclusionary society that Zionism has built is thus on the decline, being slowly replaced by a liberalized nation, both economically and politically" (Bashir, 2007).

Some political elements of Americanization which challenge traditional Israeli notions are visible regarding Israel's move from the their previous Westminster-derived model of parliamentary democracy to a more US model which has an incomplete separation of powers between those who are elected and its premier (Aronoff, 2000). Further, Americanization can be recognizable within various cultural patterns throughout "spheres of Israeli culture, from language and names to work patterns, physical structures, and more" (Rebhun & Waxman, 2000, p. 65). It is important to keep in mind that the US' "cultural industry and its commodities are functional to the US empire's political-economic dominance" (Mirrlees, 2006, p. 217). The spread of the US' cultural values and its commitment to free markets, liberal democracy, and neoliberal values are crucial to the maintenance of US dominance.

If one were to assume Israel is a force multiplier of US imperialism, one would nonetheless have to admit that Israel offers a unique case study which should not sit comfortably with reductionist ideas or one-sided understandings of the relationship between Israel and the US. That relationship is not driven only by oil geopolitics and other quests for commercial gain, nor is Israel simply imbibing US ideals and wielding them on the global stage. On the other hand, one must also remember to factor in the reality of over 200,000 current US citizens living in Israel, and the fact that an even larger number is of US ancestry, which blurs the demographic, cultural, and political lines that are used to draw the Israel and the US as two, neatly separate entities, and which strengthens the perspective of Israel as a colonial settler-state. Thus we have different descriptive options for arguments that see Israel in a subordinate role: a tool, an extension, or a minion. However, there is another option, one that differs from either Israel as a commander of US foreign policy, or Israel as a servant of the US, and that is the figure of the protégé.

Israel as a US Protégé

What I previously explored are the two most prominent explanations of the US-Israeli relationship: one was that there is a significant and powerful pro-Israel lobby in the US which has a grappling hold on the US congress, media, and universities (also, see Figure 1.6). The second assumed Israel was, and is, in a strategic position to protect the US' imperial political and economic interests. However, the US is neither simply a pawn of a powerful lobby, nor are its projects strictly rational and based on cost/benefit analysis. Here I outline the prospect that the relationship is one that has resulted in the production of a protégé. I do not state the US is purposely creating a protégé; rather it only came as a result of historical ties and each state's goals. This aspect of the US-Israeli relationship can prove to be reciprocal in the sense that it is mutually beneficial. However, it can also explain how sometimes they significantly oppose each other in order to serve their own imperial interests.

Figure 1.6: Big Brother Visits His Israeli Protégé

On October 3, 2010, a delegation of former US NBA basketball players visited the Hatzerim Air Force Base and met with Israeli Air Force soldiers of the Desert Birds Squadron, who operate US-made UH-60 Black Hawk helicopters. The visit to Israel was organized by the American Israeli Public Affairs Committee (AIPAC) and also included visits with President Shimon Peres. The visit by the US basketball players to the base involved interacting with Israeli soldiers, and allegedly "learning" about "Israel's security situation". (Photo: Cpl. Iris Lainer, Israel Defence Force Spokesperson's Unit)

Within the scope of imperialism we find nationalism, colonialism, exceptionalism, state violence, heavy militarization, and the creation of a state of emergency. If Israel is acting as a protégé, its engagement in each of these areas must be clearly understood. Clearly the US does not have a monopoly on the politics of violent domination as, "the human catastrophe of the Palestinian people under Israeli occupation and repression resembles quite closely the callous way that the US has acted around the globe" (Urie, 2014).

For the US, Cold War threats and now the "War on Terror" managed to create a forum in which the rhetoric of international security was justifiable. These emergencies became both descriptors and prescriptors for their own imperial action. Following suit, Israel has managed to use its "victim of history" discourse (Meerman, 2007) to create its own state of emergency. It was the horrors of Nazi Germany that drove many Jewish individuals to Palestine. Historically speaking, the view is that Israel has had to endure the wars that are occurring in the Middle East simply because they are a "Jewish state in the midst of an Arab world" (Chomsky, 1999, p. 99). This victim/emergency discourse allows for the rhetoric of security to become rampant in both media propaganda and as a justification for both the occupation of Palestinian land and potential further bombardments of Palestinian territory and neighbouring nations.

Creating a state of emergency in its conflict with Palestine generates a fear of, and opposition to, the Palestinian people and their cause. The successful media campaign in Israel has painted the Palestinians not as a people facing the colonial violence of Israel, but rather as aggressors. The rhetoric of Israel "feeling 'isolation,' 'under siege,' and 'suffering daily attack'" (Said, 2001, p. 31), exists to ensure support and sympathy for Israel while giving no voice to the Palestinians. Just as the US dominates discourse with the rhetoric of saving US lives, so does Israel in the name of Israeli safety. Both the US and Israel most recently purport "counter terrorism" as a basis of their actions; their ability to control the way the media presents this message is a critical part of their success. Here it becomes tenable that the presence of a strong pro-Israel lobby influencing media and educational institutions in the US is in fact a working body of Israeli imperial efforts. Important to note is that despite their relative proximity to Palestinians, "Israelis will not learn much about what happens day to day inside Palestinian society, unless it concerns terrorism, a security threat, or war. They will hardly meet Palestinians, nor socialize with them" (Silverstein, 2014/10/28). This is similar to the US' ability to create a distant enemy, an other, for which US citizens cannot feel empathy.

A state of emergency involves militarization and thus engagement in violence. Militarization is a precursor to war-making and so is the violence it entails. Charles Tilly explained the interdependence between war-making and state power, however he also highlighted various domestic forms of violence that arise (Tilly, 1985, p. 181).

This state development and the resulting internal violence is also an area in which Israel bears similar markings as the US. A disconnection between a vast majority of the citizens and their government is something the public of Israel and the US share in common (Vice, 2012). An example of this is that in Israel the government does not allow free protest. Activists are upset over education, healthcare, and affordable housing, yet they are prevented from vocalizing it (Vice, 2012). Internal discourse is stifled in order to present the veneer of a monolithic nation-state, an arguably necessary tactic of imperial nations.

Out of all of the protégé's imperial actions it is Israel's external violence which is the most visible. The US is engaging in non-territorial empire development (though chapter 5 in this volume would disagree on this point), and Israel is expanding its direct territorial empire. Israel's actions thus constitute imperialism in the colonial mode. Furthermore, it is in connection with Israel's colonial mission towards Palestine and the US' empire development that we see a prominent circular chain of influence of each state on the other:

> "US support reinforces Israeli colonialism and occupation, which bolsters Israeli militarization of state and society, which generates new ideological and political justifications and breeds new religious fanaticisms, leading to further indigenous resistance and to more US interventions in the region". (Bashir, 2007)

Their colonial actions include a number of brutal tactics which furthers Israel's end goal of controlling the land. Most often Israel engages in the creation of discriminatory structures which make life difficult for Palestinians, often resulting in outright displacement. Israelis often even resort to flat out conquest, war, and murder. It is here that Israel even managed to influence US imperialism in certain respects: "Israel was the first nation to develop drones, which it uses both to spy on its Arab neighbors and assassinate undesirable Palestinians," something the US counter-terror strategy picked up and now wields ruthlessly across the Middle East (Silverstein, 2014/10/28). (However, on its own, this fact is insufficient in denying that an imperial relationship exists between the US and Israel, since colonial territories were frequently arenas where colonial powers tested new measures of policing, repression and counterinsurgency—with an excellent example being the history of the US in the Philippines [see McCoy, 2009]).

The ongoing exchange of US and Israeli imperialism is ultimately a cycle of violence. However, Israel's ability to wield this violence is dependent on the US and thus so is its colonial expansionism. Without the funding, "Israeli militarism and Jewish fundamentalism in Israel would be on the defensive" (Bashir, 2007). Despite the persistent Israeli nationalism and increasing exceptionalism, a withdrawal of US funding could lead to an "abandonment of the 'national security' ethic and the rejection of living by the sword would have a real chance of gaining political ascendancy in Israel" (Bashir, 2007). By existing as a protégé of the US through "siding with, serving, depending, and even subordinating itself to the imperatives of U.S. empire" (Bashir, 2007) the view of the US and Israel as a hostile presence in the Middle East will continue to be perpetuated.

It is also arguable that the figure of the protégé might *not* attenuate the tension in dominant analyses (such as between Mearsheimer & Walt vs. Chomsky), but rather it could reinforce one side of the debate. In this respect, we have an example of such a case in the writing of noted Israeli author, Gideon Levy:

> "We have a protégé that humiliates its patron power and a power that grovels in front of its protégé; a power that acts against its own interests and a president who acts contrary to his worldview. We have a protégé whose dependence on the power grows with its effrontery and a power's unbelievable weakness in the face of its protégé's brazenness". (Levy, 2014/10/19)

Conclusion

Given a brief exploration such as this, it is difficult to do justice to the full complexity of the phenomenon of the US-Israeli relationship. It seems there is no end in sight for US support of Israel nor an end to Israel's colonial undertakings. Seeing Israel as a protégé of the US does not preclude the risk that US empire may one day no longer need Israel, and this implies that the US ultimately has the upper hand in the relationship. Losing US support "would be a catastrophe for Israel because Israel has no other friends in the world" (Meerman, 2007).

Explaining the historical intricacies of the US-Israeli relationship was beyond the scope of this chapter, nor did this chapter do justice to explaining the struggles of Palestinians. This chapter should thus be read as an invitation or an encouragement for the reader to seek out more sources themselves. My perspective remains that Israel's attack on Gaza and the Palestinians is a war crime among an ongoing series of war crimes (Urie, 2014). When nationalism and exceptionalism are rampant, the idea that militarized security could be a basis for peace and reconciliation must be questioned.

Notes

1   For an archived list of the members of Concordia University's Board of Directors for the period in which this chapter was written and published, see:
    http://web.archive.org/web/20150831013900/http://www.concordia.ca/about/administration-governance/board-senate/governors/list.html

References

AIPAC. (2014). Our Mission. *AIPAC: America's Pro-Israel Lobby.*
    http://www.aipac.org/about/mission

Aronoff, M.J. (2000). The Americanization of Israeli Politics and Realignment of the Party System. *Israel Studies,* (5)1, 92–127.

Bashir, A-M. (2007). Israel in the U.S. Empire. *Monthly Review,* (58)10.
    http://monthlyreview.org/2007/03/01/israel-in-the-u-s-empire/

Chomsky, N. (1999). *The Fateful Triangle: The United States, Israel, and the Palestinians.* (2nd ed.). Cambridge, MA: South End Press.

———. (2006). The Israel Lobby? *Znet.*
    http://www.chomsky.info/articles/20060328.htm

Levy, G. (2014/10/19). Yankees, Go Home, for the Sake of Peace. *Haaretz,* October 19.
    http://www.haaretz.com/opinion/.premium-1.621429

McCoy, A.W. (2009). *Policing America's Empire: The United States, the Philippines, and the Rise of the Surveillance State.* Madison, WI: University of Wisconsin Press.

Meerman, M. (Director). (2007). The Israel Lobby [Documentary]. The Netherlands: VPRO, Dutch Public Broadcasting.

Mearsheimer, J., & Walt, M. (2006). The Israel Lobby and U.S. Foreign Policy.
http://mearsheimer.uchicago.edu/pdfs/A0040.pdf

Mirrlees, T. (2006). American Soft Power, or American Cultural Imperialism? In Colin Mooers (Eds.), *The New Imperialists: Ideologies of Empire* (pp. 199–228). Oxford: Oneworld.

Rebhun, U., & Waxman, C.I. (2000). The "Americanization" of Israel: A Demographic, Cultural and Political Evaluation. *Israel Studies,* (5)1, 65–91.

Right Web. (2015). American Israel Public Affairs Committee. *Institute for Policy Studies.*
http://rightweb.irc-online.org/profile/American_Israel_Public_Affairs_Committee

Said, E.W. (2001). Palestinians under Siege. In Roane Carey (Ed.), *The New Intifada: Resisting Israel's Apartheid* (pp. 27–44). London: Verso.

Sharpe. J.M. (2015). US Foreign Aid to Israel. Washington, DC: Congressional Research Service.
http://fas.org/sgp/crs/mideast/RL33222.pdf

Silverstein, R. (2014/10/28). What Israel Has to Teach Us. *Tikun Olam*, October 28.
http://www.richardsilverstein.com/2014/10/28/what-israel-has-to-teach-us/

Tilly, C. (1985). War Making and State Making as Organized Crime. In P. Evans, D.

Rueschemeyer & T. Skocpol (Eds.), *Bringing the State Back* (pp. 169–186). Cambridge: Cambridge University Press.

Urie, R. (2013). Capitalism and US Oil Geopolitics. *Counterpunch*, September 20.
http://www.counterpunch.org/2013/09/20/capitalism-and-us-oil-geo-politics/

——————— . (2014). The U.S., Israel and Oil Geopolitics. *Counterpunch*, July 17.
http://www.counterpunch.org/2014/07/17/the-u-s-israel-and-oil-geopolitics/

Vice. (2012). Israel's Radical Left [Documentary]. United States of America: Vice News.

Chapter 2

THE NEW ALLIANCE: GAINING GROUND IN AFRICA

Mandela Coupal Dalgleish

Launched in 2012, the New Alliance for Food Security and Nutrition is a framework designed to facilitate networking, or what Shah (2012) calls "cooperation frameworks" between the private sector, African governments and civil society. The New Alliance comprises 10 African countries and over 100 corporations as well as G8 governments (McKeon, 2014, p. 2) and promises to "help lift 50 million people out of poverty" by 2022 (Shah, 2012) through investments in African agriculture. This is to be accomplished with commitments from African leaders to effect policy reforms to encourage investment opportunities and drive country-led plans on food security; private sector investors; and, donor partners who will broaden the potential for what is being heralded as rapid and sustainable agricultural growth in Africa (McKeon, 2014). According to USAID administrator Shah (2012), everybody benefits from the New Alliance: "With a focus on smallholders, particularly women, the New Alliance brings African nations, international donors and private firms together to unlock real agricultural growth". While it may be true that these actors are coming together in the form of public-private partnerships (PPPs), it is disputable whether the smallholders are truly the beneficiaries.

The New Alliance has been the target of much criticism for being a mechanism whose intent is to promote the interests of multinational corporations, rather than the small-scale farmers it claims to help. This chapter seeks to demonstrate that the New Alliance is part of a greater neoliberal project in which agricultural land and resources in Africa have become the object of a new wave of capitalist expansion, led by the US. We will examine how the New Alliance is creating the conditions for the further impoverishment and disenfranchisement of African farmers, while opening African markets to multinational corporations.

Origins of the New Alliance for Food Security and Nutrition

A number of actors have paved the way toward the foundation of the New Alliance for Food Security and Nutrition, including the private sector, civil society and G8 members. Until the mid-1990s, the US deferred to the major European powers in terms of policy in sub-Saharan Africa, as they still had considerable influence over their former colonies (McCormick, 2006, pp. 344–345). But as opportunities for investment increased in the 1990s in Africa, so did US interest in the continent in what some are now calling the new scramble for Africa (Kerr-Ritchie, 2007). In 2000, the US Congress approved the African Growth and Opportunity Act (AGOA) which aims at reforming African policies to facilitate access to US markets. It supports US corporations by pressuring African countries to open their economies and build free markets, while claiming to reduce poverty by creating opportunities and jobs for Africans. However, after September 11, 2001, AGOA also became a valuable mechanism for strengthening "counter-terrorism" activities (Bush, 2001). As president Bush stated in his speech at the African Growth and Opportunity Forum on October 29, 2001: "People who trade in freedom want to live in freedom" (Government Printing Office, 2004, p. 1316). Still today, AGOA is the cornerstone of US economic policy toward sub-Saharan Africa and remains a significant policy that promotes the trade-not-aid approach to developing countries (McCormick, 2006). This trade legislation was to give preferential access to sub-Saharan countries to the American market while enhancing opportunities for investment on the African continent (McCormick, 2006, pp. 341–342).

Philanthropists also play a large role in international development programs. In 2006, the Bill and Melinda Gates Foundation and the Rockefeller Foundation founded the Alliance for a Green Revolution in Africa (AGRA). AGRA has been chaired by Kofi Annan the former head of the UN since 2007 (Bill & Melinda Gates Foundation [BMGF], 2007, p. 5). Through PPPs, it seeks to modernize African agriculture, improve access farmers have to seeds and develop breeding programs with a focus on small-scale farmers (BMGF, 2007, pp. 7, 8). At the 2009 World Economic Forum (WEF) at Davos, Switzerland, 17 multinational companies laid

down the foundations for a corporate-led approach to food security in the New Vision for Agriculture, which would serve as the
launching pad for the "Grow Africa" partnership platform, which
in turn would become an important actor in the development of
the New Alliance (McKeon, 2014, p. 7).[1] Grow Africa came into
existence at the 2011 WEF under the sponsorship of the African
Union Commission and the New Economic Partnership for African Development (NEPAD). The three main objectives of Grow
Africa are to increase private sector investments in African agriculture, implement PPPs, and promote already existing initiatives
working towards these objectives (Obenland, 2014, p. 9). Together,
AGRA and Grow Africa have made significant steps toward natu-
ralizing corporate agricultural development, a style of development
that the New Alliance has adopted on the African continent under
the guise of African owned and led initiatives (McKeon, 2014). Relationships between these various agencies and programs are
charted in Figure 2.1.

Figure 2.1: Genealogy of the New Alliance for Food Security and Nutrition

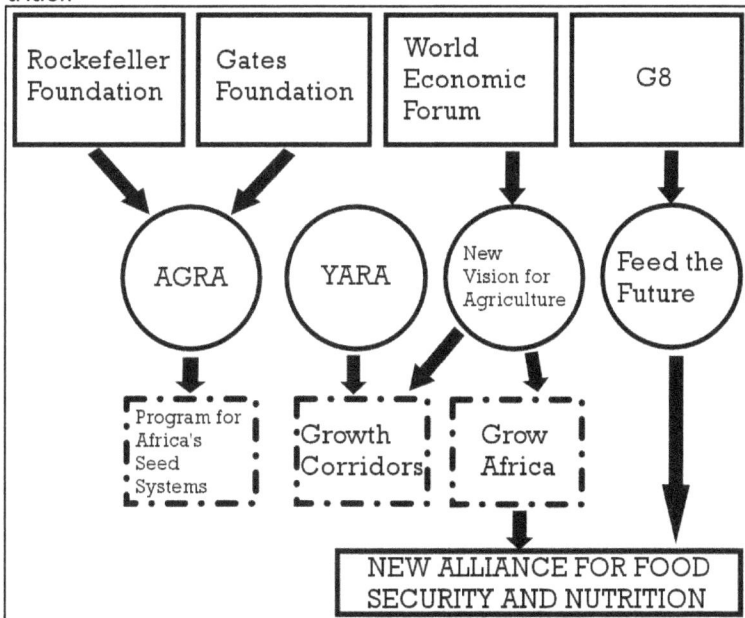

In 2009, at the G8 Summit in L'Aquila, Italy, US president
Obama pushed for a common approach towards massive investments into African agriculture and was able to leverage US 22$ bil-
lion in donor funding to support national agricultural plans in

developing countries (US Department of State [DoS], 2012, p. 1). During the same summit, the five principles that are key to the approach to investment in African agriculture, the "Rome Principles," were articulated: investment in country-led plans and processes; a comprehensive approach to food security that includes support for humanitarian assistance, sustainable agriculture development and nutrition; strategic coordination of assistance; a strong role for multilateral institutions; and, finally, a sustained commitment of financial resources (DoS, 2012, p. 1). The next year, the Feed the Future Initiative was created as the US government's global hunger and food security initiative, which is led by the US Agency for International Development (USAID). Building on Feed the Future, the New Alliance for Food Security and Nutrition was created in 2012 to usher in a new phase of global investment in Africa (White House, 2012). The New Alliance will align itself with the Comprehensive Africa Agriculture Development Program (CAADP), which is an initiative endorsed by the African Union in 2003, whose purpose is to expand national economies through agricultural development (Feed the Future, 2012).

The New Alliance comes from a multitude of similar corporate-led initiatives to industrialize African agriculture. Thus, its principles and objectives are closely related to those of AGRA and Grow Africa. The New Alliance seems to be an effort that concentrates more on sub-Saharan Africa, while strengthening the surrounding initiatives driving towards a corporate-led African green revolution.

Narrative behind the New Alliance

The New Alliance narrative lies within corporate-style agricultural development. Important concepts which are part of the New Alliance approach are modernization and productivism, both being fundamental aspects of the New Alliance narrative (McKeon, 2014, p. 8). Modernization, in the case of the New Alliance, involves the notion that traditional agricultural systems are absolute and must be modernized to fit the standard proposed by the industrial, modernized agricultural system (McKeon, 2014). In fact, the New Alliance has been pushing what it calls Enabling Actions designed to give incentives for the private sector to invest. One such Enabling Action is the Technology Platform, which aims to "assess the availability of improved agricultural technologies, identify constraints to their adoption, and create a roadmap to accelerate the adoption of these technologies among farmers" (McKenna & Shrier, 2013). So-called traditional agricultural systems must progress into modern ones, which generally leaves no room for peasant farmers. Within this modernization discourse, productivism has the single focus of increasing agricultural yield (McKeon, 2014), as expressed by Bill Gates (2013):

> "The metrics here are pretty simple. About three-quarters of the poor who live on these farms need greater productivity, and if they get that productivity we'll see the benefits in income, we'll see it in health, we'll see it in the percentage of their kids who are going off to school. These are incredibly measurable things".

To increase productivity in developing countries, the productivist discourse argues that smallholders using traditional agricultural knowledge should be pushed (or "transitioned") to modern com-modity-based production geared toward international markets (McKeon, 2014). This approach ignores local cultural realities, while also putting the power in the hands of global financiers for whom local sustainability and political autonomy are of little con-cern (McMichael, 2010). Productivism not only fails to consider cultural and social wealth in its discourse, it also excludes other forms of yield from its measurements. By promoting monocultures and genetically modified (GM) crops that require chemical pest and weed control, the productivist scheme in fact increases external in-puts that the farmer must purchase, while eroding local agricultural knowledge and crop diversity (Moahloli, 2009).

Due to the undeniable impact industrial agriculture has on the environment and local ecosystems, New Alliance protagonists have introduced the concept of "sustainable intensification" (Shah, 2014), which when looked at more closely seems to be the exact same approach as productivist industrial agriculture. USAID ad-ministrator Shah (2014) in a speech given at the Chicago Council for Global Affairs said that "game-changing technologies only ac-tually change the game when they reach farmers," that he was "in-spired by the green revolution" and that it is easy to think of new seeds as the "silver bullet". It would seem that the New Alliance is using the word "sustainable" as a way to hide their efforts at indus-trializing the agricultural systems of participating African countries.

Value Chains

Equally fundamental to the New Alliance vision is the concept of value chains, which focuses on marketing rather than production. Value chains are conceived as direct routes that link producers to the eventual consumer (McKeon, 2014), where investment, lending and the necessary infrastructures are created (Yara, 2014). The argument, according to the New Alliance, is that when there is a surplus of a crop in season, local market prices crash, which dissuades farmers from investing in technologies that would improve their yield (Obenland, 2014, p. 10). The preferred way to link farmers to new markets, or in this case the global market, is with value chains (McKeon, 2014, p. 9). Another assumption is that most farmers in sub-Saharan Africa are subsistence farmers, which is no longer the case as most farmers today are linked to diverse local markets: "As argued before, smallholder agriculture is not located outside the markets. There is no point in 'linking' smallholder agriculture to the markets. The central issue is, instead, how to invest and with which stakeholders to increase and keep more value-added at holding and territorial level" (Food and Agriculture Organization [FAO], 2013, p. 73) McMichael (2013) argues that value chain farming, or contract farming, establishes "*chains* of dependency, with smallholders entering markets over which they have no ultimate control, thereby threatening their autonomy on the land" (p. 672). Furthermore, hybrid and GM seeds supported by the value chain "individualise cropping" (McMichael, 2013, p. 679) as opposed to diversified farming. Debt also plays a large role in value chains, as smallholders are expected to buy into expensive inputs such as seeds, fertilizer and pesticides that they cannot afford while bearing the bulk of the risk, thus relying on debt to keep their farms active (McMichael, 2013). The AGRA Program for Africa's Seed Systems (PASS) finances and structures the value chain of hybrid and GM seeds through research and marketing (McKeon, 2014). GRAIN (2007) writes:

> "The logic here is staggering. The idea is to fund public breeders to develop new varieties (as the private sector does not want to do this), to fund private companies to sell these to farmers, and to provide credit to farmers for the purchase of these seeds (because otherwise they cannot pay for them). AGRA is all about creating an effective demand for its own product, prescribing a model of development that is not able to survive on its own".

One of the purposes of value chains is to create demand and dependence on the products sold by multinational corporations (Curtis & Hillary, 2012, p. 1). Once farmers stop saving their own seeds and providing their own inputs, it becomes difficult to regain that control because they are "hooked into use of external inputs through a time-bound, externally-funded programme over whose destiny they have no control" (McKeon, 2014, p. 9).

African countries participating in the New Alliance are making policy changes facilitating fertilizer and seed companies' access to national markets, as well as incentives for investment such as tax reductions. For example, Burkina Faso has committed to "facilitate private sector participation in fertilizer supply contracts" (New Alliance for Food Security & Nutrition [NAFSN], 2013b, p. 5) and to "review the seed legislation to clearly define the role of the private sector in certified seed selection, production and marketing" (NAFSN, 2013b, p. 5), while Ethiopia seeks to "increase private sector participation in seed development, multiplication, and distribution" (NAFSN, 2012a, p. 5). However, farmers in Africa are not asking for the GM and hybrid seeds corporations have to offer because "farmers have developed a very effective seed-saving system that has been in place since times immemorial. This traditional agricultural system allows farmers to access good quality seeds year after year through inter-farmer exchanges and in-crop selections of vigorous seeds" (Coulibaly, 2009, p. 11). As 90% of seeds in Africa are local varieties, the privatization of that component of the value chain is fundamental for maximum profit (McMichael, 2013). Plans to fast-track seed varieties have also been implemented in Tanzania where the "time required to release new varieties of imported seeds from outside the region [is] to be reviewed and benchmarked with international best practices" (NAFSN, 2012d, p. 5). But as McMichael (2013) stated that "fast-tracked seeds dispense with adequate local testing, shifting risk to farmers at the same time as the latter take on debt to buy such commercial varieties" (p. 685). Whether African farmers need the inputs offered by corporations or not, the biotech industry intends nonetheless to penetrate the market, as they have invested immensely in Africa (Bassey, 2009).

Growth Corridors

Led by private corporations, "agricultural growth corridors" combine industrial agricultural production models and value chains to gain maximum "effectiveness". The purpose of growth corridors is to attract investors by converting land into industrial agriculture, and building infrastructure such as roads, railways, ports and processing plants (Paul & Steinbrecher, 2013). Growth corridors were launched by Yara, a fertilizer company, at the 2008 WEF New Vision for Agriculture, "to develop underutilized land areas in Africa that have great potential to enhance food production and economic growth" (Yara, 2014), and have become an official component of the New Alliance framework. What tends to happen instead is smallholders become outgrowers working mainly for multinational corporations, thus reinforcing the dependence of farmers on foreign markets and inputs (Curtis & Hillary, 2012), as stated by EuropAfrica (2013, p. 23):

> "when family farmers enter the commodified market they become part of a commodified chain, losing autonomy and control of the resource base, local markets and jobs. Control is handed to agribusiness, who hold market power through their ability to determine prices for both commercial inputs and produce".

Once again, smallholders and their communities are supposed to be beneficiaries alongside corporations through access to credit, inputs and land rights, yet the "corridor proposals suggest that production is more likely to focus on commodities for international markets, rather than helping local communities practice agriculture for food security/sovereignty, placing them in a role of contract farmers and outgrowers rather than independent food providers" (Paul & Steinbrecher, 2013, pp. 5).

Growth corridors bring together PPPs and the value chain into an effective instrument to foster and promote private investment. The two best known growth corridors are Beira Agricultural Growth Corridor (BAGC) in Mozambique and the Southern Agricultural Growth Corridor of Tanzania (SAGCOT). Corporations intend to open new markets for their proprietary seeds, fertilizer, and machinery along the entire supply chain, thus likely creating the conditions for land appropriation (Paul & Steinbrecher, 2013).

Cooperation Frameworks

The 10 African countries who have joined the New Alliance have signed Cooperation Framework Agreements (CFAs), which include commitments by host countries, G8 nations, public donors and by corporations, national and transnational (Obenland, 2014). The

CFAs are particular to each hosting African country, yet there are important similarities between all of them. African countries are expected to make policy changes to encourage and facilitate private investment, as can be read in the New Alliance (NAFSN, 2012d, p. 3):

> "The Government of Tanzania intends to focus its efforts, in particular, on increasing stability and transparency in trade policy; improving incentives for the private sector; developing and implementing a transparent land tenure policy; developing and implementing domestic seed policies that encourage increased private sector involvement in this area; and aligning the National Food and Nutrition Policy with the National Nutrition Strategy".

This commitment makes it clear that the intention of the Tanzanian government is to help the private sector, "in particular", to penetrate the Tanzanian agricultural market. The discourse surrounding such policy reforms is that smallholders will increase their yields and productivity once they have access to modern irrigation and farming technology, hybrid and GM seeds and synthetic fertilizer (Moahloli, 2009).

However, there is little mention of the commitments governments and investors have made to support smallholders. In nearly all 10 Cooperation Frameworks, the only commitment which invokes smallholders is for the "delivery of tangible benefits to smallholders, including women", which remains a vague statement at best (NAFSN, 2012d, p. 3). Terms such as "inclusive economic growth" and "responsible agricultural investment" are systematically used in every Cooperation Framework, while providing little to no precision as to what these mean (Obenland, 2014, p. 13). However, given the neoliberal orientations of the program, one may surmise that "inclusive" means inclusive of the private sector and large foreign concerns, and responsible means that the investments respond to the interests of the latter parties.

The only country that has an ostensibly different Cooperation Framework is Benin. Benin's commitments seem more focused on the small-scale farmer by working to "improve Benin's agricultural performance so that it is able, in a sustainable way, to ensure food sovereignty for the population and to contribute to the economic and social development of Benin" (NAFSN, 2013a, p. 2). Benin is also the only country to mention gender equality and environmental issues. That being said, Benin will revise tax and regulatory legislation to "encourage and favour investment in the agricultural sector" (NAFSN, 2013a, p. 6). In addition, given that Benin aims at realizing the Millennium Development Goals more rapidly through agricultural development, this too furthers the goals of neoliberal restructuring, as explained in detail by Cammack (2006).

Public-Private Partnerships (PPPs)

The New Alliance is a "multi-stakeholder partnership initiative" which is implemented through public-private partnerships (PPPs), and represents what the Introduction to this volume explains in terms of the "force multipliers" and "connected capitalism" concepts. The World Bank defines PPPs as, "a long-term contract between a private party and a government agency, for providing a public asset or service, in which the private party bears significant risk and management responsibility" (World Bank, 2012, p. 11). PPPs are touted as a win-win for all parties involved since it becomes possible for the state to benefit from the resources of the private sector and transfer some of the risk to them, while most of the accountability rests in the public sector (McKeon, 2014). However, what generally happens is accountability tends to disappear, while corporations avoid most of the risk by imposing changes in policy and regulations that may put them in a position of risk (McKeon, 2014). AGRA and Grow Africa are both precursors of the New Alliance, and both solidified corporate-led development with PPPs as central components to their approach (McKeon, 2014), and they have been criticized for excluding policy frameworks that were formulated jointly with African peasant farmers and producers (Cissokho, 2012).

Similarly observable in the Cooperation Framework Agreements of the New Alliance, the commitments that host countries must make are much more exhaustive, describing how they intend to create an investment-friendly environment for the private sector, while corporations simply need to write Letters of Intent stating that "they will prepare and execute, and intend to advise, shape, and participate in broad, inclusive and sustained private sector consultative mechanisms with the host government" (NAFSN, 2012d, p. 3). What becomes clear is that the brunt of the risk is shouldered by smallholders who are not included in the PPPs, yet they are the ones most affected by changes in regulations and laws regarding agriculture (McKeon, 2014). Smallholders are to rest easy while corporations and governments have their best interests at heart, so it seems.

Amid the diverse actors that are engaged in the New Alliance, the use of the word "partnership" can be misleading, as it creates an image where all actors are equal and conceals any conflict there may be between them (Obenland, 2014, p. 14). It seems clear that the interests of smallholders and those of corporations are at odds, as they both compete for markets, natural resources, agricultural commodities and profit, with corporations having more influence and financial power, thus making the playing field uneven (Obenland, 2014, p. 14). According to the CFA for Nigeria, "G8 members, the Government of Nigeria, and the private sector intend to review their collective performance under this document through an annual review process to be conducted jointly" (NAFSN, 2012c, pp. 3). Smallholders, those who are the intended beneficiaries of the New Alliance, are not included when the time comes for accountability. Furthermore, the notion of accountability within the New Alliance does not mean liability for one's actions when excesses may occur, such as land grabbing, but rather "to review progress toward jointly determined objectives on the basis of jointly determined benchmarks" (NAFSN, 2012c, pp. 3). Each CFA states that part of the joint objectives or "benchmarks" is to help fulfill each host country's CAADP investment plan (NAFSN, 2012c, pp. 3). The agricultural component of NEPAD, the CAADP, is an African-owned development plan to invest in agriculture and orient priorities and programmes nationally. According to Cissokho (2012), the initiatives born from NEPAD and the CAADP, "generated significant hopes and expectations on the part of the social movements and the networks of peasants and producers, who saw agriculture regaining its position at the heart of the political agenda". That statement suggests that the CAADP was initially a much more inclusive initiative for smallholders and that it aligned itself more closely with farmers and their vision for African agriculture. Nonetheless, the CAADP rapidly degenerated (Cissokho, 2012) and due to a top-down approach and inadequate communication between governments and farmers, the National Agricultural Development Programmes, "appeared to be above all occasions for negotiating new aid" (Cissokho, 2012). CAADP became an instrument directed at acquiring external aid rather than relying on domestic resources in an efficient way (McKeon, 2014).

Land Grabs and the New Alliance

On a global scale, there has been a renewed effort to grab productive lands, but this is especially true in Africa. A World Bank report recently estimated that, "approximately 56 million hectares worth of large-scale farmland deals were announced even before the end of 2009," when up to 2008 only 4 million hectares of agricultural land were acquired (Deininger & Byerlee, 2010, p. xiv). The same report also notes that 70% of that new demand has been in Africa, the target area of the New Alliance, where "countries such as Ethiopia, Mozambique, and Sudan have transferred millions of hectares to investors in recent years" (Deininger & Byerlee, 2010, p. xiv).[2] The appropriation of this land is happening jointly with transnational and national corporate investors, governments and local elites for the purpose of producing commodities for international and domestic markets (Margulis, McKeon & Borras, 2013). The United Nations Food and Agriculture Organization (FAO), the Committee on World Food Security (CWFS), the World Bank and the African Union have been working on solutions. In 2012, the CWFS adopted the Voluntary Guidelines on the Responsible Governance of Tenure of Land, Fisheries and Forests, which according to GRAIN (2013, p. 6) are a "bottom-up consultation and are acclaimed for putting emphasis on the rights and needs of women, indigenous peoples and the poor". However, the Voluntary Guidelines are just that, voluntary. The CFAs of the New Alliance "take account" (NAFSN, 2012c, p. 3) of the Voluntary Guidelines, while also taking into account the Principles of Responsible Agricultural Investment (PRAI), which were formulated by the World Bank and International Fund for Agricultural Development (IFAD). The PRAI have been criticized for creating so-called responsible levels of land grabbing instead of working to end them completely (Transnational Institute, 2011). The Transnational Institute (2011) argues that the PRAI is an attempt to create the illusion that power imbalances are lessened between those grabbing the land and those who live and work on it by making land acquisition deals more transparent, while failing to address the problem these land grabs truly pose, that is the loss of the land itself.

As discussed earlier, African countries in the New Alliance, as part of their Cooperation Frameworks, have made commitments with the purpose of reinforcing land right laws and intellectual property rights. In Malawi, the government will release 200,000 hectares of land for large scale commercial agriculture by June 2015 (NAFSN, 2012b); Ghana will produce a database of suitable land for investors with the objective of compiling 10,000 hectares by December 2015 (NAFSN, 2012e); Burkina Faso will "adopt and disseminate a policy framework for resettlement in the developed areas taking into consideration all types of farmers, small and large-scale" (NAFSN, 2013b, p. 6); and, Tanzania will secure land right certificates for smallholders and investors, demarcate village land in the Kilombero district as well as in the SAGCOT region (NAFSN, 2012d). These are some of the policy requirements for investment in the CFAs. While strengthening land rights could have positive consequences in the right context, such as the recognition of women's ownership rights and collectively managed land, it will most likely create the conditions for land grabs (Paul & Steinbrecher, 2013). As Paul & Steinbrecher (2013) put it: "In this context, land titling is only part of the answer, because without the right policy context it can simply lead to land being sold, either voluntarily or under pressure, resulting in concentration of land in the hands of the most powerful players" (p. 11).

Practically speaking, land and its subsequent wealth is being transferred from those who live on it to corporations. Africa is seen as a new frontier for agribusiness corporations, who are committing investments in exchange for risk-free conditions that are undermining the resources and further impoverishing the inhabitants of the land.

Analysis

The New Alliance claims that it will bring 50 million people out of poverty in sub-Saharan Africa, yet it is built upon past initiatives and partnerships that have proven to be detrimental to African farmers. The New Alliance is yet another corporate-led, top-down development initiative that benefits the interests of corporations rather than the people it claims to help. The New Alliance is setting the stage for large agricultural companies to swoop into risk free investment environments that African countries must create, while the smallholders who produce the majority of the national food supply receive little to no benefits. Land tenure laws adopted under the New Alliance are leading to land grabs, laws on inputs such as seeds and fertilizer are causing loss of diversity in crops and farming techniques, while value chains and growth corridors are ushering in a new wave of industrial agriculture. Farmers in Africa have the agricultural knowledge and the genetic diversity (seeds) that they need to produce their own food in a sustainable way while generating enough profit to sustain themselves. As Zitto Kabwe stated in an article by Provost, Ford & Tran (2014): "It will be like colonialism. Farmers will not be able to farm until they import, linking farmers to [the] vulnerability of international prices. Big companies will benefit. We should not allow that".

Notes

1   According the World Economic Forum, the "New Vision" project is led by 28 of its "global partner companies," including: Agco Corporation, Archer Daniels Midland, BASF, Bayer AG, Bunge Limited, Cargill, CF Industries, The Coca-Cola Company, Diageo, DuPont, General Mills, Heineken NV, Kraft Foods, Louis Dreyfus Commodities, Maersk, Metro AG, Monsanto Company, Nestlé, PepsiCo, Rabobank, Royal DSM, SABMiller, Swiss Reinsurance Company Ltd., Syngenta, The Mosaic Company, Unilever, Wal-Mart Stores Inc., and Yara International (Paul & Steinbrecher, 2013, p. 2).

2   While Margulis, McKeon, and Borras (2013) posit that the land grab phenomena is most clearly discernible in the history of imperialism—they do not see the current land grabs as fitting within the classic North-South axis of prior imperialism. However, as these numbers demonstrate, there is a definite North-South axis that persists; moreover, the New Alliance itself stems from the actions and decisions of agencies and states of the global North, such as the Rockefeller Foundation, the Gates Foundation, and the G8, which diminishes the "polycentric" emphasis which Margulis, McKeon, and Borras, unsuccessfully labour to construct.

References

Bassey, N. (2009). AGRA—A Blunt Philanthropic Arrow. In A. Mittal & M. Moore (Eds.), *Voices From Africa: African Farmers and Environmentalists Speak Out Against a New Green Revolution in Africa* (pp. 16–17). Oakland, CA: The Oakland Institute.

Bill and Melinda Gates Foundation (BMGF). (2007). Annual Report. http://www.gatesfoundation.org/~/media/GFO/Documents/Annual-Reports/2007Gates-Foundation-Annual-Report.pdf?la=en

Bush, G.W. (2001). U.S., Africa Strengthening Counter-Terrorism and Economic Ties: Remarks to the African Growth and Opportunity Forum. Washington, DC: US Department of State.

Cammack, P. (2006). U.N. Imperialism: Unleashing Entrepreneurship in the Developing World. In Colin Mooers (Ed.), *The New Imperialists: Ideologies of Empire* (pp. 229–260). Oxford: Oneworld.

Cissokho, M. (2012). Letter from African Civil Society Critical of Foreign Investment in African Agriculture at G8 Summit. *GRAIN*, May 23.
http://www.grain.org/es/bulletin_board/entries/4507-letter-from-african-civil-society-critical-of-foreign-investment-in-african-agriculture-at-g8-summit

Coulibaly, I. (2009). GMOs Do Not Address the Needs or Concers of African Farmers. In A. Mittal, & M. Moore (Eds.), *Voices From Africa: African Farmers and Environmentalists Speak Out Against a New Green Revolution in Africa* (pp. 11–12). Oakland, CA: The Oakland Institute.

Curtis, M., & Hillary, J. (2012). The Hunger Games: How DFID Support for Agribusiness is Fueling Poverty in Africa. London: War on Want.
http://www.curtisresearch.org/The%20Hunger%20Games,%20December%202012.pdf

Deininger, K. & Byerlee, D. (2010). Rising Global Interest in Farmland: Can It Yield Sustainable and Equitable Results? Washington, DC: The World Bank.

EuropAfrica. (2013). Family Farmers for Sustainable Food Systems: A Synthesis of Reports by African Farmers' Regional Networks on Models of Food Production, Consumption and Markets. *EuropAfrica*.
http://www.europafrica.info/file_download/86/FamilyFarmers4SustFoodSystems_europAfrica_EN_web.pdf

Feed the Future. (2012). G8 Cooperation Framework to Support the "New Alliance for Food Security and Nutrition" in Tanzania. Washington, DC: Feed the Future.
http://feedthefuture.gov/sites/default/files/resource/files/Tanzania_web.pdf

Food and Agriculture Organization (FAO). (2013). Investing in Smallholder Agriculture for Food Security: A Report by the High Level Panel of Experts on Food Security and Nutrition, June 13. Rome: Committee on World Food Security, United Nations Food and Agriculture Organization.
http://www.fao.org/3/a-i2953e.pdf

Gates, B. (2013). Agricultural Productivity is Key to Reducing World Poverty. *Farmers Feeding the World*.
http://www.agweb.com/article/bill_gates_agricultural_productivity_is_key_to_reducing_world_poverty/

GRAIN. (2007). A New Green Revolution for Africa? *GRAIN*, December 17.
http://www.grain.org/article/entries/74-a-new-green-revolution-for-africa

————— . (2013). Modernising African Agriculture: Who Benefits? GRAIN, May 17.
https://www.grain.org/bulletin_board/entries/4727-modernising-african-agriculture-who-benefits

Government Printing Office (GPO). (2004). Public Papers of the Presidents of the United States, George W. Bush, 2001, Book 2, July 1 to December 31, 2001. Washington, DC: Government Printing Office.

Kerr-Ritchie, J. (2007). The New Scramble for Africa. *Nature, Society &*

Thought, 20(2), 205–212.

Margulis, M.E.; McKeon, N.; & Borras, S.M. (2013). Land Grabbing and Global Governance: Critical Perspectives. *Globalizations*, 10(1), 1–23.

McCormick, R. (2006). The African Growth and Opportunity Act: The Perils of Pursuing African Development through U.S. Trade Law. *Texas International Law Journal*, 41(2), 339–384.

McKenna, T., & Shrier, J. (2013). A Year of Progress under the New Alliance for Food Security and Nutrition. *Feed the Future*, May 30.
http://feedthefuture.gov/article/year-progress-under-new-alliance-food-security-and-nutrition

McKeon, N. (2014). The New Alliance for Food Security and Nutrition: A Coup for Corporate Capital? TNI Agrarian Justice Program, Policy Paper. Amsterdam: Transnational Institute (TNI).
http://www.tni.org/files/download/the_new_alliance.pdf

McMichael, P. (2010). Contesting Development: Critical Struggles for Social Change. New York: Routledge.

——————— . (2013). Value Chain Agriculture and Debt Relations: Contradictory Outcomes. *Third World Quarterly*, 34(4), 671–690.

Moahloli, M. (2009). Are New Technologies an Answer to the Needs of Small-Scale Farmers?. In A. Mittal & M. Moore (Eds.), *Voices From Africa: African Farmers and Environmentalists Speak Out Against a New Green Revolution in Africa* (pp. 30–31). Oakland, CA: The Oakland Institute.

New Alliance for Food Security and Nutrition (NAFSN). (2012a). G8 Cooperation Framework to Support the New Alliance for Food Security & Nutrition in Ethiopia.
https://www.gov.uk/government/uploads/system/uploads/attachment_data/file/208053/new-alliance-progress-report-coop-framework-ethiopia.pdf

——————— . (2012b). Country Cooperation Framework to support the New Alliance for Food Security & Nutrition in Malawi.
https://www.gov.uk/government/uploads/system/uploads/attachment_data/file/208059/new-alliance-progress-report-coop-framework-malawi.pdf

——————— . (2012c). Cooperation Framework to Support the New Alliance for Food Security & Nutrition in Nigeria.
https://www.gov.uk/government/uploads/system/uploads/attachment_data/file/208216/new-alliance-progress-report-coop-framework-nigeria.pdf

——————— . (2012d). G8 Cooperation Framework to Support the New Alliance for Food Security & Nutrition in Tanzania.
https://www.gov.uk/government/uploads/system/uploads/attachment_data/file/208218/new-alliance-progress-report-coop-framework-tanzania.pdf

——————— . (2012e). G8 Cooperation Framework to Support the New Alliance for Food Security & Nutrition in Ghana.
https://www.gov.uk/government/uploads/system/uploads/attachment_data/file/208055/new-alliance-progress-report-coop-framework-ghana.pdf

——————— . (2013a). G8 Cooperation Framework to Support The New Alliance for Food Security and Nutrition in Benin.
https://www.gov.uk/government/uploads/system/uploads/attachment_data/file/22

4984/Cooperation-framework-Benin.pdf

——————— . (2013b). Cooperation Framework to Support the New Alliance for Food Security & Nutrition in Burkina Faso. https://www.gov.uk/government/uploads/system/uploads/attachment_data/file/20 8030/new-alliance-progress-report-coop-framework-burkina-faso.pdf

Obenland, W. (2014). Corporate influence through the G8 New Alliance for Food Security and Nutrition in Africa. *Global Policy Forum*. https://www.globalpolicy.org/images/pdfs/GPFEurope/Corporate_Influence_throu gh_the_G8NA.pdf

Paul, H., & Steinbrecher, R. (2013). African Agricultural Growth Corridors and the New Alliance for Food Security and Nutrition: Who Benefits, Who Loses? *EcoNexus*, June. http://www.econexus.info/sites/econexus/files/African_Agricultural_Growth_Corri dors_&_New_Alliance_-_EcoNexus_June_2013.pdf

Provost, C.; Ford, L.; & Tran, M. (2014/2/18). G8 New Alliance condemned as new wave of colonialism in Africa. *The Guardian*, February 18. http://www.theguardian.com/global-development/2014/feb/18/g8-new-alliance-condemned-new-colonialism

Shah, R. (2012). Remarks by Administrator Rajiv Shah at the New Alliance Event, September 26. Washington, DC: United States Agency for International Development.

——————— . (2014). Remarks by Administrator Rajiv Shah at the Chicago Council for Global Affairs, May 22. Washington, DC: United States Agency for International Development.

Transnational Institute. (2011). It's Time to Outlaw Land Grabbing, Not to Make it "Responsible"! Transnational Institute. https://www.tni.org/files/RAI-EN-1.pdf

US Department of State (DoS). (2012). L'Aquila Food Security Initiative (AFSI): 2012 Report. Washington, DC: US Department of State. http://www.state.gov/documents/organization/202922.pdf

White House. (2012). Fact Sheet: G-8 Action on Food Security and Nutrition. Washington, DC: The White House. https://www.whitehouse.gov/the-press-office/2012/05/18/fact-sheet-g-8-action-food-security-and-nutrition

World Bank. (2012). Public-Private Partnerships: Reference Guide Version 1.0. Washington, DC: The World Bank.

Yara. (2014). Agricultural Growth Corridors. http://yara.com/sustainability/how_we_engage/africa_engagement/growth_corridors /index.aspx

Chapter 3

COCAINE BLUES:
THE COST OF DEMOCRATIZATION UNDER
PLAN COLOMBIA

Robert Majewski

C olombia has had continuous relations with the US since
1822, yet US interest in the country increased during the
Cold War era when insurgent groups emerged and became
a threat to the kind of democratic model that is preferred
by the US (Bureau of Western Hemisphere Affairs, 2013). Particularly, the *Fuerzas Armadas Revolucionarias Colombianas* (Revolutionary
Armed Forces of Colombia, or FARC) has been the stated source
of worries for US officials. The FARC was seen as a threat to the
established political order and has continuously been accused of
having a direct link to drug production operations (Labrousse,
2005). Following decades of covert and overt interventions justified
by counterinsurgency missions and anti-drug campaigns, US president Bill Clinton and Colombian head of state Andrés Pastrana
combined their efforts into a plan that aimed to eradicate drug
production once and for all and stabilize the Colombian economy
while strengthening the country's democracy (Council on Foreign
Relations [CFR], 2000). Plan Colombia was introduced in 2000 and
was unsuccessful in attaining its goals for the reduction of drug
production, yet it has had repercussions on the economic, political
and social spheres of the country. Economically, it assures a free
flow of capital between the global South and the global North, ensuring that Colombia enters successfully into the free market, thus
pleasing US investors and aligning with imperialist interests. What
US foreign policy fosters, as perpetuated under Obama, is "a complex balance between stability and instability that maintains the region's overall dependence and, therefore, its status as a source of

U.S. wealth and power" (Delgado-Ramos & Romano, 2011, p. 93). Politically, it ensures through militarization a strong counterinsurgency program for fighting actors that pose a threat to the US-backed model of democracy and the neoliberal agenda (Delgado-Ramos & Romano, 2011; Mondragón, 2007; Villar & Cottle, 2011). More tangibly, fumigation of peasant crops and massive displacement have also affected the population and can be interpreted as a symptom of Plan Colombia and more generally, imperialism itself (Ballvé, 2009).

In this chapter I will therefore argue that US-Colombian relations have been shaped by the imperialist project of the US: through the humanitarian discourse of help and cooperation, and the battle against the FARC under the umbrella of the "war on drugs," the US has legitimized its military intervention in Colombia to ensure its legitimacy and its presence in South America. Furthermore, through US-style democratization and the implementation of the rule of law, the US has ensured in Colombia a safer haven for foreign capital and opened the doors for the implementation of a free market system.

Setting the Scene: Colombian Internal Conflict

Colombia's geographic position makes it a strategic point of control over the South American continent and more particularly its neighbouring countries. Indeed, bordering Venezuela, Peru, Ecuador, Bolivia and Brazil, Colombia presents itself as the entry way to South America and the launching point of many US military operations in the region (Salazar & Acosta, 2001). Furthermore, in the entire region and also in Colombia, since the end of WWII leftist movements have blossomed due to disenchantment with the promises of industrialization and the burgeoning national security states, and offered alternatives that took into account peasant struggles and the demands of the impoverished masses. The Cold War era saw a dichotomy between the growing capitalist force of the US and the communist politics of the Soviet Union. So-called "Third World" countries witnessed a rise of revolutionary movements that offered alternatives to right wing politics. An example of this is the FARC, which was formed as a result of peasant military organization that had previously fought during *La Violencia* (Metelits, 2010, p. 93). This period of violence (1948-1966) cost more than 200,000 lives, and was a result of the political confrontations between the Conservative and Liberal Parties (Sánchez in

Metelits, 2010, p. 88). Policies on land issues were heavily contested, which led to the dramatic turning point of the assassination of Liberal party member Jorge Eliécer Gaitán. Gaitán had been pushing for land reforms and wealth redistribution, causes that gained popularity among the masses (Metelits, 2010, p. 88). During this period, peasants were forced to leave their lands and many of them joined guerrilla groups that took up arms to fight against large landowners (Metelits, 2010, p. 91). These groups gained political importance as they grew into a menace for the governments in place. In 1964, the FARC was officially formed and quickly established its political legitimacy as a revolutionary group defending peasant rights and as a force fighting against the political elite.

US officials rapidly acknowledged that the FARC was a force to be reckoned with and that the political power they held was a direct menace to US imperial dominance in Colombia that also had implications for the rest of Latin America. Parallel to the rise of the FARC, narco-traffickers were also gaining ground. Indeed, the 1980s in Colombia were characterized by a rise in cocaine production along with drug traffickers finding their way into Colombian political, financial and legal institutions (Villar & Cottle, 2011, p. 55). The lines were blurred between the government and the drug cartels; the new "narco-state" opened the way for the "narco-bourgeoisie" whose interests were in turn protected by the Colombian state. Having acquired great wealth through the drug economy, this new economic class was the main investor in Colombia. The money generated was subsequently laundered in US financial institutions (Villar & Cottle, 2011, p. 55). Yet another important actor arose to protect the drug cartels: the paramilitary forces created by the drug cartels themselves were an even more violent alternative to the Colombian army, both having similar interests in protecting the dominant class. Opposing these groups were the FARC who were targeted and depicted as a threat by the governments of Colombia and the US.

The Colombian military in the 1970s and 1980s was funded in large part by the US government. The military training and assistance that the US provided were allegedly used to counter political opponents such as the FARC rather than the emerging drug lords (Villar & Cottle, 2011, p. 45; also see "foreign internal defense" in the Introduction to this volume). The CIA on the other hand played an important role in centralizing drug traffickers through meetings that they organized in Colombia resulting in the creation of the important Medellín drug cartel led by the infamous Pablo Escobar (Villar & Cottle, 2011, p. 47). Escobar's rule did not last long as he was killed in 1993 and replaced by Carlos Castaño from the Calí drug cartel, also with the help of the CIA (Villar & Cottle, 2011, p. 78). This change of actors further engrained drug production into the Colombian political system and opened the door for the strengthening of relations between drug cartels and US agents (Villar & Cottle, 2011, p. 79). Seven years later, Plan Colombia was authorized by Bill Clinton, legitimizing and authorizing US interventions in Colombia under the same banner of the drug war.

Historical Development of Plan Colombia

Former Colombian president Andrés Pastrana Arango introduced in 1998 a national development plan called "Cambio para construir la paz" (Change to construct peace). This plan aimed to promote the economic, social and environmental conditions necessary to achieve national peace (Salazar & Acosta, 2001, p. 44). In the following year a second version of the plan was proposed and included elements of political reform and projects for alternative agricultural development for coca producers. In September of the same year, the third draft was presented but was skewed significantly toward responding to US internets in the region. Rather than social development, the emphasis was put on exposing the links between drug production and rebel groups such as the FARC (Salazar & Acosta, 2001, p. 45). Furthermore, strengthening Colombia's armed forces and assuring the rule of law were also put in the foreground as solutions for resolving the country's political crisis (Avilés, 2008, p. 418). As Avilés (2008) argues, these changes were in fact "pragmatic shifts in emphasis in order to obtain US support" (p. 419). It is in this context that we can understand the fourth draft of the plan, officially named "Plan Colombia" and backed by the US. Officially the Plan promoted, "an integrated strategy to meet the most pressing challenges confronting Colombia today—promoting the peace process, combating the narcotics industry, reviving the Colombian economy, and strengthening the democratic pillars of Colombian society" (CFR, 2000).

Economic Democratization

"The current round of imperialism," writes Mooers (2006, p. 5), "has as its goal the export and entrenchment of capitalist social-property relations throughout the world; it is about the universalization of capitalism". When reading Plan Colombia's objectives of "reviving the Colombian economy, and strengthening the democratic pillars of Colombian society" (CFR, 2000), there is a need to delve deeper into the true meaning of these objectives. The first matter of interest will be the latter part of this objective (reviving the Colombian economy). In order for foreign corporations to be interested in Colombia as a potential ground for investment, it must be perceived as "safe". As Wood (2006, p. 14) notes, "a stable global system of multiple states" is required "to maintain the kind of order and predictability that capitalism—more than any other social form—needs". The promotion of democracy in the war on drugs can also be understood as part of the expansion of international trade and implementation of a free-market economy (Avilés, 2008, p. 415). Yet, as Wood further argues, benefits are to be had from the instability of national economies, permitting exploitation of resources and cheap labour (Wood, 2006, p. 14). There is thus a subtle negotiation of security/insecurity that takes places to maximize foreign investment, while upholding conditions of constant instability.

In the case of Plan Colombia, it is therefore not surprising to find investors and representatives of transnational corporations (TNCs) on boards and committees selected to draw up policies of intervention (Avilés, 2008). An example of this is the Council on Foreign Relations (CFR), whose members have upheld an agenda directed towards capitalist globalization and economic development in the developing world (Avilés, 2008, p. 420). Domhoff explains that the "CFR obtains most of its resources from contributions from TNCs and business leaders make up the greatest proportion if its memberships" (as cited in Avilés, 2008, p. 420).

The case of Occidental Petroleum (OP), a US-based oil company, demonstrates the nature of the priorities of the US in Plan Colombia. The Department of Putumayo in the south of Colombia was chosen as a pilot zone for testing the efficiency of Plan Colombia. The region was indeed controlled mainly by the FARC and had a high concentration of coca crops, yet it was also a region in which the US had many interests. OP was also developing an exploration project in this region where a high density of natural resources can be found (Salazar & Acosta, 2001, p. 46). The company had been subject to attacks throughout the 1990s and reached out to the US government for help. OP spent US $8.6 million between 1996 and 2000 in lobbying the US government to boost its military presence in Colombia. The fruit of this investment was seen some years later when President George W. Bush

granted the company a US $100 million subsidy for forming a pro-
tection brigade for the company's pipeline (Avilés, 2008, p. 425).
As argued by Panitch and Gindin (2006, p. 21), contemporary US
imperialism,

> "is characterized above all by economic penetration and informal
> incorporation of other capitalist states, but at the same time it
> both permits and requires imperial policing and military
> intervention in a 'rogue state' which has not been incorporated
> into the neoliberal capitalist order".

While Colombia as a nation-state was never identified by the US as
a "rogue state" (reserving such terms for outright "enemies" such
as North Korea), Colombia was however deemed insecure and in
need of policing, because of internal "rogue" elements such as the
FARC. The military aid sponsored by USAID was intended for
that matter. Speaking in US terms, what renders a state unsafe or
"rogue" is amongst other things "terrorism". To quote the US Bureau of Public Affairs (2008): "strong law enforcement institutions,
rooted in democratic principles and protective of human rights, are
vital to preventing transnational threats, from drugs to organized
criminal activity to terrorism". Thus it can be understood that an
effective way of fighting terrorism is promoting democracy.

After 9/11, counter-terrorism became a paramount preoccupation for the US government. Moving from a counter-narcotics intervention in Colombia, US officials explicitly described Plan
Colombia as a counter-insurgency initiative that would defeat the
FARC (Elhawary, 2011, p. S393; see Figure 3.1). Groups such as
the FARC would no longer be framed as guerrilla movements, but
would instead be described as, "terrorist movements financed by
the drug trafficking" (Pizarro & Gaitán, 2006, p. 61). Direct combat against such groups could thus be easily legitimized by the US
state (Pizarro & Gaitán, 2006, p. 62). In this process of demonization, the FARC was described by Francis X. Taylor, coordinator
for the State Department's Office of Anti-Terrorism, as the "most
dangerous international terrorist organization based in the hemisphere" (Pizarro & Gaitán, 2006, p. 62). The perception by the
former Colombian President Álvaro Uribe that the guerrilla group
moved away from its formally promoted political motivations towards an exclusively profit-oriented logic led to the cessation of
negotiations and to an openly counter-terrorist action plan (Elhawary, 2011, p. S394). By framing the FARC as a terrorist group, the
US also succeeded in putting through the idea that the intervention
in Colombia was an issue of national security. Indeed, military in-

tervention abroad is often justified by problems at home, as it is the case with Colombia: "the social consequence of drug abuse in the USA (crime, unemployment, addiction, etc.) has earned it a place as a national security threat and US hegemony allows its perceived national security interests to dictate counter-narcotics policy for Latin America" (Avilés, 2008, p. 411).

Figure 3.1: Colin Powell Supporting Plan Colombia

Then US Secretary of State, retired General Colin Powell is shown on an official visit to Colombia in 2004 in support of "Plan Colombia" (Photo: The White House.)

Democracy was to be instated as an effective way to fight against the "terrorist" group that controlled a considerable part of Colombian territory containing valuable natural resources and bordering with neighbouring countries (Pizarro & Gaitán, 2006, p. 56). These territories were also framed as "lawless," where the state's tentacles could not reach (Marcella, 2009, p. 13). The US thus vowed to bring law and order to Colombian society, by the same channels instituting the legal means to implant their dreamed-of democratic system.

Rule of Law

A major objective that the US aimed to achieve in its intervention in Colombia was the implementation of the rule of law. In its quest of creating a US-style justice system, the US has provided over US $150 million in aid in order to create conflict resolution centres, training of public defenders and other juridical activities (US Government Accountability Office [GAO], 2008, p. 57). As righteous as they may seem, these measures fall under the banner of cultural imperialism at the juridical level, where Colombia is perceived to be a lawless society in need of the correct (i.e., US-constructed) judicial reform. It is indeed not easy to oppose such an ideal, for "the rule of law is the kind of idea that everybody places on a sacred pedestal, protected and defended on almost every side" (Mattei, 2010, p. 91). As Mattei further explains, the notion of the rule of law is entirely malleable, ranging from the protection of the weak and exploited to the defence of transnational companies that have acquired land thanks to privatization measures (2010, p. 92). Indeed, in the Colombian case, "the rule of law" has been understood as "acceptance of investment guarantees, protection of property rights, and the sanctity of contracts" (Mattei, 2010, p. 93). The idea is understood as both the protection of (individual) human rights and of property rights, where capital accumulation through possession of property is to lead to liberty on the personal level, liberty here being understood, amongst other things, as the freedom of consumption. In the imperialist and neoliberal logic, human rights are presented as synonymous to capital accumulation and supersede other freedoms such as the protection of basic human needs. This logic leads to scenarios where for example natural resources in the "Third World" are being privatized by transnational companies who are protected by property rights (Hanieh, 2006). Unfortunately for "basic human needs," the rule of law has been in most cases understood as the legal defense of the free market, capital accumulation and liberal democracy (Waldon, 2011, p. 3).

The prestige around the ideal stems, at least in part, from its seemingly benevolent and successful implementers— the US, for example—who at least appear to have a strong and well-rooted constitution and whose idealized democracy was historically upheld by law and order (Mattei, 2010, p. 91). The US has emerged as a hub for lawyers, where US law schools are highly praised worldwide and the perception of the US lawyer in many older Hollywood movies is one of prestige, integrity, and an intrepid determination to get at the truth. Law is so deeply engraved in US (high) society, such that lawyers "enjoy a legal culture and discourse that is broader than jurisdictional limits" (Mattei, 2003, p. 391). Mattei (2003) further frames the rule of law as an *imperial law*, one that is a dominant layer of the world-wide legal system whose best ally and vehicle is predatory economic globalization (p. 383). In the case of Colombia, the implementation of the imperial rule of law was not entirely "forced" upon the country in any direct sense. Indeed, a professional elite was already in place to back such hegemonic policies that they internalized beforehand as being in their own interests (Avilés , 2008, p. 413). Though this measure of Plan Colombia was aimed at giving resources to those "in need of law," Ginsburg (2011) frames the issue in the opposite way, "even if a country would be better off without support, the ruling coalition will certainly not be. There is little political incentive to 'graduate'" (p. 229).

In short, "the rule of law" is the discourse that legitimizes a given international dynamic of power (Mattei, 2003, p. 386). In our present system, where capitalism grew and is still growing towards world economic domination, nations must "change the law according to western standards in order to get access to the international market and to remain economically viable" (Mattei, 2003, p. 383). Yet to avoid forceful implementation of capitalism and shun resistance, the necessary tools must be in place:

> "Imperialism requires an 'imperial ideal', a stronger ideological apparatus that can be reached only by means of strong and well-developed 'ideological' institutions. The ideals of a global market, of international human rights, of freedom throughout the world, and most notably of the 'rule of law' perform this ideological role". (Mattei, 2003, p. 402)

Although there is ideological acceptance from the elite spheres of society, the rest of the population also has to be convinced, this being often done in a forceful and thus unconvincing manner.

The US-Colombia Free Trade Agreement

Flowing from the installation of the "rule of law," in 2012 the US and Colombia officially implemented a free-trade agreement or FTA (Embassy of Colombia, 2013). Negotiations had commenced in 2006, yet before signing the official version Colombia was forced to comply with a number of US demands for securing the ground (Office of the United States Trade Representative [USTR], 2014). Many issues since 2006 arose in the public sphere addressing concerns about the economic disadvantage that Colombia had relative to the US, namely, US farmers benefit from government subsidies giving them an unfair advantage in the context of international trade, so that products exported from the US end up being cheaper than those produced locally. It also has the effect of inhibiting exports coming from Colombia to the US (Garay Salamanca et al., 2009, p. 27). In short, while the susbsidized competitiveness of US farmers is rising, Colombian *campesinos'* vulnerability is also on the rise. A brief glance at the past can be relevant in predicting the future. The economic neoliberal transitions that affected Colombia in the 1980s and 1990s and the country's steady integration into the global capitalist market caused a severe drop in coffee prices, the main national export, and forced many agrarian workers to turn to the cultivation of coca crops (Avilés, 2008, p. 417). The peasant movement that is voicing its concerns with the FTA in Colombia is gaining ground and is slowly being recognized by the government as one that has legitimate concerns. Nevertheless, the Colombian state continues to fail to satisfy the demands formulated by peasants. Notably, most peasants are concerned with the impact that the FTA will have on local economies and rural Colombia as a whole. As one farmer testifies, importing a chicken from the US is cheaper than one that is Colombian-raised (Ospina-Valencia, 2013). Local groups such as the *Red Colombiana de Acción Frente al Libre Comercio* (the Colombian Action Network against Free Trade, or RCAFLC) are organizing both on the ground but also producing academic work with the aim of trying to find alternatives to the FTA, showing that solutions are being developed from within (RCAFLC, 2014).

With farmers relying on their crops as their main source of income, the FTA is directly inhibiting the chances of farmers to live off the land. Furthermore, Law 9.70 under the intellectual property rights integrated in the FTA, forced farmers to buy seeds from state approved companies and criminalized keeping seeds from one year to another. This is a clear example of how the "rule of law" can act to the detriment of lower classes and disregards traditional understanding of agriculture (for related and parallel cases in Africa, see chapter 2 in this volume). A series of protests and strikes were held in the country to oppose the commodification of seeds. The strikes succeeded in suspending law 9.70. These events pay tribute to the grassroots mobilization that can take place locally to solve local problems (Charles, 2013). The case of the intellectual property rights law implemented by the US with the FTA serves as a clear example of the contradiction between one of the legislative acts under the FTA and Plan Colombia. On one side, the US promotes rural development and alternative economies to coca crops through Plan Colombia, yet it then does the contrary through its actions with the FTA. Indigenous and Afro-Colombian peasants were particularly concerned with the passing of the FTA as it would impact the relative autonomy from which they benefited and would change the way in which they relate to their crops and their land (US Office on Colombia, 2011). If small farmers see their harvest devalued by competing foreign products, they will have to turn to alternative ways of subsistence. Again a look to the past is telling of possible outcomes of such aggressive legislation. The alternative economic development proposed by Plan Colombia consisted in subsidizing mega agro-projects such as the palm oil industry (Mondragón, 2007, p. 24). Large land owners were encouraged to partner up with *campesinos* and offer them an alternative to coca production. The benefits for the US of encouraging palm oil production in Colombia can be explained by the fact that half the production is exported to the US and Europe (Mondragón, 2007, p. 26). Furthermore, it has been shown that palm oil companies such as Urapalm have not only cultivated stolen land previously taken away from peasants by narco-paramilitaries, but have been an effective way for narco-traffickers to launder their drug money (Mondragón, 2007). Indeed, paramilitaries have forcefully removed peasants from their land to make way for coca cultivation (Quintero & Posada, 2013, p. 374), but they have also been displaced by "paramilitaries paid by rich African oil palm growers, [who are] intent on expanding their holdings and increasing their production for world markets" (Escobar, 2004, p. 19). Along with fumigation, coca production and palm oil plantations have caused massive displacement of rural people in Colombia, as shown by Escobar (2004, p. 19):

> "It is little known that Colombia today has about three million internally displaced people, constituting one of the largest refugee crises in the world. Over 400,000 people were internally displaced in 2002 alone. A disproportionate percentage of the displaced are Afro-Colombians and indigenous people, which makes patently clear a little discussed aspect of imperial globality, namely, its racial and ethnic dimension. One aspect of this is of course that, as in the case of the Pacific, ethnic minorities often inhabit territories rich in natural resources that are now coveted by national and transnational capital".

In light of the history of previous measures of economic liberalization and the regrettable realities that vulnerable populations have to face in the name of development, it is doubtful that the FTA could ever bring a viable solution for Colombian problems. It is far more likely that it will only benefit the higher classes of society and exploit those who seem to have less and less. Briefly, the US is benefiting economically from palm oil plantations and the fact that such companies are indirectly fuelling drug production does not seem to be understood as any sort of contradiction with Plan Colombia that is financing and promoting such operations.

Militarization and the Privatization of the Conflict

Borrowing from one of Louis Althusser's basic theses, we can understand that when the ideological state apparatus is not sufficient in fully inculcating the ideas it authorizes, use of force is called upon to enforce hegemony (Althusser, 2006). Most of the funding for Plan Colombia was directed to military and police assistance. With its aid, the US contributed greatly in militarizing the Colombian conflict. Indeed, between 1997 and 2003, the military component of US aid to Colombia amounted to over US $2.36 billion. These funds were directed towards the education and training of the Colombian army by US forces (Pizarro & Gaitán, 2006, p. 68). Yet as the US is pouring money into the Colombian military it seems to be somewhat disregarding the fact that this army has a long history of collaboration with the Colombian paramilitary organizations, and by the same token, major narco-traffickers (Avilés, 2008, p. 412). In addition, Private Military Security Companies (PMSCs) are embedded with the Colombian military to enforce laws and carry out military missions. As noted by Peacock, US $3.1 billion were spent by the US government between 2005 and 2009 on counter-narcotics programs in Latin America, DynCorp being one of the principal beneficiaries receiving more than US $1.1 billion for its operations in Latin America (Hobson, 2014, pp. 1443, 1444). DynCorp was one of 25 PMSCs acting in the country by 2006 (Hobson, 2014, p. 1444). The intervention in Colombia was framed as a testing ground from which lessons were to be learned regarding challenges that the US government would face elsewhere (US Embassy, Bogota [USEB], 2009/10/23) this particularly applying to private military contractors (Hobson, 2014, p. 1442).

The secrecy of these companies is highly praised by the governments that contract them, especially as the media coverage of their activities is fairly limited and they are not held accountable to the same laws that state militaries are—they can even benefit from total immunity (Hobson, 2014, p. 1446). The results of this immunity are found in cases of various abuses of which DynCorp employees have been accused, such as rape, recording pornographic material with minors, and the importation of bottles of liquid laced with cocaine (Hobson, 2014, p. 1446).

The advantage of PMSCs is that they can be employed by anyone with the resources to do so; the higher bidders always get the upper hand. With a large amount of capital at their disposal, the US state and transnational corporations have not hesitated to employ PMSCs to defend their properties and carry out missions which often result in harmful impacts for civilians, such as aerial fumigation (for a different face of Coca-Cola's "connected capitalism," as discussed in the Introduction to this volume, see Foster [2010] who highlights the company's use of paramilitaries in Colombia). Indeed the collaboration between PMSCs, paramilitary groups and the US government in securing zones where companies like OP had interests because of their energy and mineral-rich territory has been shown (Ramírez Cuellar, 2005, p. 36). These heavily contested zones were endowed with US military bases from which US-supported forces could act to secure a given area (Ramírez Cuellar, 2005, p. 36). The securing of private property and accumulation of capital works to the detriment of populations long rooted in those lands.

A major contract that DynCorp received had as an objective the fumigation of coca crops in Colombia (Bonds, 2013, p. 96). The toxic war that the paramilitaries waged against coca growers, where strong herbicides have been used as a weapon, has resulted in numerous cases of lost subsistence crops and contaminated land and water (Bonds, 2013). Though fumigation is indeed consistent with one of the objectives of Plan Colombia, it is completely contradictory to others. Rural coca growers become the targets of military strikes and see their subsistence and coca crops being destroyed, ones that they were often forced to harvest in the first place and that constituted their only source of revenue (Quintero & Posada, 2013, p. 375).

DynCorp, defending its work in Colombia, boasts of carrying out a number of humanitarian actions in the regions in which they act. These include the financing of school supplies for Colombians around the military bases used by DynCorp. The company's website includes testimony of a DynCorp instructor stating in a compassionate manner that "helping children is the most marvelous thing in the world" (DynCorp, 2013). With "democracy" being instated, legally upheld by the rule of law and militarily defended by PMSCs and the US-trained Colombian military, the environment in Colombia has of course become more welcoming for foreign investment. This translated into the implementation of measures such as the signing of the Free Trade Agreement (FTA) between Colombia and the US, thus closing the loop between the political, juridical, and military dimensions of US dominance in Colombia.

Cornered In

In the end, the "war on drugs" is far from being an actual war on drugs but rather an excuse for the expansion of US-style liberal democracy and global capitalism, which the US aims to impose through both military and ideological apparatuses. Slowly and painfully, the US is implanting its preferred structures in Colombia. In light of the Colombian situation—the country with one of the most skewed income distributions in the world (Escobar, 2004, p. 19), with the FARC controlling part of the territory, and where the amounts of cocaine being produced are so huge they seem almost unimaginable—Colombia may appear as a humanitarian disaster in severe need of intervention. On the other hand, US presence in the country has proven to be ineffective in alleviating the pains for which it is partly responsible. Internally, examples of small rural communities such as the Comunidad de Paz de San José de Apartadó (2006) organize and resist against national and foreign threats in refusing any cooperation with any party involved in the conflict. This example of resistance is one of many Colombian initiatives that have found their place in the sometimes inhospitable rural areas. Regretfully, local initiatives by local actors who are better placed to understand their own realties and who are conscious of their needs are silenced by seemingly benevolent actors who claim to know better what must be done (Ginsburg, 2011, p. 230). Currently (in 2014), the Colombian head of state Juán Manuel Santos is in the midst of peace negotiations with the FARC. In an interview he gave for Euronews, he asked the European Union for both political and financial support for Colombia. He further stated that peace would benefit not only Colombia but the whole world (Euronews, 2014/11/6). The question to be asked is how to attain this peace? Based on available evidence, it seems unlikely that a renewal of plans of imperial intervention can or will produce any viable peace. Is peace even the actual goal of the states in question? Since the world seems to be in a permanent state of warfare and aggressive, imperialist apparatuses are gaining ground. Our aim then becomes dismantling the entanglements of the different methods that imperialism uses to further root itself in societies. In exploring different angles, subtle and not-so-subtle manifestations of imperialism, it will eventually be cornered in from all sides.

References

Althusser, L. (2006). Ideology and Ideological State Apparatuses. In Aradhana Sharma & Akhil Gupta (Eds.), *The Anthropology of the State* (pp. 86–111). Oxford: Blackwell.

Avilés, W. (2008). US Intervention in Colombia: The Role of Transnational Relations. *Bulletin of Latin American Research*, 27(3), 410–429.

Ballvé, T. (2009). The Dark Side of Plan Colombia. *Nation*, 288(23), 22–32.

Bonds, E. (2013). Hegemony and Humanitarian Norms: The US Legitimation of Toxic Violence. *Journal of World-Systems Research*, 19(1), 82–107.

Bureau of Western Hemisphere Affairs. (2013). *U.S. Relations with Colombia*. Washington, DC: US Department of State. http://www.state.gov/r/pa/ei/bgn/35754.htm

Bureau of Public Affairs. (2008). Diplomacy: The U.S. Department of State at Work. Washington, DC: US Department of State. http://www.state.gov/r/pa/ei/rls/dos/107330.htm

Charles, D. (2013). Forcing Farmers to Plant Genetically Modified Seeds: Colombians Revolt Against Seed Control and Agricultural Tyranny. *Global Research*, October 2. http://www.globalresearch.ca/colombians-successfully-revolt-against-seed-control-and-agricultural-tyranny/5352534

Comunidad de Paz de San José de Apartadó. (2006). Declaración Relativa a la Comunidad de Paz de San José San José de Apartadó. http://cdpsanjose.org/?q=/node/9

Council on Foreign Relations (CFR). (2000). *Plan Colombia*. http://www.cfr.org/colombia/plan-colombia/p28004

Delgado-Ramos, G.C., & Romano, S.M. (2011). Political-Economic Factors in U.S. Foreign Policy: The Colombian Plan, the Mérida Initiative, and the Obama Administration. *Latin American Perspectives*, 38(4), 93–108.

DynCorp. (2013). INL Air Wing Charity in Colombia - Because it's the Right Thing To Do. *DynCorp International*. http://www.dyn-intl.com/news-events/press-release/inl-air-wing-charity-in-colombia-because-its-the-right-thing-to-do/

Elhawary, S. (2010). Security for Whom? Stabilisation and Civilian Protection in Colombia. *Disasters*, 3(34), S388–S405.

Embassy of Colombia, (2012). U.S.-Colombia Free Trade Agreement. Washington, DC: Embassy of Colombia. http://www.colombiaemb.org/FTA

Escobar, A. (2004). Development, Violence and the New Imperial Order. *Development*, 47(1), 15–21.

Euronews. (2014/11/6). Juan Manuel Santos, président colombien: « La paix bénéficiera au monde entier ». *Euronews*, November 6.
http://fr.euronews.com/2014/11/06/dans-une-interview-exclusive-le-president-colombien-juan-manuel-santos-affirme-/

Foster, L. (2010). Soft Drink: Hard Power. In Maximilian C. Forte (Ed.), *Militarism, Humanism, and Occupation* (pp. 181–192). Montreal: Alert Press.

Garay Salamanca, J.G.; Barberi Gomez, F.; & Cardona Landínez, I. (2009). Impact of the US-Colombia FTA on the small farm economy in Colombia. *Oxfam America*.
http://www.oxfamamerica.org/static/oa3/files/colombia-fta-impact-on-small-farmers-final-english.pdf

Ginsburg, T. (2011). In Defense of Imperialism? The Rule of Law and the State-Building Project. In J.E. Fleming (Ed.), *Getting to the Rule of Law* (pp. 224–240). New York: New York University Press.

Hanieh, A. (2006). Praising Empire: Neoliberalism under Pax Americana. In C. Mooers (Ed.), *The New Imperialists: Ideologies of Empire* (pp. 167–198). Oxford: Oneworld Publications.

Hobson, C. (2014). Privatising the War on Drugs. *Third World Quarterly*, 35(8), 1441–1456.

Labrousse, A. (2005). The FARC and the Taliban's Connection to Drugs. *Journal of Drug Issues*, 35(1), 169–184.

Mattei, U. (2003). A Theory of Imperial Law: A Study on U.S. Hegemony and the Latin Resistance. *Indiana Journal of Global Legal Studies*, 10(1), 383–448.

———— . (2010). Emergency-Based Predatory Capitalism: The Rule of Law, Alternative Dispute Resolution, and Development. In Didier Fassin & Mariella Pandolfi (Eds.), *Contemporary States of Emergency* (pp. 89–105). New York: Zone Books.

Marcella, G. (2009). Democratic Governance and the Rule of Law: Lessons from Colombia. *Strategic Studies Institute*.
http://www.strategicstudiesinstitute.army.mil/pdffiles/PUB955.pdf

Metelits, C. (2010). *Inside Insurgency: Violence, Civilians, and Revolutionary Group Behavior*. New York: New York Press.

Mooers, C. (2006). Introduction: The New Watchdogs. In C. Mooers (Ed.), *The New Imperialists: Ideologies of Empire* (pp. 1–8). Oxford: Oneworld Publications.

Mondragón, H. (2007). Democracy and Plan Colombia. *North American Congress on Latin America*, 40(1), 42–45.

Office of the United States Trade Representative [USTR]. (2014). *Labor in the U.S.-Colombia Trade Promotion Agreement*.
http://www.ustr.gov/uscolombiatpa/labor

Ospina-Valencia, J. (2013/9/4). Protestas en Colombia: la paz pasa por el campo. *Deutsche Welle News Network*, September 4.
http://www.dw.de/protestas-en-colombia-la-paz-pasa-por-el-campo/a-17067650

Panitch, L., & Gindin, S. (2006). Theorizing American Empire. In A. Bartholomew (Ed.), *Empire's Law: The American Imperialist Project and the "War to Remake the World"* (pp. 21–43).Toronto: Pluto Press.

Pizarro, E., & Gaitán, P. (2006). Plan Colombia and the Andean Initiative: Lights and Shadows. In B. Loveman (Ed), *Addicted to Failure: U.S. Security Policy in Latin America and the Andean Region* (pp. 53–79). Lanham, MD: Rowman & Littlefield Publishers Inc.

Quintero, S., & Posada, I. (2013). Estrategias políticas para el tratamiento de las drogas ilegales en Colombia. *Revista Facultaria Nacional de Salud Pública*, 31(1), 373–380.

Ramírez Cuellar, F. (2005). *The Profits of Extermination: How the U.S. Corporate Power is Destroying Colombia.* Monroe, ME: Common Courage Press.

Red Colombiana de Acción Frente al Libre Comercio (RCAFLC). (2014). Quénes Somos? http://www.recalca.org.co/quenes-somos/

Salazar, I.Y., & Acosta A.C. (2001). El Plan Colombia: Punta de Lanza de Estados Unidos en la Región Andina. *Tribuna del Investigador*, 8(1), 43–62.

US Government Accountability Office (GAO). (2008). *Plan Colombia: Drug Reduction Goals Were Not Fully Met, but Security Has Improved; U.S. Agencies Need More Detailed Plans for Reducing Assistance.* Washington, DC: United States Government Accountability Office. http://www.gao.gov/assets/290/282511.pdf

US Embassy, Bogota (USEB). (2009/10/23). Telling Colombia's Story: From Failing State To Stable Ally [Diplomatic cable]. Bogota, Colombia: US Embassy. [09BOGOTA3362]. https://wikileaks.org/cable/2009/10/09BOGOTA3362.html

US Office on Colombia. (2011, June 20). *Impact of the FTA with Colombia on Afro-Colombian and Indigenous Communities* [Video file]. https://www.youtube.com/watch?v=9Q7NOY8Axf4

Villar, O., & Cottle, D. (2011). *Cocaine, Death Squads, and the War on Terror: U.S. Imperialism and Class Struggle in Colombia.* New York: Monthly Review Press.

Waldon, J. (2011). The Rule of Law and the Importance of Procedure. In J.E. Fleming (Ed.), *Getting to the Rule of Law* (pp. 3–31). New York: New York University Press.

Wood, E.M. (2006). Democracy as Ideology of Empire. In C. Mooers (Ed.), *The New Imperialists: Ideologies of Empire* (pp. 9-24). Oxford: Oneworld Publications.

Chapter 4

BULGARIAN MEMBERSHIP IN NATO AND THE PRICE OF DEMOCRACY

Lea Marinova

T he 10th anniversary of Bulgaria's admission as a member in the North Atlantic Treaty Organization (NATO) occurred in 2014. Bulgaria was one of several new NATO members in 2004, joined by Estonia, Latvia, Lithuania, Romania, Slovakia and Slovenia (NATO, 2004). Also, 2014 marked 25 years since the fall of the Berlin Wall. In 1991, the first democratically chosen government was elected in Bulgaria. Bulgaria's entrance in NATO is praised by government officials, and generally by a large part of the population. It is proclaimed as an important step for Bulgaria in the route towards democracy and independence. It is interesting to note that Bulgaria's membership in NATO and the EU (joined in 2007) has not really resulted in the improvement of the standard of living in Bulgaria. Bulgarian accession to NATO resembles membership in an "elite club" (Slatinski, 2012), a prestigious network of white men who have a hobby of shopping for new weapons. Whether the weapons are of mass destruction or more mundane, these weapons are intended for "the new hybrid war, which combines conventional methods with guerrilla, cybernetic and information war" (Bulgarian Ministry of Defence [MoD], 2014a; for more on "hybrid war" as discussed in US military documents, see the Introduction to this volume). In the context of a country whose gross domestic income is one of the lowest in Europe as of 2006, around 2.6% of the budget is invested in the military. This percentage of military investment surpasses that of richer NATO members like Austria and Germany by 1.5%. (Chobanov, 2007). Furthermore, as reported by the EU's risk analysis team, Bulgaria is not identified as being in any danger of external attacks (Chobanov, 2007). The biggest issue, as listed by numerous sources, is organized crime within the country, viewed as an important problem by 96% of Bulgarian respondents (Bertelsmann Stiftung, 2014, pp. 2, 5). Foreign threats, real or imagined, are often used as an attention-grabbing tactic to distract a population from the internal problems of a country. This was a technique that was well elaborated during the socialist era in Bulgaria, a time when the West and all that was connected to it were considered the enemy. Today, a similar technique is used by the US, and is known as the risk of a terrorist attack (Harvey, 2003, p. 12). The question remains then, if there is no actual risk of foreign attack, why is all the funding for military equipment needed? If Bulgaria's membership in NATO is not really serving the Bulgarian people by facilitating development, then how does Bulgaria benefit from such an association? This chapter focuses on NATO's use of Bulgaria as an instrument of US imperialism. It is argued here that the main goal of the instrumentalization of Bulgaria is to augment US power and influence through the addition of allies, or "force multipliers" as explained in the Introduction to this volume. This chapter will thus broadly discuss the importance and nature of Bulgaria's NATO membership. Furthermore, it will investigate Bulgaria's *responsibility* as a member of NATO, as well as its participation in NATO's military operations.

Historical Predisposition

A dichotomy between pro-Russian and anti-Russian sentiments has "a long history" in Bulgaria (Andreev & Cekov, 2014/3/26). According to Bulgarian anthropologist, Ivaylo Dichev (cited in Andreev & Cekov, 2014/3/26), in the Bulgarian media one finds commentary that predominantly favours "the interests of the EU and NATO, while the [pro-]Russian perspective remains underrepresented and even demonized". This separation thus still structures popular opinion and can play an important role when painting a picture of the domestic political situation, one that echoes with the rhetoric of the Cold War and provides a historical predisposition that opened the way for NATO membership.

In her ethnographic study, Eleanor Smollett remarked on what she found was a certain "infatuation" of Bulgarians with the USA. Some of the youth with whom she talked said that they could not believe that unemployment could possibly exist in countries like the US, opinions which Smollett characterizes as an expression of ignorance, and repudiation of the socialist regime (Smollett, 1993,

p. 10). Such popular opinions did not appear organically from thin air, but rather were formed in a consistent manner. In other words, the pro-Russian and anti-Russian dichotomy exists because it has been imposed.

For a very long time, the only alternative to socialist news sources was Radio Free Europe, and it was largely funded by the CIA and private US donors (Johnson, 2008). Today, similarly there are not many media outlets that are free of private foreign funding or other interests. Educational institutions, such as the American College of Sofia,[1] a prestigious secondary institution founded by US missionaries in the 1869s, and the American University in Bulgaria at Blagoevgrad, founded in 1991,[2] were instances of US influence in education. First, American missionaries were sent to educate children, who later took working positions in the administration of the country. The work of the missionary schools was suspended in 1940. Throughout the 1990s in Bulgaria, there was also the appearance of numerous NGOs and think tanks that were largely funded by the US (Center for the Study of Democracy, 2010, p. 14). All these sources shaped not only Bulgarian public opinion, but the military community is also highly inspired by NATO ideology and the US Army. Interestingly, the historical binary opposition of pro-Russian and anti-Russian is used in official documentation and political discourse, especially as an argument for certain political decisions, such as the project named "Vision 2020".

Vision 2020

Vision 2020 is a project that was put into place by the Bulgarian Ministry of Defence and NATO. Its aim is to upgrade all of Bulgaria's military equipment by replacing older Soviet and Russian equipment with US-made weapons. The upgrade of military equipment ties into the larger project of adding to the US' network of allies, through membership in NATO. The central intention is to expand the budget Bulgaria spends on military equipment every year, until reaching 2.6% of GDP projected for 2020. The central argument for the increase in spending is security. In the last meeting between the Bulgarian Defence Minister Velizar Shalamanov and the Assistant Secretary General for Defence Policy and Planning, Heinrich Brauss, it was claimed that the modernization of the Bulgarian army is necessary because there is a "real risk for us to be outwitted by our enemies" (Novinite, 2014/10/13). Brauss warned

that if the Bulgarian government failed to follow the realization of
Vision 2020, there would be a penalty procedure against Bulgaria
initiated by NATO headquarters in Brussels. In terms of who and
what Bulgaria must defend itself against, this Vision 2020 document frames its logic in terms of the Russian conflict in Ukraine
and its "illegal annexation" of Crimea, classing this as a "negative
development [that] has direct implications for Bulgaria's security"
(MoD, 2014a, p. 3). Here the pro-Russian, anti-Russian dichotomy
becomes very useful even if inaccurate, or at least insufficient. In
her 2008 report on Bulgaria and Southeast Europe, Antoinette
Primatorova[3] discussed the central issues surrounding the development of Bulgaria in a "globalizing world". She identified climate
change, energy issues, internal corruption and organized crime as
the central issues in the country. Primatorova argued that the Bulgarian political context, after the collapse of the Berlin Wall, was
simply not ready for participation in any exterior, international decision making, adding:

> "The political agenda in Bulgaria has been defined in recent
> years mostly so as to comply with demands from or blueprints
> delivered by international organizations and bodies—be it the
> Council of Europe, the European Union, NATO, the
> International Monetary Fund, the World Bank". (Primatorova,
> 2008, p. 5)

Given that Russia still controls the energy supply, this refrains Bulgaria from participating in the creation of a common European
policy for energy. Otherwise, since the collapse of the Soviet bloc,
the driving forces behind reforms in Bulgaria have been NATO,
the EU and the Council of Europe, and they have shaped to a great
extent the political and economic decisions for the last 14 years or
so (Primatorova, 2008, p. 8).

It is important to note that the EU and NATO have been central in shaping the Bulgarian socio-political context since the collapse of the Soviet-backed government. However there has not
been enough critical questioning of the work of these organizations, simply because they are globally influential and thus taken-
for-granted. Through the freedom and democracy discourse promoted by NATO and the soft power of the EU, those institutions
appear as if they are arriving in Bulgaria for nothing else but to save
the day. But such an outlook is rather naïve. Through the insertion
of a set of values, the remaking of every possible system within a
society, be it journalism, the army, or the official erection of private
interests over public ones, these structures slowly create an ally in

the likeness of NATO and the EU. NATO is interested in the up-grading of the Bulgarian army, not out of an altruistic impulse, but because it would be greatly beneficial if Bulgaria could participate in NATO's "peace missions" and thus effectively perform as an ally—or, as a "force multiplier," as conceived by the US military strategists discussed in the Introduction to this volume (see Figures 4.1 and 4.2). The geopolitical position of Bulgaria permits easier entry to three important geographical regions: the Middle East, Russia, and Europe. Bulgaria forms part of south-eastern Europe and is situated next to the Black Sea, where the Middle East, Russia, and the rest of Europe connect. As Dr. Slatinski emphasizes in his analysis of Bulgarian membership in NATO, the accession of Bulgaria to the Alliance is not so much a sign of Bulgaria's development after the fall of the Berlin Wall, but rather "the result of an already determined geopolitical tendency" (translated from Slatinski, 2012). Today, Bulgaria plays a subordinate role in NATO. In 2013, NATO Secretary General Anders Fogh Rasmussen commented on Bulgaria's role, saying the country was to be "praised for its [sic] contributions to the Alliance and its commitment to transatlantic security" (NATO, 2013). The number one threat to the NATO alliance's security is identified as global terrorism (NATO, 2014a). Since 9/11, NATO has officially declared itself in support to the US in the "global war against terrorism," thus enforcing the US' right to increase security, to impose the US military presence in facilities in allied countries, and to demand foreign assistance in its campaigns. One of these forms of assistance is NATO's "peacekeeping missions". As a member of NATO, Bulgaria is left with no choice but to follow the steps of US imperialism.

Figure 4.1: NATO Training Bulgaria for "Interoperability"

This photo from May 15, 2014, shows members of Bulgarian Special Operation Forces conducting combat marksmanship training in preparation for "Exercise Combined Resolve II" at Grafenwoehr Training Area, Germany. It also provides a graphic sample of the meaning of the "force multiplier" concept. "Combined Resolve II" is a US Army Europe-directed multinational exercise, including more than 4,000 participants from 15 allied and partner countries including special operations forces from the US, Bulgaria, and Croatia, that involves "interoperability training" to promote "security and stability among NATO and European partner nations". (US Army photo by Visual Information Specialist Gertrud Zach)

Afghanistan, Iraq, Kosovo, Somalia, Yemen and the War on Terrorism

Bulgaria is actively participating in several of NATO's "peace-support" missions. As presented in the objectives set out by Bulgaria's Ministry of Defence, Bulgarian participation in these missions is essential for the enhancement of the country's "international prestige" (MoD, 2014b). In Afghanistan, the Bulgarian mission has reached its third stage already, that is, the participation of Bulgaria in training the Afghan Army. In Kosovo, attached to the Dutch contingent, the Bulgarians participated mostly in the building of facilities for the local population. The mission in Bosnia and Herzegovina had a similar mandate. Currently, Operation Active Endeavour consists in detecting and protecting against terrorism in the Mediterranean. Also, Bulgaria is part of NATO Training Mission-Iraq (NTM-I), as of 2014, which aims at the "relief and reconstruction of Iraq" (MoD, 2014b).

What is common to all of these missions? They all follow a similar model of intervention. NATO justifies such intervention as a means of countering terrorism, or potential terrorism. NATO thus claims to be bringing peace by facilitating the eradication of terrorism (NATO, 2014b). Such missions are part of the larger spectrum of crisis-management operations, in which the US and NATO collaborate, "from combat and peacekeeping, to training and logistics support, to surveillance and humanitarian relief" (NATO, 2014c). Peace-support is a euphemism for combat.

The "counter-terror" cover can also serve as a useful pretext for placing US forces in proximity to Russia. This justificatory logic is echoed in the report, "International Involvement in the Western Balkans," where Georgi Kamov deduces that, "probably the only real motive for more than symbolic US presence in the Western Balkans is the anti-terror campaign and the possibility of intensified terrorist activity in the near future" (Kamov, 2005, p. 10). The actual danger of such terrorist attacks and the meaning of them are details omitted in this report, as is the case in all others. Plamen Pantev discusses in his article "Bulgaria in NATO and the EU: Implications for the Regional Foreign and Security Policy of the Country," how Bulgarian policy is manipulated in order to fit in the larger paradigm of the war on terrorism:

> "The wisdom of the last 16 years of the country's foreign and security policy that contributed to the appearance and effective performance of a network of partnerships in a difficult period of wars and high tensions requires refreshing. This already happens with the clear Bulgarian commitments to focus on 'completing the job' in the Western Balkans and taking simultaneously responsibilities in dealing with the geopolitical obligations as a NATO and soon EU country in the Black Sea area and in the fight on terrorism and stabilising war-torn societies in the broader Middle East. The *purpose of 'Europeanising' the Balkans with the instrumental involvement of EU and NATO and preserving positive US interest* will constitute the contents of Bulgaria's foreign and security policy in a region, considered a high security priority for the country". (emphases added, Pantev, 2005, p. 5)

This statement openly accepts that such organizations as NATO and the EU are instruments operating to transform societies and inject US interests. From this perspective, it is clearer what is meant by an enemy. All of those who are perceived as enemies of the US, are also enemies of the members of their "elite clubs". For the past decade or so, the enemy has been "terrorism". Perhaps a brief review of the history of the Bulgarian relationship with this perceived phenomenon might shed some light on what exactly is meant by the controversial term "terrorist".

Terrorism and Bulgaria

In July of 2012 a bus exploded close to the airport of Burgas, a city on the shore of the Black Sea. The bus was filled with Israeli tourists according to a BBC report (BBC, 2013/2/5). The article reporting the event cites numerous times different official sources such as the Israeli Prime Minister, the Bulgarian Prime Minister and Interior Minister, the Canadian Prime Minister, the Lebanese Prime Minister, the director of Europol, and the US Deputy National Security Advisor for Homeland Security and Counterterrorism who was also Assistant to the US President. Soon after the explosion, it was claimed that the attack was a terrorist act committed by the Lebanese Hezbollah. The argument was that there are "obvious links" leading investigators to Hezbollah (even implicating Iran), links which were then framed as merely part of a "reasonable assumption". The individuals identified as the attackers, held Australian and Canadian passports, which raises questions about the so-called "obvious link to Lebanon"—especially since their reportedly Lebanese driver licenses were revealed to be fakes (Barnett, 2013/2/5). It was claimed that the link to Hezbollah had been established because of certain data showing a financial connection to Lebanon and therefore to Hezbollah. The nature of that data however is not explained. US President Barack Obama did not wait long to qualify the act as being a "barbaric terrorist attack" (CNN, 2012/7/18). As soon as it was known that there was a Canadian passport holder involved in the explosion, the Canadian foreign minister declared that beyond a shadow of a doubt Hezbollah was responsible for the attack and that it needs to be internationally listed as a terrorist group (Barnett, 2013/2/5). The reactions of all these actors have something in common: the advancement and preservation of their own geopolitical interests. The event in Burgas was used to reassert the word "terrorism," at a time when the EU was refusing to class Hezbollah as a "terrorist" group. References to Iran, Lebanon, Hezbollah, terrorism, and "heinous attack" were cast about in the media space as key words in place of substantive evidence and critical questioning. Still, even after the official report was released by Bulgarian investigators, there is no more information surrounding the sources of their information, the nature of the data acquired, or even details about the investigation itself—but there is ample evidence of Israeli, US, and Canadian authorities capitalizing on the event to pressure the EU to designate Hezbollah a terrorist group.

Another aspect of Bulgarian history which contributes to its present relationship with the issue of "Islamic terrorism" is its relationship with Turkey and its Muslim majority. Five hundred years of Ottoman rule (or "the Turkish yoke" as commonly heard in Bulgaria), which ended with the Russian-Ottoman war, have intensely marked the Bulgarian consciousness. Around 10% of the total population are Turks living mostly in the rural areas of southeastern and north-eastern Bulgaria. In addition to Bulgarian television news at 8:00 pm every evening, there is a broadcast of the news in Turkish at 5:00 pm. Also, a large number of imported TV series are from Turkey. The rest is inspired or directly comes from the US. Recently, a heated public debate surrounded the appearance of a Turkish language bill, obliging Turkish students to study Turkish in schools as a second language (World Bulletin, 2014). One of the influential parties in the Bulgarian parliament, The Movement for Rights and Freedoms (Dvijenie za Prava i Svobodi, DPS) is an ethnic party that aims to defend the interests of the minority Turk population. This party appeared in 1990, a year after the fall of the Soviet-backed government. In the 1980s, the Bulgarian Communist Party initiated the so-called "national revival process" (Vasileva, 1992; Tavanier, 2010). That process consisted of forced deportations to Turkey, and the negation of Muslim and Turkish cultural identification such as changing Turkish names into Bulgarian ones. During this time there was also the creation of ghettos for the Roma people who were constantly ostracized by the rest of the population. After the end of the regime, the Turkish language was banned from schools.

The Turkish and Roma Bulgarians have been used to produce an image of the other. Scapegoating the other reinforces the totalizing and very negative image of the "Arab" or the "Muslim". In recent reports, some Syrian migrants have claimed to be victims of abuse by border police in Bulgaria (McCall, 2014/9/26). There are numerous examples of how xenophobia and racism are constantly being inflamed within the population in the public sphere. Casual racism towards Roma, Turkish or simply those known as Arab and/or Muslim populations has even become even the goal of certain political parties, such as Ataka.

Ethnic tensions in the country have also been discussed in the broader context of Bulgaria's membership in NATO and the democratization process, in which quelling ethnic divisions is seen as an instrumental task to strengthen counter-terrorism:

"Stabilizing and democratising the area, overcoming the ethnic
animosities   and   belated   economic   and   infrastructure
modernization of the broader Balkan region, strengthening the
state institutions in all countries of the region are key [antidotes]
in the fight with terrorism". (Pantev, 2005, p. 17)

However, in adapting national politics to the US-led "war against
terrorism," when in the Bulgarian context it is precisely the idea of
terrorism that is matched with the profile of a population that has
been criminalized and marginalized on principally ethnic grounds,
we face an aggravation and escalation of such tensions. How is the
fight against terrorism helping to overcome ethnic animosities?

The Price of Democracy

The counter-terrorist agenda of the US curiously fits into the context of ethnic tensions in Bulgaria. In a country which is the poorest of the EU, the desire to join a global force such as NATO is
immense. On the one hand, it provides status as a democratic
country and masks the worms of the recent past and present, that
is, the deeply embedded socio-economic problems. On the other
hand, Bulgaria becomes an ally in the "war on terror". Bulgaria is in
a unique position, with Greece, as a European country having a
border with Turkey, and thus providing an entrance to the rest of
the Middle East. In 2014 Turkey politely declined participation in
the US-led attack on ISIS in Iraq. Bulgaria is a country which cannot refuse such demands. It has to remain an ally of NATO, leaders think, for the sake of its own survival. Pantev argues that
Bulgarian membership in NATO, and consequently its participation in NATO's military campaigns, are essential for the democratization of the country:

"if we are serious in our intentions and declarations of joining
NATO and the EU, we need to prove we can be ourselves
vehicles of transition, reform, progress, development and
integration. That is why *Bulgaria is not, and no country from the region
should be, afraid of 'getting infected' by a temporary 'culture of dependency'.*
While dealing with the issues of change, using the external
support of the EU, NATO and the USA the 'know-how' of
being modern and up-to-date in social, economic and political
performance can be internalised and turned into a building-block
and basic motivation of new Bulgaria, member of NATO and
the EU [*sic*]". (emphases added, Pantev, 2005, p. 24)

The discourse of democracy, freedom and equality that NATO uses to justify its military interventions is in striking contrast with actual actions. Nonetheless, imperialism needs the support of as many "allies" as possible, in order to perpetuate its existence. In return, protection and prestige are offered, and sought by some.

Figure 4.2: The US Inspects Bulgaria's "Modernization"

The original caption for this photograph was: "Secretary of Defense William Cohen (right), accompanied by Bulgarian Minister of Defense Georgi Ananiev (left), inspects the joint service Bulgarian honour guard assembled at the airport in Sofia for his arrival welcoming ceremony, July 12, 1997. Cohen visited the former Soviet satellite nation to see for himself the governmental reforms and planned programs of modernization which have elevated Bulgaria to the forefront among those countries seeking NATO membership". (Photo: US Department of Defense, via Wikimedia Commons)

Conclusion

In 2009, former Prime Minister Sergei Stanishev stated in the *Harvard International Review*,

> "After years of social and political transformation, Bulgaria has uniquely positioned itself among the countries of the Balkans and the Black Sea region. Not only does it currently enjoy unprecedented economic growth and the full trust of foreign investors, but its accession to the European Union and its NATO membership have made it an even more critical strategic player in regional and international relations". (Stanishev, 2009)

Besides the fact that this statement is false in its asserted facts, it also rests on the fallacy that participation in international relations is positive for the internal development of Bulgaria. As the poorest country of the EU, not only has Bulgaria not improved its economic standing but it is also headed towards greater expense which is far from necessary. As stated earlier, 2.6% of the GDP invested in the military is a budgetary decision that not even countries like Austria and Germany have taken, even though their economic growth is significantly greater than Bulgaria's. It is important for Bulgarians to be critical of any significant socio-political changes in Bulgaria at any moment, no matter if they are introduced by influential organizations such as NATO and the EU, and to examine how any policy (or change in policy) may influence the internal politics of the country. Bulgaria needs to take an independent position, oriented towards its own well-being, in order to become something different than its already established status as a vassal of empire.

Notes

1   For more details presented by the American College, see: http://www.acs.bg/Home/About_ACS/History.aspx
2   For a minimal presentation of the chronology behind the establishment of the American University in Bulgaria, see: http://www.aubg.edu/quick-facts
3   Antoinette Primatorova was a Deputy Minister of Foreign Affairs and later the Bulgarian ambassador to the European Communities: http://www.cls-sofia.org/en/our-staff/antoinette-primatarova-32.html
4   Ataka is renown in the public sphere as an extreme-nationalist party, which early gained greater visibility by using the motto, "Bulgaria for the Bulgarians". For a statement of the principles of this party, see: http://www.ataka.bg/en/index.php?option=com_content&task=view&id=14&Itemid=27

References

Andreev, A., & Cekov, N. (2014/3/26). The Two Faces of Russia in Bulgaria (Bulgarian title: Двете лица на Русия в България). *Deutsche Welle*, March 26.
    http://dw.com/p/1BVpU
Barnett, D. (2013/2/5). Bulgaria: Hezbollah behind Burgas terror attack.

Long War Journal, February 5.

http://www.longwarjournal.org/archives/2013/02/bulgaria_hezbollah_b.php

BBC. (2013/2/5). Hezbollah Linked to Burgas Bus Bombing in Bulgaria. *BBC News*, February 5.

http://www.bbc.com/news/world-europe-21342192

Bertelsmann Stiftung. (2014). BTI 2014: Bulgaria Country Report. Gütersloh: Bertelsmann Stiftung.

http://www.bti-project.de/fileadmin/Inhalte/reports/2014/pdf/BTI%202014%20Bulgaria.pdf

Bulgarian Ministry of Defence (MoD). (2014a). Vision 2020: Bulgaria in NATO and the Defense of Europe (Bulgarian title: Проект Визия 2020: България в НАТО и в Европейската отбрана). Sofia, Bulgaria: Ministry of Defence.

http://www.clubz.bg/ckfinder/userfiles/files/20140826_Vision_2020.pdf
(English version available at:
http://www.government.bg/fce/001/0234/files/Vision%202020.pdf)

——————— . (2014b). Missions and Operations. Sofia, Bulgaria: Ministry of Defence of the Republic of Bulgaria

http://www.md.government.bg/en/tema_MissionsOperations.html

Center for the Study of Democracy. (2010). Civil Society in Bulgaria: Trends and Risks. Sofia, Bulgaria: Center for the Study of Democracy.

http://wap.southeasteurope.org/artShow.php?id=15480

Chobanov, D. (2007). Defence Spending and the Future of the Army (Bulgarian title: Разходите за отбрана и бъдещето на армията). *Institute for Market Economics (И.П.И.)*, September 11.

http://ime.bg/bg/articles/razhodite-za-otbrana-i-bydeshteto-na-armiqta/

CNN. (2012/7/18). Israelis Killed in Bulgaria Bus Terror Attack, Minister Says. *CNN*, July 18.

http://www.cnn.com/2012/07/18/world/europe/bulgaria-israel-blast/

Harvey, D. (2003). *The New Imperialism*. Oxford: Oxford University Press.

Johnson, A.R. (2008). Then And Now: Free Media in Unfree Societies. *Radio Free Europe/Radio Liberty*.

http://www.rferl.org/info/history/133.html

Kamov, G. (2005). International Involvement in the Western Balkans. Sofia, Bulgaria: Institute for Regional and International Studies (IRIS).

http://www.iris-bg.org/files/International%20Involvement.pdf

McCall, J. (2014/9/26). Syrian Migrants Claim Abuse by Bulgarian Border Police. *Al Arabiya*, September 26.

http://english.alarabiya.net/en/perspective/features/2014/09/26/Syrian-migrants-claim-abuse-by-Bulgarian-border-police.html

North Atlantic Treaty Organization (NATO). (2004). NATO Welcomes Seven New Members. *NATO Update*, April 2.

http://www.nato.int/docu/update/2004/04-april/e0402a.htm

——————— . (2013). Bulgaria Praised for Its Commitment to the

Alliance. *NATO*, June 20.
http://www.nato.int/cps/en/natohq/news_101540.htm

———— . (2014a). Countering Terrorism. *NATO*, July 6.
http://www.nato.int/cps/en/natohq/topics_77646.htm?

———— . (2014b). NATO and Afghanistan. *NATO*.
http://www.nato.int/cps/en/natolive/69772.htm

———— . (2014c). NATO Operations and Missions. *NATO*.
http://www.nato.int/cps/en/natohq/topics_52060.htm?

Novinite. (2014/10/13). NATO to Observe Closely Bulgaria's Military Modernisation. *Novinite*, October 13.
http://www.novinite.com/articles/164028/NATO+To+Observe+Closely+Bulgaria%27s+Military+Modernisation

Pantev, P. (2005). Bulgaria in NATO and the EU: Implications for the Regional Foreign and Security Policy of the Country. Institute for Security and International Studies (ISIS). Sofia, Bulgaria.
http://www.isis-bg.org/Publications/research_reports/RS12.pdf

Primatorova, A. (2008). Shaping a Globalized World. Sofia, Bulgaria: Center for Liberal Strategies.

Slatinski, N. (2012). The Role and Place of Bulgaria in NATO in the Changing World: Military Violence as a Factor in International Life and the Bulgarian Political Elite. (Bulgarian title: Ролята и мястото на България в НАТО в условията на променящия се свят. Военното насилие като фактор в международния живот и българският политически елит, translated by L. Marinova). *Strategy, Synergy, Security (Стратегия Синергия Сигурност)*.
http://nslatinski.org/?q=bg/node/441

Stanishev, S. (2009). Building Cooperation: Bulgaria's Essential Role in Regional Integration. *Harvard International Review*, 30(4), 84.

Smollett, E. (1993). America the Beautiful: Made in Bulgaria. *Anthropology Today*, 9(2), 9–13.

Tavanier, Y.B. (2010). Ottoman Past Dogs Sofia-Ankara Relations. *Balkan Insight*, December 22.
http://www.balkaninsight.com/en/article/ottoman-past-dogs-sofia-ankara-relations

Vasileva, D. (1992). Bulgarian Turkish Emigration and Return. *International Migration Review*, 26(2), 342–352.

Chapter 5

FORCED MIGRATIONS:
AN ECHO OF THE STRUCTURAL VIOLENCE OF
THE NEW IMPERIALISM

Chloë Blaszkewycz

The past three decades have been characterized by a "new" form of domination in the world. It is a form of political, economic and social domination, one that might be more subtle but equally or more destructive than colonialism. The new imperialism led by the US superpower is often conceptualized as a non-territorial empire. The US new imperialism understood as a global hegemonic power (Harvey, 2003) can rule from its own country without necessarily having a physical presence in the dominated territory, especially through various "force multipliers" (see the Introduction to this volume). Much of the scholarship on the new imperialism does indeed stress its non-territorial character, as one distinguishing it from the old colonial imperialism. On the other hand, the historical movement of US borders, through expansion (see Figure 5.1), calls into question this non-territoriality. Nevertheless, the phenomenon is still more complex. The spatial substitutes for the territorial, especially around borders. Trouillot thus spoke of borders, "of the space between centralized governments with national territorial claims, where encounters between individuals and state power are most visible" (2001, p. 125), while Scott (1998) pointed to the ways in which a state enforces its power through the placement of people and control over their movement. Here I am concerned with the "spatialization effect" of an imperial state, with the production of boundaries and jurisdiction (Trouillot, 2001, p. 126). At present, with campaigning US politicians calling for the building of a wall along the US border with Mexico, or Hungary frantically trying to complete a fence to keep out refugees, we should be reminded of the extent to which "the protection of borders becomes an easy political fiction with which to enlist support from a confused citizenry" (Trouillot, 2001, p. 133).

Even though the new imperialism guided by the US demonstrates its capacity to rule from a distance, this protagonist also has a military presence in 156 countries, with more than 700 military installations (including full bases) in at least 63 countries (Dufour, 2007/7/1). The new imperialism has pushed through neoliberalism virtually worldwide, resulting in different degrees of social and economic violence. Integrated into neoliberal thinking is a tendency to cast the West as superior, breathing new life into ideas of white racial superiority that have entailed more violence directed against non-Westerners. Stemming from this, we see the extensive, historical militarization of the US border with Mexico and thus the rest of the Latin American land mass (see Figures 5.2, 5.3, and 5.4).

This chapter intends to demonstrate the different forms of structural violence caused by the new imperialism, with special attention paid to the forced migratory movement that exists in the contemporary world. In doing so, I rely on Harsha Walia's concept of "border imperialism" as a starting point. In *Undoing Border Imperialism*, Walia (2013) argues that Western imperialism is dispossessing communities in order to secure land and resources for state and capitalist interests in maximizing profits. Dispossessed persons often attempt to migrate to the same centres of power responsible for their dispossession. However, those people are often stopped at strongly protected borders. This movement is explained by different scholars as the "pull and push" phenomenon. Makaremi (2008) points out that those migratory movements are subject to political management built on a framework of exclusion, a framework that follows the outline of the division of the world between the global North and South, and is a system of political management that reaffirms the state's control over the movement of persons. In this chapter I will illustrate how, to borrow the words of David Bacon (2008, p. 2), "U.S. policies have both produced migration and criminalized migrants".

Figure 5.1: A Mobile US Border

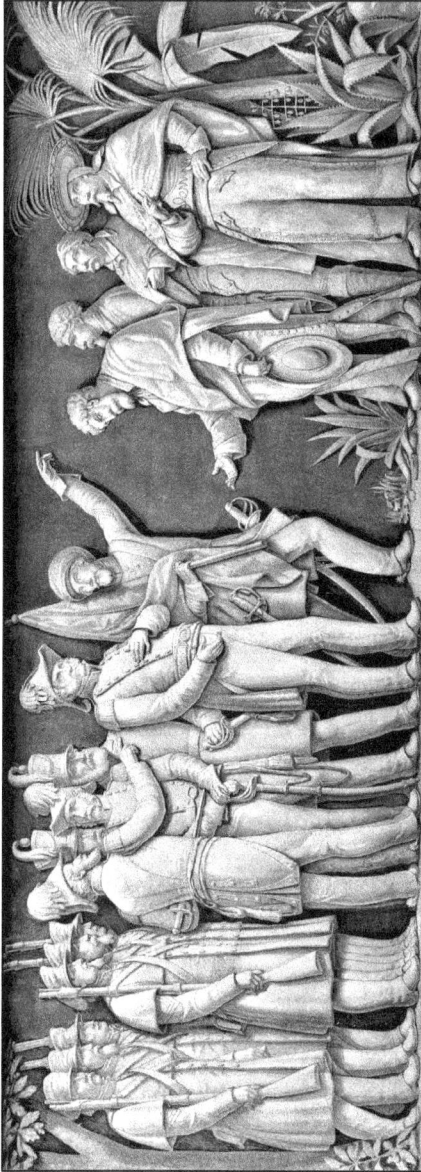

General Winfield Scott is shown during the Mexican War, entering the Mexican capital. The Treaty of Guadalupe Hidalgo of 1848 fixed the Mexican-American border at the Rio Grande and recognized the US annexation of Texas. The treaty also extended the boundaries of the US to the Pacific. This scene was painted by Filippo Constaggini in 1885, and is part of an official Architect of the Capitol photograph.

Figure 5.2: A History of Militarizing the US-Mexican Border, 1916

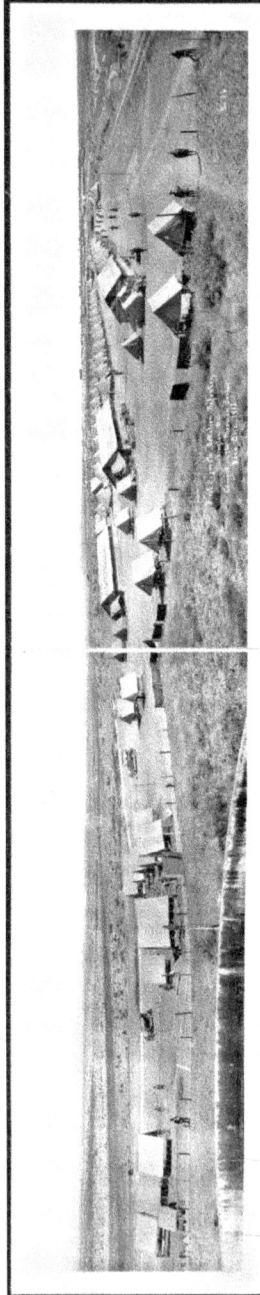

This photograph from 1916 shows the First Separate Battalion Infantry, camped on the Mexican border at Naco, Arizona. (Photo from the Library of Congress)

Figure 5.3: Militarizing the US-Mexican Border, 2015

US Border Patrol agents escort four undocumented immigrants captured near the US-Mexico border on April 23, 2015. A Mississippi Army National Guard LUH-72 Lakota helicopter helped locate the men beneath a tree along a mountainside near Nogales, Arizona. Six soldiers with the 1st Battalion, 185th Aviation Regiment of Tupelo, Mississippi, are assigned to Task Force Raven, which works with multiple federal agencies in patrolling the border. (Photo: Staff Sgt. Scott Tynes, Mississippi Army National Guard)

Figure 5.4: An Imperial Border

Shown here is a portion of the fence between the US and Mexico along the Pacific Ocean just south of San Diego—it was taken at what is in fact named "Imperial Beach" at "Border Field State Park". (Photo via Wikimedia Commons by Tony Webster)

Why Force Matters

"The essence of empire," Matthew Connelly (2006) maintains, "is not military force, but the exercise of untrammeled power" (p. 32). Michael Ignatieff, one of the leading ideological proponents of US dominance, also relegates military power to a lesser status when he wrote, "the 21st century imperium is a new invention in the annals of political science, an empire lite, a global hegemony whose grace notes are free markets, human rights and democracy, enforced by the most awesome military power the world has ever known" (Ignatieff, 2003/1/5). Despite grace notes and abstract power, one cannot deny the rise of the US' "new empire," especially after the Cold War, as anything but an aggressive expansion of its presence in world affairs, achieving the position of an unrivalled military superpower. This force is a crucial element of the power from which the US benefits. As Gonzalez et al. (2004) argue, "in the geopolitical sphere, the most powerful of nations and unparalleled promoter of neoliberalism—the U.S.—constructed the most dominant and war-ready military machinery in history, all under the guidance of the highly centralized state" (p. xi). The US is using and pushing forward its military power to dominate, because it cannot rely primarily on its economic power due to its phenomenal level of indebtedness, the decline of domestic manufacturing, and persistent trade deficits, among other factors.

The US is one of the key actors causing as well as controlling the migratory phenomenon that results, amongst other things, from accumulation by dispossession. In addition, Gordon and Webber (2008, p. 65) argue that, "the creation of new spaces of accumulation is not an innocuous process; it inevitably involves the forceful and violent reorganization of peoples' lives as they are subordinated to the whims of capital". Those economic determinants and their repercussions are extremely important in understanding migratory movement.

Freedom of Capital versus Border Control

One can examine the contradiction between freedom of capital and the "unfreedom" of migrants. On the one hand, neoliberal states are seeking to create free trade agreements to push forward the opening of markets and privatization. On the other hand, talk of freedom and openness does not generally apply to people, apart from the movement of executives and a select few technical specialists. After September 11, 2001, Canada and the US created the "smart border" accord in order to reaffirm that even if they would be increasing control of immigration, it would not affect the free flow of capital, goods and services across borders (Walia, 2013). States regulate immigration as much as they can but let some people cross their borders with legal or illegal status to satisfy particular interests. The example of seasonal workers with no permanent residency demonstrates a dynamic of differential inclusion and exclusion. Harvey (2003) explains the inside-outside dialectic of capitalism, arguing that capitalism necessarily and always needs something outside of itself, thus using a pre-existing "outside" or creating its own "other". Sharma (2005) argues that the neoliberal doctrine celebrates the mobility of capital and some bodies, while the bodies of others, in this case migrants, face ever growing restrictions and criminalization.

States, Neoliberalism, and Corporate Movement

Nowadays, the state and the neoliberal doctrine go hand in hand. The Canadian and US states are increasingly facilitating the institutionalization of neoliberal doctrine while reducing social programs as much as possible (Walia, 2013). There are too many examples to count that show that both states facilitate the movement and entrance of private corporations into others countries, and their own. Therefore, the Canadian state is legally backing private Canadian companies such as mining corporations, especially in Latin America but also elsewhere. To illustrate this argument, Kerr (2012/3/30) affirms that, "over 75% of the world's exploration and mining companies are headquartered in the country [Canada, and] in 2008, these 1293 companies had an interest in 7809 properties in over 100 countries around the world".

Security, Borders and Migration

Numerous scholars have discussed "globalization" in terms of an increasing flow of goods, capital, services and people (Piché, 2005; Bellier, 2009). However, those movements are not arbitrary but coordinated by the US among others. As mentioned above, the dispossession bred by the system is forcing people to migrate and simultaneously there is a strong regulation of the influx of migrants. It is an important issue for many countries especially the US as the fortification of borders seems to increase (Piché, 2005;

Walia, 2013), with the wall between the US and Mexico and the involvement of the US in the construction of the wall between Israel and Palestine being clear examples (see Figure 5.5). On November 9, 2014, the 25th anniversary of the fall of Berlin wall was celebrated; nonetheless, the world has never been as filled with the construction of walls dividing countries and so many restrictions on migrations. Sharma (2005) uses the powerful concept of global apartheid to describe the world's response towards migration. One can see a contradiction in official narratives about the West being open to migration. The US government and NGOs use a humanitarian discourse when speaking of untenable situations in other countries, using moral arguments to legitimize their intervention in those countries (Fassin, 2010). Yet this is part of what we might call a double discourse on the part of the US, which is supposedly very conscious about the lives of Others elsewhere, but not letting them in as immigrants into the US when such an option is needed. The US-led invasions and military occupations of Afghanistan and Iraq have created some of the world largest refugees communities (UN High Commission for Refugees [UNHCR], 2011). Afghanistan, occupied by the US, was the top most producer of refugees in the world up to 2013, even 12 years after the start of the occupation, while Somalia, where the US indirectly intervenes (sometimes directly), being the third largest producer of refugees (UNHCR, 2013). Today, what some call a human tidal wave of refugees from Iraq, Afghanistan, and Syria, is overwhelming border control points from Greece to Macedonia, Serbia, and Hungary, as tens of thousands make their way through the Balkans (see Smale, 2015/8/24). Nevertheless, the chief protagonist in producing the conditions for those mass displacements, the US, only accepted 328 Afghan people in 2009 (Walia, 2013, p. 42). In fact, it has been left up to developing countries to shoulder most of the burden, hosting 86% of the world's refugees, up from 70% a little over a decade ago (UNHCR, 2013). The mobility and the "illegal situation" of migrants is hard to capture in statistics but it still becomes apparent that the majority of refugees are not in those countries that promote the discourse of humanitarian aid and "helping others," but are to be found rather in countries such as Pakistan, the Islamic Republic of Iran and Lebanon (UNHCR, 2013). Though the UNHCR presents the statistics that provide the pattern outlined here, the organization itself fails to ever really explain the causes of such displacements.

Figure 5.5: The US Army: Walling Off Mexico

US Army Specialist Michael J. Westall uses a motorized boom lift to get into position to weld the reinforcement of the primary steel border fence along the US-Mexico border, on June 7, 2007. Westall is attached to the 188th Engineer Company, North Dakota Army National Guard and assigned to Task Force Diamondback. Task Force Diamondback's mission is to erect and reinforce segments of the border fence and the construction of obstacles to along the US-Mexico border. (Photo: Senior Master Sgt. David H. Lipp, US Air Force)

Migrant Detention in the US

As David Harvey put it, "military activity abroad requires military-like discipline at home" (2003, p. 193). The Department of Homeland Security detains 400,000 immigrants in over 250 facilities

across the US at an annual cost of more than $1.7 billion (Deten-
tion Watch Network [DWN], 2012). The world of detention systems is also a lucrative one, with increased privatization and the
formation of a detention industry. Companies such as the Corrections Corporation of America [CCA] boast of having a capacity of
85,000 (CCA, 2013). The CCA represents another example of the
"public-private partnership" scheme, heralded as a force multiplier
(see the Introduction to the volume, and chapter 2).

September 11, 2001, was a crucial moment to reorganize, reaffirm and articulate a way to deal with what some politicians in the
US have been calling one of the biggest national threats: illegal immigrants. In 2003, the immigration-control apparatus was reorgan-
ized, with what existed being replaced by three new agencies, under
the Department of Homeland Security: US Immigration and Customs Enforcement, US Citizenship and Immigration Services, and
Customs and Border Protection (Gavett, 2011/10/18). With this
reorganization, "the line between criminal and civil enforcement of
immigration issues becomes blurred" (Gavett, 2011/10/18). The
landscape of immigration law has changed dramatically as the traditional boundaries between the criminal and immigration spheres
have eroded (Frey & Zhao, 2011, p. 281). Others have also noted
that since the late 1980s one can observe an increasing convergence
between the criminal justice and immigration control systems
(Kanstroom, 2004, p. 640). With the frequent cooperation from
mass media and private groups, the anti-immigrant rhetoric has
strengthened the pejorative construction of immigrants "illegals"
and therefore "criminals". This group is thus perceived as a national threat (Frey & Zhao, 2011). The attempt to create deviants
can be seen as a way to legitimize the exercise of US domination
over migrants. This control relies upon "'geostrategic discourses' of
external threat and internal safety" (Martin, 2011, p. 477). In addition, the reality facing migrants is of much more severe treatment
by US border control agencies. Frey and Zhao (2011, p. 281) indicated that the US Congress, "increased the number of immigration-
related criminal offenses as well as the severity of punishment, expanded the number of criminal offenses that require deportation,
and delegated more immigration enforcement to state and local law
enforcement officers". All non-citizens in the US are "subject to a
complex, ever-changing, relatively insular, flexible, and highly dis-
cretionary legal regime called immigration law" (Kanstroom, 2004,
p. 641). Detention centres are not an isolated practice but are part
of a complex system of trying to efficiently block entry to undocumented migrants. Other strategies include sending trained

agents from the US and Canada abroad for interdiction purposed, stopping migrants even before they succeed in entering in those countries (Davidson, 2003, p.5). Makaremi (2008) argues that in Western countries, border control and the construction of detention centres and refugee camps are a testimony of the new distribution of power regulated by access to mobility.

Labor, Migration and New Imperialism

States control movements across borders by documented and undocumented migrants, in order to protect or advance certain interests. Among these interests are the will to secure a work force that can accept very precarious conditions that few Americans would accept, such as very low income without any social security. Walia (2013) argues that the state which admits migrants, in those conditions, therefore, "legalizes the trade in their bodies and labor by domestic capital" (p. 70). Furthermore, the precarious position of migrants can diminish their motivation to protest against employers since they do not have the necessary legal status or protections. In addition, their vulnerability can open them to different forms of abuse. Walia (2013) proposes that "the state denial of legal citizenship to these migrants ensures legal control over the disposability of the laborers, which in turn embeds the exploitability of their labor" (p. 70). In her analysis, migrants and seasonal workers are "the flip side of transnational capitalism" (Walia, 2013, p. 70). Refusal to grant legal status is also a way to maintain migrants in a position where they can be perpetually displaceable and therefore maintained in a "wandering" situation (Walia, 2013; Makaremi, 2008).

The imposition of structural adjustment policies, such as the reduction in employment in the public sector and the privatization of lands, has severely affected the lives of many around the world. Such policies, added to attacks on trade unions and labour legislation, are seen as having, "led to the massive conversion of workers into unemployed, underemployed, and low-paid self-employed street vendors and itinerant laborers" in the Latin American case (Petras, 2003, pp. 14–15). These radical changes, such as land privatization, mostly affect peasants and/or indigenous communities that already have a precarious situation and a hard time receiving recognition from States. Petras adds that many communities living in urban or rural areas affected by this system have been forced to move. They therefore become a significant part of a larger pattern of "large-scale out-migration to urban slums" and "emigration overseas" (Petras, 2003, p. 18). On the same note, the impact of the North America Free Trade Agreement (NAFTA) signed in 1994 by the US, Canada and Mexico, is also devastating peasant and indigenous communities in Mexico. Petras claims that, "over two million peasant families—mostly small farmers and Indians have been forced off the land since NAFTA was implemented" (2003, p. 17). This is largely due to the falling price of corn, which renders it unprofitable to produce in Mexico. Fanjul and Fraser (2003, p. 2) show that "prices for Mexican corn have fallen more than 70 per cent since 1994," while US corn exports to Mexico have expanded by a factor of three. Furthermore, the corn consumed in Mexico which is imported from the US, comes from farms mostly cultivated by Mexican migrants, who have been forced off their own fields by land privatization. Structural reforms thus lead them to their competitors, which are massive, industrialized and foreign. This situation captures the irony and the violence of the neoliberal imperialist system. These new economic dynamics which are drawn from neoliberal policies strengthen the new imperialist superpower.

Mexico's case is not isolated, but is part of a broad range of countries, communities and people worldwide that are at the receiving end of neoliberal violence. A similar example to that of Mexico's happened during the implementation of neoliberal reforms in Colombia, ushered in with the US-Colombia Trade Promotion Agreement (CTPA) in 2006 (for more, see chapter 3 in this volume). The structural reforms forced peasants to cease growing their original crops and instead opt for the cultivation of coca. The reforms, plus the war against drugs, created massive internal displacement in Colombia and promoted flight abroad. Avilés (2008, p. 417) explained the situation in a very concise way:

> "The decline in the international price of coffee, intensifying agricultural competition from global producers, and the privatisation of state-owned enterprises have contributed to rural landlessness and economic inequality. It also contributed to thousands of Colombians committing themselves to growing and selling more profitable crops—coca and opium poppies—in the decade following the beginning of Colombia's embrace of neoliberalism (the 1990s)".

Racism and the New Imperialism

Border imperialism and the new imperialism share roots in ideologies of racism. The reliance on either contracted or undocumented migrant workers has produced a large rural labour force for the US. Exploitation by the US needs to rest on some kind of discourse or ideology to legitimize this practice; this is when racial propaganda begins to matter. Through arguments and processes that construct migrant workers as inferior, or as deviants, and not privy to "naturalization," the state and the media advance an essentially racialized rhetoric in the hope that citizens will internalize patterns of superiority and acquiesce to the exploitation of others (Walia, 2013, p. 62). The concept of imperialism as a syndrome (see the Introduction) is reflected in the narratives of the state and the media. It is therefore relevant because one can see that the values, ways of living, social hierarchies, ways of producing, consuming and much more are conveyed through those narratives. They are then internalized and replicated into everyday social relations without questioning the patterns of the oppressive system.

This is a crucial moment where the global structure and ideologies of border imperialism enter a more intimate place, that is, the domain of interpersonal relationships. Certain practices towards migrant people in this case are starting to be accepted and normalized. Moreover, Walia (2013, p. 40) also notes that, "simultaneously, the reinforcement of physical and psychological borders against racialized bodies is a key element through which to maintain the sanctity and myth of superiority of Western civilization". In the same vein, the widespread representation of "illegal immigrants" as stealing jobs is a direct strategy to construct migrants as a potential threat to the citizen (Sharma, 2005). However, a majority of migrants who are able to legally immigrate partly due to their education level then find that their educational qualifications are not recognized by the authorities, after they have arrived in the country. As for "illegal" migrants they end up working in sectors and conditions that would hardly appeal to citizens. It is clear that non-Western workers who have been heavily oppressed by older patterns and processes of colonialism and racism are now represented as the "enemies", the ones to restrain and control (Sharma, 2005; Walia, 2013). In addition, the US' structural change, in shifting the matter of undocumented migrants from civil law to criminal law, shows the method whereby the state creates deviants to exercise and legitimize its domination. Due to past colonial history, liberal states avoid the risk of being seen as openly racist and thus avoid overtly targeting one particular ethnic group (even though the post 9-11 period has especially targeted Arabs and Muslims for "profiling"). Instead, the state personifies itself as a victim that needs protection against the "criminals," in this case the "illegal" migrants (Walia, 2013). Therefore, this trick enables the state to strengthen physical and psychological borders in order to protect itself, that is, to protect its domination.

Conclusion

Border imperialism theory is contiguous with new imperialism theory. It adds a focus on aggressive territorial control comprised by borders. Spatial elements are not perhaps as important in the new imperialism theory, which tends to emphasize "empire without colonies". However, through this essay I hope it has been shown that migration control means territory still matters. It was also demonstrated how neoliberal structural reforms are directly targeting people, often the ones that have suffered a long history of domination from colonialism. Therefore, new imperialism seems to be the new expression of domination in the contemporary world. Paying special attention to the ideology of cultural imperialism shining through mainstream media, shows how a system of migrant exploitation is legitimized. Also, through narratives of panic and crisis, conceptualized as a permanent state of emergency (Pandolfi, 2010), the US is able to apply some significant changes in law towards migrants, namely by producing a narrative that creates an imperative to build spaces in order to restrain and control the "terrible" flows of persons who instantly become "criminal" by virtue of their arrival in the US.

References

Avilés, W. (2008). US Intervention in Colombia: The Role of Transnational Relations. *Bulletin of Latin American Research*, 27(3), 410–429.

Bacon, D. (2008). *Uprooted and Criminalized: The Impact of Free Markets on Migrants*. Oakland, CA: The Oakland Institute.

Bellier, I. (2009). Globalisation et fragmentation : l'anthropologie au défi des mondes contemporains. In Francine Saillant (Ed.), *Réinventer l'anthropologie? Les sciences de la culture à l'épreuve des globalisations* (pp. 45–65). Montréal: Liber.

Corrections Corporation America (CCA). (2013). Welcome to CCA: Public-Private Prison Partnerships.
http://www.cca.com/

Connelly, M. (2006).The New Imperialists. In Craig Calhoun, Frederick Cooper, & Kevin W. Moore (Eds.), *Lessons of Empire: Imperial Histories and American Power* (pp. 19–33). New York: The New Press.

Davidson, R.A. (2003). Spaces of Immigration "Prevention": Interdiction and the Nonplace. *Diacritics*, 33(3/4), 2–18.

Detention Watch Network (DWN). (2012). About the U.S. Detention and Deportation System.
http://www.detentionwatchnetwork.org/resources

Dufour, J. (2007/7/1). The Worldwide Network of US Military Bases: The Global Deployment of US Military Personnel. *Global Research*.
http://www.globalresearch.ca/the-worldwide-network-of-us-military-bases/5564

Kerr, S.E. (2012/3/30). CIDA Under Fire for Partnering with Mining Company. *Alternative International Journal*, March 30.
http://www.alterinter.org/spip.php?article3786

Fanjul, G., & Fraser, A. (2003). Dumping without Borders: How US Agricultural Policies are Destroying the Livelihoods of Mexican Corn Farmers. Oxfam Briefing Paper.

Fassin, D. (2010). Heart of Humaneness: The Moral Economy of Humanitarian Intervention. In Didier Fassin & Mariella Pandolfi (Eds.), *Contemporary States of Emergency: The Politics of Military and Humanitarian Interventions* (pp. 269–293). New York: Zone Books.

Frey, A. B., & Zhao, X. K. (2011). The Criminalization of Immigration and the International Norm of Non-Discrimination: Deportation and Detention in U.S. Immigration Law. *Law and Inequality*, 29, 279–312.

Gavett, G. (2011/10/18). Map: The U.S. Immigration Detention Boom. *Frontline*, October 18.
http://www.pbs.org/wgbh/pages/frontline/race-multicultural/lost-in-detention/map-the-u-s-immigration-detention-boom/

Gonzalez, G.G.; Fernandez, R.A.; Price, V.; Smith, D.; & Trinh Võ, L. (2004). Globalization: Masking Imperialism and the Struggles from Below. In Gilbert G. Gonzalez, Raul A. Fernandez, Vivian Price, David Smith, & Linda Trinh Võ (Eds.), *Labor versus Empire: Race, Gender and Migration* (pp. x–xxviii). New York: Routledge.

Gordon, T., Webber, J.R. (2008). Imperialism and Resistance: Canadian Mining Companies in Latin America. *Third World Quarterly* 29(1), 63–87.

Harvey, D. (2003). *The New Imperialism*. Oxford: Oxford University Press.

Ignatieff, M. (2003/1/5). The Burden. *The New York Times Magazine*, January 5.
http://www.nytimes.com/2003/01/05/magazine/05EMPIRE.html

Kanstroom, D. (2004). Criminalizing the Undocumented: Ironic Boundaries of the Post-September 11th 'Pale of Law'. *North Carolina*

Journal of International Law and Commercial Regulation, 29, 639–670.

Makaremi, C. (2008). Pénalisation de la circulation et reconfigurations de la frontière : le maintien des étrangers en « zone d'attente ». *Cultures & Conflits*, 71 (automne), 55-73.

Martin, L. (2011). The Geopolitics of Vulnerability: Children's Legal Subjectivity, Immigrant Family Detention and US Immigration Law and Enforcement Policy. *Gender, Place & Culture: A Journal of Feminist Geography*, 18(4), 477–498.

Pandolfi, M. (2010). From Paradox to Paradigm: the Permanent State of Emergency in the Balkans. In Didier Fassin & Mariella Pandolfi (Eds.), *Contemporary States of Emergency: The Politics of Military and Humanitarian Interventions* (pp.153–172). New York: Zone Books.

Petras, J. (2003). Empire and Labour: U.S. and Latin America.
http://petras.lahaine.org/b2-img/030327empire_labor.pdf

Piché, V. (2005). Immigration, mondialisation et diversité culturelle : comment « gérer » les défis? *Les Cahier du GRES*, 5(1), 7–28.

Scott, J. (1998). *Seeing Like a State: How Certain Schemes to Improve the Human Condition Have Failed*. New Haven: Yale University Press.

Sharma, N. (2005). Anti-Trafficking Rhetoric and the Making of a Global Apartheid. *NWSA Journal*, 17(3), 88–111.

Smale, A. (2015/8/24). Migrants Push Toward Hungary as a Border Fence Rises. *The New York Times*, August 24.
http://www.nytimes.com/2015/08/25/world/europe/migrants-push-toward-hungary-as-a-border-fence-rises.html

Trouillot, M-R. (2001). The Anthropology of the State in the Age of Globalization: Close Encounters of the Deceptive Kind. *Current Anthropology*, 42(1), 125–138.

UN High Commission for Refugees (UNHCR) .(2011). A Year of Crises: UNHCR Global Trends, 2011.
http://unhcr.org/4fd6f87f9.html

————— . (2013). War's Human Cost: UNHCR Global Trends, 2013.
http://www.unhcr.org/5399a14f9.html

Walia, H. (2013). *Undoing Border Imperialism*. Oakland, CA: AK Press.

Chapter 6

HUMANITARIAN RELIEF VS. HUMANITARIAN BELIEF

Iléana Gutnick

"The most important exclusion, however, was and continues to be what development was supposed to be all about: people. Development was—and continues to be for the most part—a top-down, ethnocentric, and technocratic approach, which treated people and cultures as abstract concepts, statistical figures to be moved up and down in the charts of 'progress'". (Escobar, 1995, p. 44)

Famines in Africa, wars in the Middle East, and tsunamis in Japan: the world seems to have gone haywire. Are these a sign of God's final punishment? Or are they simply reminders of the ordinary, redundant poverty or misfortune that exists because the world is just an unfair place? This uneasy mix of desperate and ambivalent rhetoric seems to characterize the main discourse of a variety of Western non-governmental organizations (NGOs): no one can specifically be held accountable for how the world works, but with your money and your kindness, we can end poverty today.

However, this rhetorical skew is actually a lot more than a simple attempt to get inside people's wallets. It actually contributes to the decontextualization of poverty, and in a context of neoliberal structural adjustment under globalization, failing to mention it is like ignoring the odds that the floor will give way because of the huge purple elephant in the room. If one truly sets out to end poverty, overlooking essential factors that have several times been pointed out seems quite odd. In this case, to purposefully omit the role of underlying structures from the public discourse conceals the fact that they actually are part of the problem. It therefore does not seem unreasonable to assume that these organizations are driven by some kind of political agenda. But what on earth could well-intentioned, white, Western, rich and developed organizations want from the rest of the world?

This chapter will argue that humanitarian aid discourse is intentionally misleading in that it shifts the public's focus of attention toward seemingly immediate yet irrelevant ways of coping with global poverty and underdevelopment. If "lack of fertile land, war and political strife, government corruption, unfair trade policies, disease, and famine" (The Life You Can Save [TLYCS], 2014a) are the main causes of poverty, I will argue that such situations are intentionally generated by Western states in order to, as Susan George (1988, p. 5) bluntly puts it, keep the "Third World" in line. The underlying political agenda of NGOs is therefore ironically very similar to that of the powerful states that back them, that is, to impose a foreign presence in order to advance imperial political and economic interests, in the name of development. In this perspective, "humanitarianism is nothing more than a virtuous disguise for reasons of state" (Fassin, 2013, p. 275). One NGO whose discourse will be at the focus of my examination is The Life You Can Save, which describes itself as "a movement of people fighting extreme poverty" (TLYCS, 2014b), and is useful as an average example of the kind of humanitarian rhetoric typically used by NGOs seeking visibility and funding from the Western public (TLYCS, 2014c).

Helping Others

Donating to a Good Cause

The Life You Can Save is based on the creator Pete Singer's philosophy, which he calls "Effective Altruism". Effective Altruism is defined as "[combining] both the heart and the head": donating money is therefore a feel-good initiative as well as one that is reasonable and legitimate. If every Western individual donated a couple of dollars, then together we would have the financial resources to end poverty. This particular focus on Western individuals is also a big part of the rhetoric aimed at convincing potential donors. The Life You Can Save claims that "giving makes us happier," an apparent fact backed up by the mention of a certain Harvard study (TLYCS, 2014c). "Giving is tax deductible" (TLYCS, 2014c), which means it is possible to "reduce the cost of your donation" (TLYCS, 2014c). Finally, "giving is in our nature" (TLYCS, 2014c): humans feel naturally compelled to help those who suffer, and experience guilt when they do not.

Placing the burden of ending world poverty on individuals completely obliterates donor states' responsibility for the social consequences of their foreign aid to recipient states. As Agier (2008) puts it, humanitarian aid can be considered as the empire's left arm. It kills with the right, and cares with the left (p. 296). So while US $30 billion lands in Africa through foreign aid, US $192 billion leaves the continent in the form of debt servicing, tax evasion, and multinational companies' profit, to name a few examples (Health Poverty Action et al., 2014). Aid is typically granted by countries that benefit from Africa's resource exploitation. If "giving makes us happier" and is a universal part of human nature, then the ambivalence generated by NGOs' humanitarian rhetoric can be striking. Since wealthy states and international financial institutions are exploiting the "underdeveloped" world, while performing superficial altruism often in tandem with NGOs, then the moral standards of giving are not that universal after all, and for those who benefit most from Africa's exploitation, taking is what apparently makes them happier than giving.

Neither the international financial institutions nor powerful states have managed to diminish poverty. Not only do they fail to fulfill their moral duties on an international scale, they are also as unsuccessful at home, on a national level. According to the US Census Bureau (2013), 14.5% of US citizens are living in poverty (2013), a number that is higher in other studies that take into account different factors, such as rising household debt and decreased income available for services. Poverty rates for children in the US are amongst the highest in the industrialized world (American Psychological Association [APA], 2006, p. 2). On average, every adult in the US owes roughly US $11,000 in consumer debt, excluding real estate loans (Pressman & Scott, 2009, p. 127). That figure also excludes the per capita share of public debt. Consumer debt has risen annually at a 4.1% rate over the past 20 years, while median household income has remained essentially the same (Pressman & Scott, 2009, p. 127), which has pushed more and more people below the poverty line. Those at the top 5% of the income distribution ladder have benefited from a significant increase in their incomes, while the bottom 40% has not, gradually widening the gap between the rich and the poor (APA, 2006, p. 1). Basically, while the rich get richer, the middle class and the poor get poorer. In this context, informing the majority at the bottom of the income scale of "how powerful [their] pocket change can become when pooled together" (TLYCS, 2014c), seems quite unethical and insensitive. Placing the burden on Western individuals obliterates the state's economic responsibility regarding the socio-economic inequalities that affect the well being of their own citizens. "You don't have to be a millionaire to make a significant difference" (TLYCS, 2014c), is preached to people who have experienced the negative "significant difference" that has been wrought by millionaires.

Going Abroad: The White Savior

Not only is helping the needy abroad a moral obligation, it is also as easy as the click of a button, we are commonly told by humanitarian aid agencies. The most obvious way of "helping" is by donating a couple of dollars to a charity every month. But for the most adventurous of us, our moral duty feels like it needs to be fulfilled by *actually doing something*. One must travel to the troubled zone, which suggests problems lie elsewhere, and are in no way connected to the northern/western hemisphere. By assuming this is the case, humanitarian rhetoric exempts the global North from blame. It instead legitimizes and promotes non-governmental intervention, by adopting the moral principle that any privileged individual not only has the duty to help the weak, but is also competent enough to do so just because of his or her material advantage. Useful assistance is therefore depicted as "[requiring] nothing more than the presence of a Western Volunteer" (Biehn, 2014, p. 82). Assuming that any Western foreigner is equipped to understand, evaluate and act upon local issues suggests that the locals themselves are not so equipped. Locals are depicted as being unaware and incapable of assessing their own needs, and their capacity to fulfill them according to their own value- and belief-systems.

Locals are also often erased from the list of main motives for volunteers to venture abroad. The emphasis is not put on the actions that potentially help the poor, but rather on the "experience of a lifetime" that volunteering can be. As Biehn points out, the feeling of cultural immersion is often one of the promises made to volunteers by organizations (2014, p. 80). This seeming celebration of multiculturalism is furthermore constructed through the images published on NGO websites, which mostly range from smiling non-white children to sad non-white women wearing "exotic" clothing. Rather than to celebrate, these images essentialize and ghettoize societies by stamping each and every individual with "Help me! I'm poor" on their foreheads. This representation further reproduces the same discourse offered by development theories, which portray the "Third World" using terms like "powerlessness, passivity, poverty, and ignorance" (Escobar, 1995, p. 8). The individual internalization of this rhetoric does nothing more than to reproduce at a personal level the North/South power relations that this rhetoric entails. If resourcefulness is enough to justify one's competency, then we should be asking ourselves why locals do not have those resources. It therefore becomes fundamental to recontextualize poverty.

Saving Lives at Gunpoint:
The Militarization of Humanitarian Intervention

War, sometimes justified as a humanitarian intervention, is itself one of the many justifications for humanitarian intervention: war is bloody and endangers human lives, the same lives that some NGOs claim they strive to save. In the case of intervening in a conflict zone, NGOs regularly insist that they adopt a neutral framework, meaning that they consider all civilian lives to be worthy of protection, regardless of political allegiance. In reality, the humanitarian approach is often not as impartial as it claims to be. More often than not, humanitarian aid is deployed "in a context where political and economic interests, the logics of states and agencies, and imperial and nationalist ideologies are at work" (Fassin, 2013, p. 270). The same nation-states that engage in armed intervention are those which generate the humanitarian aid. In addition, those living in countries that possess profitable resources frequently appear to be more worthy of saving than those who do not. Perhaps NGOs can find a way to argue that they cannot be everywhere at once. However, even within countries where NGOs are at work, the principle of neutrality still does not apply. It turns out life does have a cost, and that is the cost of state security. To ensure state security, it is agreed upon within international law that some human suffering is necessary and inevitable (Orford, 2010, p. 338).

Some might wonder what military violence has to do with humanitarian aid. They actually have a lot more in common than some might wish to consider. First, humanitarian and military personnel both act within a limited timeframe and extraordinary circumstances—that is to say, an "emergency" framework—which leads them to "consider their own role [as being] above the common law" (Fassin, 2013, p. 284). It is important to emphasize how similar this type of framework can be to that of colonial rule. Furthermore, as stated above, humanitarian morality is used to legitimize foreign presence, which is most often military. It is therefore not surprising to see NGO personnel and the military continue to collaborate once they are in the shared "theatre of operations". First and maybe more obviously, humanitarian workers need protection from armed forces in order to deliver help. This means they must adhere to (and benefit from) military logistics and organization to manage sites, such as "corridors of tranquility" (Anderson, 1996, p. 343), living quarters and refugee camps (Fassin, 2013, p. 284), but also to manage which lives are to be saved, how and on what basis. If humanitarian aid and military intervention are deployed in countries that are of strategic interest to the West, it should come as no surprise that they pursue the same political objectives. In this case, analysis should focus on how foreign interest has shaped and contributed to the occupied countries' political situation that is used to justify further occupation, and how this incapacitates locals from self-determination. Given what has been presented here, one can see the case that is made by military writers in framing NGOs as "force multipliers" (see the Introduction to this volume).

Recontextualizing Poverty

In the Name of Development

"Without stable institutions like efficient banks, a reliable police force, functioning schools and fair criminal justice systems, it is very difficult to compete on a global scale" (TLYCS, 2014c). It is no secret that development is at the heart of many NGOs' concerns: for more than 50 years, it has been the basis of foreign action of Western institutions and considered the only way in which "the American dream of peace and abundance [can] be extended to all the peoples of the planet" (Escobar, 1995, p. 4). Seen in this light, it makes sense that developed nations would help underdeveloped nations.

The notion of development following a universal model stems from the belief that Western society and culture have evolved into ones that are better-equipped and therefore more efficient in dealing with satisfying basic needs. Apart from being evidently ethnocentric and condescending, this interpretation assumes efficiency is of advantage to the poorest. The concept of efficiency is now embedded in Western culture: cars go faster than donkeys, and four-minute microwaveable foods are less-time consuming. The removal of time-related constraints allows for one's time to be used efficiently: "they can work, they can go to school, they can contribute to their household income, and they don't take someone else's time and capacity to work by requiring care" (TLYCS, 2014c). In this perspective, the goal of efficiency, understood as the conceptualization of time in terms of economic value (simply put time equals money), is to create workers and consumers. And technological innovation is what makes efficiency possible. Indeed, development promotes a type of progress that favors technological advancement and industrialization. Since development is praised for its practical superiority, it becomes legitimate to impose this progress onto others, supposedly for their own good. Setting the conditions in which development can thrive, subsequently becomes a priority. The cultural traits, values and political ideals that set the stage for development processes must then be exported in order to impose a framework in which it becomes advantageous and desirable for locals to (literally) clear the way for the establishing of foreign institutions. Modern technology makes the globalization of culture much easier.

The privatization of national telecommunication infrastructures in the 1970s, strongly urged by US corporations and governments, meant the US could broadcast US values, ideologies and images on a truly global scale (Mirlees, 2006, p. 199). The US ideals that are transmitted both implicitly and explicitly tend to suggest that living by "possessive individualism" and "excessive consumerism" is bound to lead to a preferable and more adequate existence (Mirlees, 2006, p. 200). US-style democracy is also extensively featured as being of superior moral nature, as it presents individuals as being free and equal under the law. However, what is claimed as a universal ideal of individual liberty also has as an effect to "[reduce] all types of people to interchangeable units of labour" (Wood, 2006, p. 11). Television, computer and mobile screens become the conveyors of a world where the US becomes a template for an avowedly beneficial global culture, and does so by exporting the means that strengthen its political and economic values (Mirlees, 2006). So much for multiculturalism.

The reaching of new audiences and therefore potential consumers becomes instrumental in laying the basis for a system that eventually "allows the systematic creation of objects, concepts and strategies; [and] determines what can be thought and said" (Escobar, 1995, p. 40). These regulating objects, concepts and strategies are embodied by "efficient banks, a reliable police force, functioning schools and fair criminal justice systems" (TLYCS, 2014c) argued to be the basic foundations of overcoming poverty. It is to be noted that the economy, defense, education, the implementation of rule of law and the promotion of democracy are cited as NGOs' top priorities in their fight against poverty, especially in the case of The Life You Can Save. In this sense, NGOs' interventions on foreign territory are themselves another object that participates in the creation of a set of relations between "institutions, socioeconomic processes, forms of knowledge, [and] technological factors" (Escobar, 1995, p. 40) that form the system that creates workers and consumers. However, increased modernization comes with many increased costs, which is minimized in the discourse of NGOs such as The Life You Can Save.

External Debt: Eternal Debt

Extreme poverty as defined in NGO narratives is often explained in terms of individual daily spending. TLYCS' Extreme Poverty Report states that 65% of the global population lives on less than US $2 a day, implying this is not enough to meet basic necessities such as food and shelter (TLYCS, 2014d). Regardless of the merits of the implication, the report leaves out the part about "Third World" countries being heavily indebted to their Western counterparts, which is one of the reasons they are financially insecure in the first place. Although The Life You Can Save mentions "unfair trade policies" as harmful to "Third World" development, it never contextualizes them, nor does it provide a basis of action to counter them.

Whether development is implemented in order to raise "Third World" living standards to match the West's, or whether development reflects the fact that, "Third World economies were only integrated to the global capitalist system in order to serve the Centre's needs" (Mushkat, 1975, p. 42), might be open to debate. When one analyzes the way in which the development model actually works, there appears to be less room for debate: historically development has neglected the majority to the advantage of the few, justifying this by endorsing the "'trickle-down' process" (George, 1988, p. 15), which would somehow eventually improve everyone's living conditions by first improving the conditions of the wealthy, and as experience has taught us, fails to generate economic growth, greater investment, or job creation. In addition, in the name of development, "Third World" countries have been now swamped in debt: the West lends money for them to develop their economies by exploiting their resources, to meet the needs of the developed centre, and to benefit the wealthy that are the first concern of trickle-down development policies.

We can summarize some of the key features of development policies and projects that should raise questions about NGO discourses that may blur the causes of poverty. First, the pattern of foreign investment in development is not one that is driven by the needs of the majority, of course, as much as it by the profit concerns of investors. Typically investors have focused on the extraction of resources that fuel Western consumption (George, 1988). In some cases development loans have been used to finance "hardly profitable and useless projects" (Guillén & Gandy, 1989, p. 37). One must also remember that the basic purpose of lending is for creditors to gain capital through (rising) interest. It therefore seems safe to assume that when a disaster such as famine is pointed out as being one of the leading causes of poverty, it is not necessarily a natural phenomenon, but rather one with a long political and economic genealogy. Loans are used to finance rapid industrialization, not diminishing rapidly growing hunger. When loans are not directed towards productive and/or income-generating activities, backlashes such as food shortages and food riots have occurred. Furthermore, because of free trade agreements, such as NAFTA's implementation in 1994, some peasants are forced off their lands, while others are forced to change crops because they cannot compete with the prices offered by multinational corporations (Janvry et al., 1995). In 2009, fertile land made available to foreign investors amounted to 56 million hectares around the world (Oakland Institute, 2011, p. 3). Banks are involved in this global economic land coup, since they are the ones financing these corporations (George, 1988, p. 36).

Local government elites play their part as the force multipliers of global capitalism, with many receiving payments for ensuring the undisturbed establishment of multinational corporations in their territories. These elites protect themselves, hire armies, and kill. They are also guilty of transferring loan money into foreign bank accounts (George, 1988, p. 19), allowing interest rates to pile up over their citizens' heads while they drink champagne— in 2013, Nigeria had the second fastest growing champagne consumption rate in the world (Hirsch, 2013/5/8). As Hirsch puts it, "not everyone in [a] country where 63% live on less than $1 a day is impressed with the $50m and rising spent each year on fizz" (Hirsch, 2013/5/8). However, just as champagne bottles are usually shared, corruption is a game played by two (or ten, or hundreds), and is not always called corruption when it is structurally legitimized by international financial organizations as well as market (de)regulations.

The International Monetary Fund (IMF) officially bills itself as, "an organization of 188 countries, working to foster global monetary cooperation, secure financial stability, facilitate international trade, promote high employment and sustainable economic growth, and reduce poverty around the world" (IMF, 2014). Official statements aside, the fundamental role of the IMF, which is largely organized around US interests given its dominant share of votes in the organization, is to promote trade by ensuring that debts will be repaid to creditor banks (George, 1988, p. 47). It imposes what are called structural adjustments, which administer national economies in order to "guarantee that countries will continue to have the means to pay" (George, 1988, p. 49)—in other words, the focus is on short-term debt servicing rather than ensuring the well-being of the majority. Austerity measures are supposed to increase income and reduce spending (George, 1988, p. 52) in order to save money to pay debts back quickly. The most common measures imposed and undertaken by structural adjustment programs include, "devaluation of currency, wage freezes, increased privatization, removal of tariffs and other 'protectionist' measures, and reduced government spending and employment" (Bradshaw, 1991, p. 322). These adjustments most often lead to reduced quality of life, severe cuts in social spending (such as food subsidies or medical care), and usually increase both unemployment and poverty (Bradshaw, 1991, p. 322). Bearing in mind "Third World" countries already lack the financial resources required to meet their citizens' basic needs (a fact that is at the heart of NGOs' concerns and interest), reducing their access to services in order to reduce spending is directly responsible for creating a "need" market for NGOs. Furthermore, if countries do not comply with IMF measures, they will not be deemed as "acceptable credit risks" (Bradshaw, 1991, p. 321), which means they will not be able to borrow to pay back their debts. Considering "Third World" countries often depend on new loans only to service old ones (George, 1988, p. 13), it becomes impossible even for countries that are not governed by corrupt elites to step out of the game. This would mean no more foreign cash flow (Bradshaw, 1991, p. 325), which is crucial to their economies. To better contain the threat of a popular social backlash, the IMF imposes austerity measures on social spending, but not on military expenditures (George, 1988, p. 22).

War and Political Strife: Militarizing the "Third World"

NGOs repeatedly point to war, political strife and government corruption as being some of the main reasons of poverty. However, as mentioned earlier, it is difficult to imagine how heavily indebted "Third World" countries find the millions necessary for seemingly endless wars. The IMF has shown little interest in the issue, justifying this inattention by claiming it does not want to interfere with government sovereignty (George, 1988, p. 22).

Rather than a straightforward question of sovereignty, what is at play is a highly lucrative international arms trade. The US was responsible for 79% of the weapons sold to developing countries in 2011 (Grimmett & Kerr, 2012, p. 25). On top of owing billions in debt, "developing" countries that by definition possess limited financial resources are the main recipients of arms trade agreements (Grimmett & Kerr, 2012, p. 31). Weaponry imports have in turn functioned as "a significant contributory fact to Third World indebtness" (Looney quoted in Dunne, 2004, p. 128). Military expenditure is yet another example of debt being used for unproductive activities: "[arms purchases] produce no wealth and, when not manufactured locally, they don't even create jobs or inject money into the local economy. They are nothing but pure consumption" (George, 1988, p. 24). Funds allocated to military expenditure in Africa and the Middle East often take priority over those allocated to health and education (World Council of Churches, 2005 p. 15).

Repoliticizing Poverty

Despite the prevailing NGO narrative as reproduced by The Life You Can Save, poverty is a politically constructed phenomenon, and not just at the local level. NGOs are increasingly leading the way in popular representations of "Third World" countries in commercial media in the West; advertisements are filled with poor, powerless and passive individuals awaiting foreign help. Such an approach obscures Western states' responsibility in creating or aggravating socioeconomic disparities. By asking for personal donations, NGOs place the burden of saving the poor on individuals, many of whom are themselves already strained by austerity measures, instead of on those who impose these measures worldwide.

This is justified in the name of development, described by Susan George as "a myth-word in whose name any destruction, and any expenditure, may be undertaken with impunity" (1988, p. 15)

References

Agier, M. (2008). *Gérer les indésirables: Des camps de réfugiés au gouvernement humanitaire*. Paris: Flammarion.

American Psychological Association (APA). (2007). *Report of the APA Task Force on Socioeconomic Status*. Washington, DC: American Psychological Association.
http://www.apa.org/pi/ses/resources/publications/task-force-2006.pdf

Anderson, M. (1996). Humanitarian NGOs in Conflict Intervention. In Chester Crocker, Fen Hampson & Pamela Aall (Eds.), *Managing Global Chaos* (pp. 343–354). Washington, D.C.: United States Institute of Peace Press.

Biehn, T. (2014). Who Needs Me Most? New Imperialist Ideologies in Youth-Centered Volunteer Abroad Programs. In Maximilian C. Forte (Ed.), *Good Intentions: Norms and Practices of Imperial Humanitarianism* (pp. 77–87). Montreal: Alert Press.

Bradshaw, Y.W., & Huang, J. (1991). Intensifying Global Dependency: Foreign Debt, Structural Adjustment and Third World Underdevelopment. *The Sociological Quarterly*, 32(3), 321–342.

Dunne, J.P.; Perlo-Freeman, S.; & Soydan, A. (2004). Military Expenditure and Debt in Small Industralised Economies: A Panel Analysis. *Defence and Peace Economics*, 15(2), 125–132.

Escobar, A. (1995). *Encountering Development: The Making and Unmaking of the Third World*. Princeton, NJ: Princeton University Press.

Fassin, D. (2013). Heart of Humaneness: The Moral Economy of Humanitarian Intervention. In Didier Fassin & Mariella Pandolfi (Eds.), *Contemporary States of Emergency: The Politics of Military and Humanitarian Interventions* (pp. 269–293). New York: Zone Books.

George, S. (1988). *A Fate Worse than Debt*. New York: Grove Press.

Grimmett, R., & Kerr, P. (2012) Conventional Arms Transfers to Developing Nations 2004-2011. Washington, DC: Congressional Research Service.
http://www.fas.org/sgp/crs/weapons/R42678.pdf

Guillén, A. & Gandy, R. (1989). Crisis, the Burden of Foreign Debt, and Structural Dependence. *Latin American Perspectives*, 16(1), 31–51.

Health Poverty Action et al. (2014). Report: Honest Accounts? The True Story of Africa's Billion Dollar Losses. Report by Health Poverty Action et al.
http://www.healthpovertyaction.org/wp-content/uploads/downloads/2014/07/Honest-Accounts-report-v4-web.pdf

Hirsch, A. (2013/5/8). Nigeria's Love of Champagne Takes Sales Growth to Second Highest in World. *The Guardian*, May 8.
http://www.theguardian.com/world/2013/may/08/nigeria-champagne-sales-growth-second-highest

International Monetary Fund (IMF) (2014). About the IMF.
http://www.imf.org/external/about.htm

Janvry, A.; Sadoulet, E.; & Davis, B. (1995). NAFTA's Impact on Mexico: Rural Household-Level Effects. *American Journal of Agricultural Economics*, 77(5), 1283–1291.

Mirlees, T. (2006). American Soft Power, or, American Cultural Imperialism? In Colin Mooers (Ed.), *The New Imperialists: Ideologies of an Empire* (pp. 199–227). Oxford: Oneworld.

Mushkat, M. (1975). Sous-développement en Afrique: Une situation imposée par des éléments extérieurs? *Africa: Rivista trimestrale di studi e documentazione dell'Istituto italiano per l'Africa e l'Oriente*, 30(1), 39-45.

Oakland Institute (2011). Understanding Land Investment Deals in Africa—Country Report: Ethiopia. Oakland, CA: The Oakland Institute.
http://www.oaklandinstitute.org/sites/oaklandinstitute.org/files/OI_Ethiopa_Land_Investment_report.pdf

Orford, A. (2010). The Passions of Protection: Sovereign Authority and Humanitarian War. In Didier Fassin & Mariella Pandolfi (Eds.), *Contemporary States of Emergency: The Politics of Military and Humanitarian Interventions* (pp. 335–356). New York: Zone Books.

Pressman, S., & Scott, R. (2009). Consumer Debt and the Measurement of Poverty and Inequality in the US. *Review of Social Economy*, 67(2), 127–148.

The Life You Can Save (TLYCS). (2014a). *What is Extreme Poverty?*
http://www.thelifeyoucansave.org/Learn-More/What-is-Extreme-Poverty

——————— . (2014b). About Us.
http://www.thelifeyoucansave.org/About-Us

——————— . (2014c). Why Donate?
http://www.thelifeyoucansave.org/Learn-More/Why-Donate

——————— . (2014d). Extreme Poverty Report.
http://www.thelifeyoucansave.org/Portals/0/Extreme%20Poverty%20Report%20-%20General.pdf

US Census Bureau. (2013). Social, Economic, and Housing Statistics Division: Poverty, 2013 Highlights. Washington, DC: US Census Bureau.
http://www.census.gov/hhes/www/poverty/about/overview/index.html

Wood, E.M. (2006). Democracy as Ideology of Empire. In Colin Mooers (Ed.), *The New Imperialists: Ideologies of an Empire* (pp. 9–23). Oxford: Oneworld.

World Council of Churches. (2005). World Military Expenditure: A Compilation of Data and Facts Related to Military Spending, Education and Health. Geneva: Coordination Office for the Decade

to Overcome Violence, World Council of Churches.
http://www.overcomingviolence.org/fileadmin/dov/files/wcc_resources/dov_docu
ments/MilitarySpendingReport.pdf

ON SECRECY, POWER, AND THE IMPERIAL STATE: PERSPECTIVES FROM WIKILEAKS AND ANTHROPOLOGY

Maximilian C. Forte

"['Anne,' journalist at a Pentagon press conference]: Do you have any mechanism or authority to compel WikiLeaks to do as you say—as you are demanding?

"[Pentagon spokesman, Geoff Morrell]:...how do we intend to compel, what I would say there, Anne, is that at this point we are making a demand of them. We are asking them to do the right thing. This is the appropriate course of action, given the damage that has already been done, and we hope they will honor our demands and comply with our demands. If it requires them compelling to do anything [*sic*]—if doing the right thing is not good enough for them, then we will figure out what other alternatives we have to compel them to do the right thing. Let me leave it at that". (US Department of Defense [DoD], 2010b)

Speaking as a moderator for a public conversation with Julian Assange and Slavoj Žižek, Amy Goodman declared, "information is power. Information is a matter of life and death" (Goodman, 2011/7/5). "Information is power" is not just a popular cyberactivist article of faith, it is arguably a core premise in Julian Assange's theoretical repertoire. Assange thus conceptualizes WikiLeaks as a "mechanism" whose goal is to "to maximise the flow of information" which results in maximising "the amount of action leading to just reform" (Davies, 2010/7/25). This is reminiscent of the "force multiplier" idea outlined by the US military and diplomatic establishment, as discussed at length in the Introduction to this volume. Anthropologists, on the other hand, will be tempted to respond that information is not the same thing as knowledge, and neither is the same thing as meaning, and that power rests on a base that is far broader than information-control alone. Nevertheless, with the conflict between the US government and WikiLeaks there is much to be learned about the exercise of state power as it applies to secrecy and counter-surveillance, especially in terms of the actual expanse of the power of the US imperial state. The focus of this chapter is on the relationships between power, knowledge, and the social organization of the imperial state. WikiLeaks, and in particular its chief representative, Julian Assange, have a great deal to say in terms of theorizing information and power that might be of value to anthropology; likewise, most anthropologists, with extensive experience with secrecy at the local level, and especially those who have focused specifically on secrecy, have much to offer in return, given certain caveats. Unfortunately, the perspectives of those anthropologists who over the generations have served in the US' clandestine intelligence apparatus are not presented here (however, see Price 1998, 2008).

Secrecy of/as Science

One of the aims of this chapter is to present two different approaches to understanding secrecy—from WikiLeaks and anthropology—with special reference to mapping state power, and to issues of responsibility and trust (of particular concern to the state), and accountability and conspiracy (of particular concern to some critics of the US imperial state, and to WikiLeaks). (To an extent, both sides share a concern for accountability, but to different ends, and at different points along the power gradient, with the imperial state favouring accountability on the part of the weak.) The reason for the dual focus stems from an acknowledgment of the possibility that both WikiLeaks and anthropology have something to gain from each other. Anthropology is a treasure-trove of knowledge about secrecy, built up over generations of research by countless ethnographers, with many insights that offer WikiLeaks a thicker conceptual armour that could aid its practice in better understanding, scrutinizing, anticipating, and deflecting attempts by states (particularly the US) to circumscribe or even quash it. WikiLeaks, on the other hand, has much to offer in terms of putting a spotlight on how information and power are related in the imperial state, besides of course also offering a great deal of information that is useful for anyone attempting to "study up," as Laura Nader put it (1972).

At the outset we already saw the start of what appeared to be a certain "science of secrecy," which in the case of WikiLeaks, as with the US military, is a science of mechanisms that *do* things. Both WikiLeaks and the US military have an obviously intimate relationship with machines, and with machines as the prime means of achieving their goals, with the apparent result being that their conception of human action is mechanized, instrumentalized, even automated. Anthropology is not innocent of such constructs either (historically it has not been immune to scientism), nor is the conception of force multipliers alien to it, given various ideas about how to create "effective allies" for US power, in South Asia for example (see Bateson in Price, 1998, p. 381). Nor is the instrumental exploitation of Indigenous Peoples and their natural resources beyond the pale of US anthropology, especially during World War II (see Price, 2008). However, for the most part, we shall see in anthropology a different science of secrecy that focuses on meaning and social relations, more than mechanisms as such. Otherwise, there are broad connections between secrecy and social science as a whole—as a former professor and US Senator, Daniel Patrick Moynihan (1999), affirmed: "social science" is "the science of secrecy".

It may not be an accident that there are close correspondences between preferred phrases in anthropology and those used by both diplomats and intelligence agents. For example, anthropologists in North America and Britain speak of going into "the field," and "going native" (as a problem), and refer to local hosts as "informants". It is noteworthy that even as some anthropologists object to the nomenclature of the US Army's Human Terrain System (see González, 2012)—finding it objectionable that, in the military's linguistic rendering, human beings are symbolically reduced to inanimate *terrain* to be mapped and marched on like dirt—anthropologists themselves nonetheless persist in using a term related to terrain through land, that being *field*. In fact, *terrain* is also a synonym of two other key conceptual terms in anthropology: *space* and *arena*. Interestingly, forming a bridge between field and terrain are various other synonyms pertaining to the *battlefield*. While González (2012) would like to a see a linguistic analysis performed on military terminology, we should also turn that gaze back. One would in fact not have far to travel to find identical terminology in US anthropology, as when George Marcus described "multi-sited ethnography" as follows: "multi-sited ethnography is an exercise in mapping terrain" (Marcus, 1995, p. 99). In a theoretical piece of dubious value, that was nonetheless influential in US anthropology, Arjun Appadurai disaggregated the world-system into one composed of distinct "scapes" (such as mediascapes, technoscapes, etc.)—which is not too distant from the idea of "landscape," a term that approximates "terrain" (Appadurai, 1990).

It is also no accident of misrecognition that so many local communities have, as retold by generations of anthropologists, seen anthropologists as spies—many were just that (see Price, 2008). Numerous US anthropologists continue to serve as "force multipliers" in multiple formal and informal capacities. As if to cloud the air further, the American Anthropological Association even went as far as censuring one of its founding figures, Franz Boas, for having dared to condemn anthropologists working as spies during WWI, and then kept that censure in place for the next 85 years. In recent decades the AAA even excised the injunction against secret research from its code of ethics, before reinstating it in the last few years. Collaboration with the CIA is also not foreign to the AAA. At one point, collusion with the CIA, secret research, and Boas' continuing censure were all simultaneous facts—none of this can be a mere accident. More recently, the AAA's 12-member Commission on the Engagement of Anthropology with the US Security and Intelligence Communities (CEAUSSIC), charged with investigating the ethics of anthropologists working for intelligence and military agencies, included three persons[1] who were working precisely with the US military and weapons contractors, even as they served on the commission. The obvious conflict of interest, on a panel addressing ethics no less, was an irony that seemed to disturb few commentators. Apart from that, the fact that so many US and British anthropologists prefer not to write about their "field methods," with many against teaching methods courses, can only add to the aura of suspicion, suggesting that secret techniques are being used to elicit secret information. Of course, I would only be relating an open secret if I said that among the ranks of North American anthropologists there is also widespread, simmering resentment against ethics review boards, or that students reluctantly plod through ethics review applications as a mere formality.

WikiLeaks, while generally lacking a history of collusion with imperialist states, has immense practical experience with state secrecy and particularly with diplomacy and military intelligence, in ways that probably most anthropologists do not, since they rarely confront the power of the imperial US state. As anthropologists we should learn how to expand our research repertoire by including what I refer to later in this chapter as the methodology of WikiLeakism, while also revising our own ideas about the actual practice of imperial intervention to include the role of non-state actors working in combination with the imperial state, even if/when not under its formal and rigid direction. Theoretically, WikiLeaks' conflict with the US power structure affords us a glimpse into something that is different from either conspiracy theories (not intended pejoratively here) or coincidence theories, and moves us towards something like a theory of convergence, where goals are shared and understood, and agents act, but without any need for central coordination—a march without a marshal. This is likely due to the confluence of interests in the corporate-oligarchic state, which explains the nearly automatic readiness of credit card companies, banks, and Amazon.com in acting as proxy censors that debilitated WikiLeaks' operations, though not necessarily under any explicit commands from the US state.

Secrecy as Viewed from WikiLeaks, Anthropology, and Sociology

More than journalism, communications/media studies and law, the fields that have arguably dominated the bulk of public debates about WikiLeaks, anthropology can claim special expertise on the study of secrecy. While anthropologists have a wide range of in-depth knowledge about secrecy in diverse social and cultural contexts, and of the ways in which secrets are spoken in socially acceptable ways, these are usually derived from experiences in small-scale, local settings, usually outside of the cultural West, and only rarely dealing with state secrecy (however, see Price, 1998). Anthropological work has primarily been on secrecy as found in secret societies, cults of initiation, shamanic practices, worship, the installation of priests, the socio-linguistics of secrecy, all within settings of intimate inter-personal ties and dense social bonds tying the actors together. The diverse treatments of secrecy reveal multiple analytical paradigms, whether functionalist, instrumentalist, situationalist, or political-economic in the Marxist sense (see Piot, 1993). Concerns range from how social stability is maintained, to analysis of the rules of accepted behaviour around secrecy, to how power is maintained in situations of social inequality (Fulton, 1972; Little, 1949, 1966; Watkins, 1943; la Fontaine, 1977; Murphy, 1980; Ottenberg, 1989). In terms of caveats regarding care needed in applying any anthropological lessons to WikiLeaks, we need to remember the problem of a mismatch between units and scales of analysis. However, in terms of how elites work to maintain their networks and associations, and how the management of information becomes a vehicle for distributing power, there is something of value to learn from anthropology.

WikiLeaks, for its part, has given us an anthropological gift. It is a gift to core areas of anthropological concern, spanning questions of universalism-particularism, power, and knowledge. For example, WikiLeaks' clash with the US has shown us that what underpins hegemomic liberal claims to moral universalism is instead a particularist commitment that sits easily with the kind of moral turpitude exhibited by the merciless expansion and unquestioning defence of imperial power. Put in other words, the gift here is to further expose and once again put on public display the kind of moral dualism that is the practical reality of moral universalism. In this respect, the conflict generated around WikiLeaks has helped to render more visible not just specific state practices, but also the workings of the state in defence of a particular ideology that is superficial and altogether deceptive in espousing values of universal rights.

We could argue that WikiLeaks also has its own distinctive research methodology, one not readily comparable to anything we know of in the social sciences, and yet in some respects worthy of emulation. It's not fieldwork immersion and conversational interaction with informants (their informants are unknown to them). However, they learn a lot about actors through documents, and could learn even more through the actors' reactions to the release of the documents (in a way that conventional ethnography would not normally achieve). It is distinctive because WikiLeaks does not collaborate with informants, it does not send operatives into the institutions whose behaviours it unmasks, and it is not scientific lab research. It also neither steals information nor does it gain access through deception and covert action. It is neither a naturalistic nor an experimental methodology. We could thus call it *WikiLeakism* since it lacks an exact parallel in the social sciences.

What is not too persuasive is the apparently defensive counterargument of some anthropologists, who hold that "we" also have experience working with leaked classified documents and the reports of investigative journalists. WikiLeaks does not just work with classified documents and journalists, since it is the publisher of such materials and uses software, mass media, and social networking to ensure that the information is available to the public without barrier—this is not what anthropologists can generally claim to have done. The institutional context, praxis, and audiences are very different when comparing WikiLeaks and academic anthropology, particularly in the US. On a political level, the differences can be even more striking, since WikiLeaks has been willing to engage in head-on conflict with an imperial power, a power about which most US anthropologists prefer to remain silent.

WikiLeakism and Non-Local Ethnography

As a methodology, WikiLeakism shares some traits in common with more recent forms of "non-local ethnography" of the kind advocated and articulated by Feldman (2011), and older ideas of "studying up" (Nader, 1972). A range of important methodological points have been made between studying up (research that travels up the scale of power and dominance, focusing not on the traditional powerless groups but on the powerful), and non-local ethnography (which can study abstract and impersonal apparatuses that are localized nowhere or are not available to direct sensory experience). A spectrum of methods has thus opened up in anthropology that, though still marginalized (for broadly political and disciplinary reasons), places value on the use of virtual interfaces, documentary research, and media analysis, among other options. A non-local ethnography would thus research phenomena such as NATO, whose expansion and escalated aggression has largely been met with silence by US anthropologists writing on related topics. Possible reasons for this silence in current Anglo-American anthropology include the assumption that NATO policies and practices do not involve "ordinary people" and are thus for some reason "outside the purview of anthropology/ethnography" (Feldman, 2003, p. 1). NATO is therefore constructed in much of Western anthropology as if it were removed from "everyday life". Feldman summarizes some of the problems with this occlusion:
1.   It neglects the indirect social and economic impacts on ordinary people as a result of maintaining excessively large militaries designed for foreign intervention;
2.   It glosses over the identification of nation with the military;
3.   NATO is not just a military organization confined to Brussels, but "rather it is a function of socially reproduced discourses of military, state, nation and even civilization" (Feldman, 2003, p. 2); and,
4.   NATO's effects are localizable and therefore accessible to anthropologists.

The third assumption challenged by Feldman is that,

"NATO precludes ethnography because its Brussels headquarters is even more secretive than the European Commission. An anthropology of NATO necessitates ethnography at headquarters, which is not feasible. No anthropologist will gain ethnographic access to the elites working in Brussels, unlike those who have undertaken ethnographies of the European Commission". (Feldman, 2003, p. 2)

Feldman's response is that this view is an antiquated one that privileges access to specific (usually "remote") locations, rather than being in line with more contemporary arguments in anthropology that reconceptualize "the field" as multiple, interlocking social and political formations. Where Feldman came closest to producing a really challenging answer that opens up horizons, is in pursuing this line of the geographical decentering of research and what this means for participant observation:

"It is not that participant observation is irrelevant or unnecessary, but in instances where face-to-face interaction does not address the necessary research question, anthropologists should use alternative methods that focus on non-localizable sites to expose the culturally produced logic structuring unequal social-political relations" (Feldman, 2003, p. 2).

It is interesting to note in the passages above—on issues relating to secrecy, access, and NATO specifically—how much the turn to WikiLeaks precisely addresses these gaps, making it an essential resource for any non-local ethnography that studies up the imperial chain.

Indeed, secrecy is one of the problems highlighted by González (2012, p. 21), when discussing the methods to be used in studying dominant military formations, such as the Pentagon. One of these involves documentary analysis, and in his discussions González specifically mentions leaked documents, some of which came to light as a result of the work of WikiLeaks. The only point I would add here is that we may view the practice of WikiLeaks as representing either the complete obliteration of ethnography (in its localist, small-scale, direct sensory mode), rendering the latter not just marginal but almost wholly irrelevant, or an expansion of ethnography (into a non-local mode that studies up). In the latter sense, Julian Assange would have an even stronger claim to make that he is an ethnographer, more than a journalist who has not had the "privilege" of experiencing first-hand the machinations of the imperial state apparatuses, which Assange can also claim and which would take him closer to ethnography in the traditional sense of not just observation and listening but also participation.

The Problem of Secrecy

WikiLeaks is a problem—as seen from the perspective of the US state. It is specifically a problem for secrecy, for rendering state secrecy problematic, and for bringing state secrecy back within the domain of questioning and critique. Contrary to former US Secretary of State Hillary Clinton's assertion that WikiLeaks' disclosures represent an "an attack on America's foreign policy interests," and even more than that, "an attack on the international community" thus representing, in her claim, a threat to "global security" and "economic prosperity" (Kessler, 2010/11/30), Carne Ross (2010/11/30), a former British diplomat, takes a different and more analytically useful approach. For Ross, the real attack is on a mode of international diplomacy that is premised on the claim that government business is secret business, and an attack on the ability of governments to claim one thing and do another.

For others, the significant attack is on the patron-client relationship between the state and the corporate media. In exchange for access to official sources (that privileged access is itself a by-product of secrecy, and an enforced scarcity of information that allows public officials to "buy" favourable stories [see Stiglitz, 1999, pp. 11–12]) journalists promise to keep certain information out of public knowledge and to write up stories more favourable to government (also see the Introduction to the volume on the media's military analysts). The corporate media (many of which are linked to the state through their parent corporations' involvement in defence contracting) become part of the reality-management machine of the imperial state, in what some liken to Army Psychological Operations (see Politact, 2010/12/2). If information is a mechanism, as Assange maintains, then it can also be a mechanism that disrupts the force multiplication offered by the mainstream corporate media to the imperial state—information thus becomes a force diminisher, and the willingness to use it for those purposes is part of the broad "blowback" that Chalmers Johnson identified (see the Introduction to this volume).

Beyond diplomacy, and the state's relationship with the chronically embedded media, WikiLeaks also poses a challenge to the secret wars of the US imperial state. As Will Wilkinson (2010/11/29) of *The Economist* put it:

> "The careerists scattered about the world in America's intelligence agencies, military, and consular offices largely operate behind a veil of secrecy executing policy which is itself largely secret. American citizens mostly have no idea what they are doing, or whether what they are doing is working out well. The actually-existing structure and strategy of the American empire remains a near-total mystery to those who foot the bill and whose children fight its wars. And that is the way the elite of America's unelected permanent state, perhaps the most powerful class of people on Earth, like it".

WikiLeaks thus rendered visible the clash between empire's work in the shadows and democratic accountability (see Mueller, 2010/12/7). It would seem as if the careerists that Wilkinson mentioned work on the unexamined assumption that the less people know, the more they will trust the state—or, perhaps, the less people can question, the more the state gains in legitimacy. Trust cannot thrive when questions are provoked, especially when the imperial state's behaviour is shown to be based on a series of duplicitous fabrications. Legitimacy cannot flourish when critique is validated, especially when the imperial state's behaviour is shown to violate both legality and morality. But is it all about the content? Is the problem of trust and legitimacy—cornerstones of what Assange calls conspiracy—largely based on control over information flows? This takes us to some anthropological questions about secrecy.

Leaks: Sacrilege, Privilege, Social Control and Bureaucracy

Taking umbrage at *sacrilege* and *defacement*, with everything that functionaries of the US imperial state believed ought to have remained secret instead coming to light, is how we can begin to understand the sometimes shrill responses of state actors such as Hillary Clinton, or the former Pentagon spokesman, Geoff S. Morrell, or Admiral Mike Mullen, the now former Chairman of the Joint Chiefs of Staff. As Michael Taussig argues the, "[public] secret may [...] be defined as that which is generally known but cannot be spoken," and he asks that we pay special attention to:

"[T]he heterogeneity of the knowledge at stake here, with its *knowing what not to know*, its strategic absences, its resort to riddle and tone...a Swiss-cheese reality of unexpected shapes...of roller-coaster rides through the carnival grounds of 'concealment and revelation,' fuelled by the intensity of the ambivalence of active not-seeing". (Taussig, 1999, p. 50, emphasis added)

This presents us with the explanation that there are different kinds of secrets, and different ways to speak about them (which takes us to rules, below). What is open to question, having read thousands of the ordinary and mundane reports produced by US diplomats that were published by WikiLeaks, is the limited extent to which there is any solid empirical distinction to be made between public knowledge and state secrets, especially in cases where diplomats are merely writing up summaries of local news reports on a given topic of interest to the relevant US mission. Another distinction drawn by some is between the "private secret" (such as a lie) and the "public secret" (secrecy that takes on outward manifestations as in public rituals)—see Bendix (2003, p. 33) for further explanation. I find this treatment of privacy to be problematic, for assuming that we can draw comparisons between individual, public, and state phenomena, without understanding the qualitative difference between each. In practice, this has resulted in some treating Assange's assertion to a right to privacy as somehow "hypocritical" given his publication of leaked state secrets—when the two are not comparable, unless we are to confuse transparency as governmental openness with transparency as a form of personal nudity. Although, perhaps it's a case of the emperor having no clothes after all that unconsciously leads some to conflate the personal and the statal.

How we speak about secrets is crucial, for it is in naming them as such that we create them. In different words, Taussig argues "there is no such thing as a secret," being instead an "invention that comes out of the public secret" and says that "to see the secret as secret is to take it at face-value," rather than a great "as if" without which "the public secret would evaporate" (1999, p. 7).

A second important analytical point comes from something as deceptively simple as the way that Franz Boas, a founding figure in American anthropology, wrote up the transcripts of George Hunt, his Tlingit collaborator, wherein Boas frequently converted the word "secret" into "sacred". The implication of this, as Taussig explained, is that "the sense of something as secret has to be maintained at a pretty high level in the community of believers [dealing with shamanic practices here]," and "the secret itself must remain secret" (2006, p. 136). As Taussig (1999, p. 7) reminds us, "wherever there is power there is secrecy" and at the core of this power lies also public secrecy.

This explanation points to secrecy as a social practice, as a means of social control, which involves practices of inclusion and exclusion that serve to lock out competitors while locking in knowledge as a privilege. The higher the classification of information, the higher up is the level of access in a hierarchic system of control. This clearly takes us to the work of Georg Simmel (1950) in which secrecy is understood as an inherently social relationship involving those who possess and share the secret, those to whom it is permitted to divulge the secret, and those from whom the secret is concealed, and thus differences that bring power to the fore. Simmel also made the case for judging the role of the secret not by its contents, its topics, which constantly shift, but by the social rules that are employed to manufacture and contain the secret (1950, pp. 331, 335).

Leaking is therefore *not* in fact banned outright by the upper echelons of the US imperial state; rather, it is an act that is endowed with privilege. Note how General Stanley McChrystal's classified assessment on the war in Afghanistan was released in time to force Obama's hand in sending more troops (Schorr, 2009/9/23), without any hint from the White House of a hunt to find and prosecute the source of the leak (Smith, 2009/9/22). Even more striking is the now confirmed fact that former Secretary of Defense, Leon Panetta, himself leaked details of the operation to assassinate Bin Laden. As Daniel Ellsberg explained, the only leaks that US administrations condemn are those "that they haven't made themselves, that haven't actually been authorized by their own high officials, which is the greater part of leaks. Nearly all leaks to the newspapers, so-called, are actually authorized by a boss, or even by the highest officials" (Ellsberg, 2011/1/24).

As part of this broad canvas of ideas that inform anthropological and sociological approaches to power and secrecy, there is the question of what Max Weber called the "official secret," as a "specific invention of bureaucracy" (1968, p. 992) and here we come closest to some of Assange's statements on state power as conspiracy, and the ostensibly "irrational" over-classification of information, such that what was published via WikiLeaks often seemed to be of little consequence (again, this should tell us that *content* is not quite the issue in this conflict between the US and WikiLeaks). Going beyond any strictly functional interest in maintaining a secret, Weber explains that state bureaucracy is really interested in exercising rights over the secret as a means of pursuing and enhancing its power against competing entities, such as parliament or various "interest groups". Moynihan (1999) adds to this by attesting to the role of "symbolic secrecy"—secrecy that serves no actual purpose other than to advance state power as an end in itself, and is closely connected to an ideological extremism that rose to power in the Cold War (Shils in Moynihan, 1999). As Weber put it, quite sharply, "bureaucracy naturally welcomes a poorly informed and hence a powerless parliament—at least in so far as ignorance is somehow compatible with the bureaucracy's own interests" (1968, p. 993). As just one available indication of the over-classification of information in the US, of the 6,610,154 million secrets created in 1997 alone, only 1.4% were created under statute, and "the remainder are pure creatures of bureaucracy, via Executive Orders" (Moynihan, 1999). And Weber was right to be blunt, as others have explained the condition in our political system where the public has little knowledge of the extent of the state's regulation of information (from the 1997 Report of the Commission on Protecting and Reducing Government Secrecy quoted by Moynihan [1999]), and as Joseph Stiglitz argued, this reflects "a mistrust between those governing and those governed; and at the same time, it exacerbates that mistrust" (Stiglitz, 1999, p. 2). Moreover, as Stiglitz argued, secrecy not only shields bureaucrats and policy-makers from having their mistakes exposed, secrecy puts incumbents at an advantage over rivals in elections since the incumbent can always argue (thanks to secrecy, left unspoken) that the costs of change would be too high as the rivals are "unprepared" (i.e. they lack the information necessary to govern a situation) (1999, p. 12).

It is also important to understand the limits of Weberian theory, in part due to the neoliberal restructuring of government. Making government run more like a private business, contracting work out to the private sector and bringing in private consultants, clearly challenges Weber's model of bureaucracy. No longer can we argue that there are clear lines separating the state and private sectors, bureaucracy and market. Rather than an impersonal machine, state bureaucracy has in part fallen into the hands of private, personal networks, where loyalty to persons and ideological adherence matters most (Wedel, 2009, pp. 28, 102). So altered is the landscape, argues Wedel, that "the term 'governance,' a relative newcomer to the vocabulary that refers to rule by a combination of bureaucratic and market entities, now often substitutes for 'government'" (2009, p. 77).[2] This is also part of the reason for the decline in government's public accountability, and increased sequestering of information by private networks with access to public goods, that is, the public information paid for by the public. Policy, and its making, has been increasingly privatized "beyond the reach of traditional monitoring systems" (Wedel, 2009, p. 75). The "privatization revolution" of neoliberalism (Wedel, 2009, p. 33), is met by actors such as WikiLeaks, engaged in what we may call a "publication revolution".

The Power of the Secret Tellers: Anthropological Perspectives

The media publications of some non-anthropologists helped to bring certain anthropological points to mind regarding the ways that WikiLeaks has been perceived as a threat, and what that can tell us about the reality of the secret, and the manner in which the state constructs "non-authorized" actors. For some, it is not the *content* of the released documents that matters, but rather the *rules* governing the use of those documents, and this is the real centre of the conflict between WikiLeaks and the state. It is the "rupture in the rules of the game that the practitioners of US foreign policy find astonishing and threatening" (Mueller, 2010/12/7). That the conflict is around a question of rules more than content is given further weight by the public statements of former US Secretary of Defense Robert Gates. He referred to the revelations as "embarrassing" and "awkward," but with little practical effect on the conduct of US relations with foreign partners, adding that the public response has been "overwrought" (US Department of Defense [DoD], 2010a)—presumably that includes the response of his colleague, Hillary Clinton. In another instance, Gates stated that a Pentagon review had "not revealed any sensitive intelligence sources and methods compromised by the disclosure" (Levine, 2010/10/16). Likewise, the German Minister of the Interior referred to the disclosures not as a threat, but rather as "annoying" (Stark & Rosenbach, 2010/12/20). This does not mean that WikiLeaks' work had no significance; rather, it is *what* was significant that is in question, that is, whether what mattered most were rules of disclosure, the relationships and the power structure upheld by those rules, or the empirical content of the leaks.

Breaking the rules that maintain the structure of a system is a very significant act, arguably more than the leak of discrete bits of often unremarkable data. The official spokesman for the Pentagon, Geoff Morrell, confirmed as much when speaking about whether US troops could be trusted with access to information generated from higher levels. In language whose sanctimony and pompous pretence only magnifies the social effect of the "breach," Morrell declared: "we instill an incredible degree of trust and responsibility in our most junior officers and our most junior enlisted," and that clamping down on access, which would represent internal distrust, was not then being considered as officials would "not want to do anything to jeopardize the fundamental goodness of this trusting relationship that has existed for decades in the United States military" (DoD, 2010b).

In some ethnographic studies, a secret is something everybody knows, but agrees not to talk about, or not to talk about except in certain ways (Piot, 1993). This does not seem entirely applicable to the WikiLeaks case, where in many cases we did not know certain secrets, and when we did, many certainly talked about them openly. The latter fact could be seen as stemming from the public's alienation from governance, as having no real stake in the system and hence freely speaking about the open secrets, which would be another of the revelations wrought by WikiLeaks, even if the organization were not conscious of this.

If "secrets are meant to be told," as some anthropologists have contended is the case in most societies where secrecy is practiced (see Bellman, 1984), then if accurate this further distances the discussion away from content and toward rules. Secrecy thus has to do more with excluding the non-members of a social unit, than with content; language metaphorically alludes to concealed information, in societies where members agree on the rules (Bellman, 1984; see also Rosaldo, 1984, and Weiner, 1984). What defines a secret then is not its content, but *who gets to tell it* (see Brenneis & Myers, 1984; Bellman, 1984; Rosaldo, 1984).

Who gets to tell it also alludes to a body of people governed by certain rules. Secrets can help to create communal affect, by including some in knowledge of the secret, and excluding others, thus creating both boundaries and alliances (Kasfir, 2010; Gable, 1997, p. 230, fn. 7). *How the secret gets told* can involve what some call "deep talk," that is allusive, metaphoric speech (Bellman, 1984, pp. 76, 140). However, the concept of "deep talk" should be amplified with the more colloquial concept of "double talk," as when President Obama hailed himself, ironically, as "a big supporter of non-censorship," stating rather surprisingly: "I think that the more freely information flows, the stronger the society becomes, because then citizens of countries around the world can hold their own governments accountable. They can begin to think for themselves" (Branigan, 2009/11/16). One view might be that Obama was being dryly "honest": these qualities of openness, accountability, and freedom of thought are not meant for the US, where patriotism and national security reign paramount. These qualities are instead meant to be practiced by the targets of US destabilization—their absence used to justify interference, and their presence allowing for the regularization of interference.

How information attains the value of being secret is also critical. With reference to magic, some hold that the secret is a "privileged possession," and that secrecy "elevates the value of the thing concealed" making it seem "desirable" and "powerful"—magicians exploit this in order to give significance to their knowledge, and to conceal it from scepticism, indeed, to provide a means by which their own scepticism may be muted (Luhrmann, 1989, p. 161). To make knowledge unquestionable, it needs to be surrounded with "sacredness" (Rappaport, 1979).

Being initiated into a secret society requires respect for the rules of secrecy, unsurprisingly. In an extreme rendition of this principle, joining the US diplomatic corps has meant that career services offices at some US universities, and some newspapers, published notices to students advising them not to read the WikiLeaks cables, or risk any future employment prospects with the US government (Grinberg, 2010/12/8; Dortch, 2010/12/9). In this case, students had to agree to *not* know the secrets that everybody knew, in advance of joining the institutions that created the information that was now no longer secret. Clearly, secrecy and rationality are not partners. That secrecy flourishes in the presence of irrationality, can be seen in the demand made by the Pentagon spokesman, Geoff Morrell, who instructed WikiLeaks to "return" the documents—as if a physical body of original paper files that had not been received as copies of electronic data (DoD, 2010b). Adding to the apparent irrationality is the US state's injunction against staff reading the same reports—which they or their colleagues might have produced—and which were published by WikiLeaks, even when such files are available internally. Assange describes this irrationality in terms of a logic of maintaining the sanctity of classification:

> "While a given document can be read by cleared staff when it issues from classified government repositories, it is forbidden for the same staff to set eyes on the exact same document when it emerges from a public source. Should cleared employees of the national security state read such documents in the public domain, they are expected to self-report their contact with the

newly profaned object, and destroy all traces of it". (Assange, 2015)

Even without being initiated into formal membership, the other principle that comes into view is that of *responsibility*—responsibility better understood as submission, or as collusion. In order to gain legitimacy from the state, with the promise of possibly being included among its ranks of "authorized" knowledge bearers, it is important to abide by the rules of "responsibility". To be irresponsible, is also to be a threat. As Senator Joseph Lieberman commanded, "no responsible company—whether American or foreign—should assist WikiLeaks in its efforts to disseminate these stolen materials," and he referred to WikiLeaks' disclosures as "illegal, outrageous, and reckless acts" (Arthur, 2010/12/7). Similarly, Bill Keller, editor of *The New York Times* which for a while partnered with WikiLeaks in publishing these disclosures, distanced Julian Assange by referring to him merely—and inaccurately—as a "source" thus denying him membership in the club of responsible journalists (Benkler, 2011, pp. 37–38). While it called for action against Assange, the White House, according to Keller, "thanked us for handling the documents with care" (Keller, 2011/1/30).[3] The Pentagon itself seemed keen to distance the *New York Times* from WikiLeaks, stating that they doubted the former would describe itself as the latter's partner (DoD, 2010b).

Crisis, Secret Arrangements, and Neoliberal Restructuring

The WikiLeaks releases occasioned a sense of crisis among the powerful. Eric Wolf argued that, "we owe to social anthropology the insight that the arrangements of a society become most visible when they are challenged by crisis" (Wolf, 1990, p. 593). For Wolf, power is at least in part manifested in the ability to shape the "arena" in which interactions take place (1990, p. 586), and that implies the rules that govern those interactions. But power is also "implicated in meaning through its role in upholding one version of significance as true" against competing versions (Wolf, 1990, p. 591). Secrecy matters here: "To keep a secret creates the sense of the secret's power without the need for its demonstration" (Luhrmann, 1989, pp. 142–143).

Crisis may make some rules become visible, but it can also usher in a new set of invisible rules as seen in what anthropologist Janine Wedel describes in her 2009 book, *Shadow Elite*, as the restructuring of government in the US towards work done by insider-outsiders, that is, "flexians". These flexians occupy multiple roles in state, non-state and parastatal organizations such as think tanks, academia, business, the media, and military contracting, with increased power even when it comes to making policy. They are higher order "force multipliers". As private contractors, doing the work formerly done by public servants who were at least nominally accountable to the public, these flexians pursue what Wedel calls a "coincidence of interests" and have "privileged access to *official* information" (2009, pp. 1, 3). This privileged access even allows some flexians (such as the notorious neoconservatives, Richard Perle, Paul Wolfowitz, and Douglas Feith) to provide classified information to a foreign power (Israel), without ever facing prosecution (Wedel, 2009, pp. 148–149). Similarly, the White House Iraq Group, attached to Vice-President Dick Cheney, was also involved in deliberately leaking intelligence to the media (Wedel, 2009, p. 186). The result of the post-Cold War redesign of governing—"the privatization of the state by the state" (Kryshtanovskaya in Wedel, 2009, p. 7)—results in "increased authority delegated to private players" which "has enabled them to become guardians of information once resting in the hands of state and international authorities" (Wedel, 2009, p. 4).

The information security that WikiLeaks threatens, as we are told by flexians such as Geoff Morrell (who, not coincidentally, has worked both as a journalist and the Pentagon spokesman), is in fact the security of a fragmented order of power marked by the "frequent relinquishing of information by states to all manner of private players"—particularly, private players with multiple loyalties beyond the home state (2009, p. 9). Official information, previously available to both government and theoretically the public (or legally in some cases), is now increasingly privatized (2009, p. 10). As gatekeepers of inside access and knowledge, flexians are able to "brand information and control its applications" (Wedel, 2009, p. 16).

Wedel saw that state agencies such as the Pentagon had started to recruit "the next generation of workers who are tech savvy, open-minded, multi-tasking, and perhaps unprepared for command and control environments" (2009, p. 39)—which almost perfectly describes the source of the largest leaks to WikiLeaks, Chelsea Manning, as well as Edward Snowden, the source of the leaks on the National Security Agency. In the case of Snowden, we see yet another example of the force multiplier concept coming to ruin; perhaps the boomerang should have inspired Pentagon thinking instead.

What WikiLeaks threatens is this new, neoliberal order of re-designed government, and it does so by radically dropping the price of access to privileged information and returning it to the public. Cry as she might about law, security, and responsibility, Hillary Clinton herself operated as a flexian: as a private citizen, but married to then President Bill Clinton, she chaired the Task Force on National Health Reform. She was not then a public official, yet she asserted the right to conduct proceedings behind closed doors, thwarting public monitoring and accountability (for more on this see Wedel, 2009, p. 101). Of course she would feel threatened by WikiLeaks—her effort, however, is to make the rest of us believe that threats to positions such as those she wielded, are somehow threats to everyone. Yet the secrecy itself proves that the US is far from a "republic of everyone," but rather a corporate-oligarchic system (Kapferer, 2005; Gilens & Page, 2014; Guerin, 2014), where the very few presume to manage and control the great majority in the interests of the same few. "Irresponsibility" thus means the failure to obey the laws of submission, denying the role of authorities to authorize.

Julian Assange: Information Politics and Government as Conspiracy

There is some correspondence between Assange's views on information, secrecy, and state power and those of both Weberian and US libertarian inspiration, as suggested by the quote from James Madison in Stiglitz (1999, p. 5): "A popular government without popular information or the means of acquiring it is but a prologue to a farce or a tragedy or perhaps both". This creates part of the dualism of WikiLeaks: when it stresses the *content* of its leaks, it does so in a context where it defends itself as journalism; when it instead stresses its identity as one that is about freedom-of-information activism, it is inevitably dealing with the *rules* governing access to information.[4] This dual approach to its self-description reveals more than just that: it is a dual theoretical approach to confronting secret information, which arises from WikiLeaks' self-analysis, as revealed in this passage:

> "we're an activist organization. The method is transparency, the goal is justice. Part of the method is journalism. But it is our end-goal to achieve justice, and it's our sources' goals, usually, to also achieve justice". (Assange, 2010)

Julian Assange's theory of power and secrecy differs to a considerable extent from what has been presented by anthropologists thus far—and to be fair, given the age of this chapter (see the Acknowledgments below), the version of Assange's theory discussed here is primarily that which took shape up to 2011, but is otherwise a work in progress that manifests considerable change in the present (see Assange, 2015). In summary, thanks to Benkler (2011, p. 40), Assange posited that:

1) Authoritarian regimes depend on secrecy in hiding their internal communications from the public that is subject to state suppression;

2) Secrecy is vital to minimizing the potential for resistance, by essentially keeping the public ignorant of the backstage machinations; and,

3) By exposing the internal communications of authoritarian regimes, regimes will be forced to further tighten restrictions on their information, thereby slowing internal communications, and thus decreasing the ability of the regimes to work effectively.

Much of Assange's analysis of power seems to over-emphasize the instrumentality of data, to the exclusion of meaning and affect. This can lead to a misunderstanding of the proliferation of personal smear pieces in the media, and an overabundance of articles on the so-called "rape" allegations faced by Assange in Sweden. The result is that Assange may perceive this as simply designed to create an "interference pattern" (see Benkler, 2011, p. 21) in media coverage of WikiLeaks, as if designed solely to undermine or reshape the Google visibility of WikiLeaks releases. While no doubt in part correct, this perspective might not offer an adequate explanation for either the sustained nature of this production of personal coverage, and might overlook the deeper significance of the pieces: to class Assange as an irresponsible, reckless, dangerous, and even literally dirty *outsider*. (Assange himself has come to see the "contamination" undertones of the accusations launched by the US [Assange, 2015].). Articles in mainstream news coverage form rungs on a growing step-ladder of demonization, aimed at training public opinion to more and more see Assange as a serious problem—a problem that needs "fixing" by state authorities. In addition, though Assange shows some awareness at times of the multiple loyalties of those attacking him from their positions in the media, the focus on interference patterns can obscure the nature of flexian governance that he is up against. The result of Assange's analysis is a picture of an all-knowing, centralized, conspiratorial state and various dupes and sellouts (force multipliers) that serve them, which minimizes the social importance of networks whose rules of information control are challenged by WikiLeaks.

Assange's analytical emphasis is on the mechanics of information control, which is a necessary emphasis, even if incomplete on its own. Assange speaks of the need to "discover technological changes that embolden us with ways to act in which our forebears could not" (Assange, 2011). His view of power reduces to a vision of "collaborative secrecy," behaviour which, as he says, can be defined as "conspiratorial" (Assange, 2011). "Literacy and the communications revolution," he argues has,

> "empowered conspirators with new means to conspire, increasing the speed of accuracy of their interactions and thereby the maximum size a conspiracy may achieve before it breaks down. Conspirators who have this technology are able to out conspire conspirators without it. For the same costs they are able to achieve a higher total conspiratorial power". (Assange, 2011)

With a view that sees the information technology architectures of power more clearly than anything else, Assange says that,

> "our will came from a quite extraordinary notion of power, which was that with some clever mathematics you can, very simply...enable any individual to say no to the most powerful state. So if you and I agree on a particular encryption code, and it is mathematically strong, then the forces of every superpower brought to bear on that code still cannot crack it". (quoted in Obirst, 2011)

Again, this does more than just transfer the array of struggles between civil society and the state to the cyber domain; in fact, it seems to reduce all such conflict to the virtual and informational planes alone, to a question of mathematics.

At the very least, Assange has a more serious theory of "force multipliers" than anything we saw from military and political circles in the US in the Introduction to this volume. On the other hand, his theory shares something in common with the "force multipliers" notion. Here I turn to Baudrillard's (2005) critique of the fetishizing of "information" as a "machine" and its destruction of true knowledge and meaning, condemning the "immense banalization of life by the information machine" (p. 134):

> "The policing of events is essentially carried out by information itself. Information represents the most effective machinery for de-realizing history. Just as political economy is a gigantic

machinery for producing value, for producing signs of wealth, but not wealth itself, so the whole system of information is an immense machine for producing the event as sign, as an exchangeable value on the universal market of ideology, of spectacle, of catastrophe, etc.—in short, for producing a non-event. The abstraction of information is the same as the abstraction of the economy. And, as all commodities, thanks to this abstraction of value, are exchangeable one with another, so all events become substitutable one for another in the cultural information market. The singularity of the event, irreducible to its coded transcription and its staging, which is what quite simply constitutes an event, is lost. We are passing into a realm where events no longer truly take place, by dint of their very production and dissemination in 'real time'—where they become lost in the void of news and information. The sphere of information is like a space where, after having emptied events of their substance, an artificial gravity is re-created and they are put back in orbit in "real time"—where, having shorn them of historical vitality, they are re-projected on to the transpolitical stage of information. The non-event is not when nothing happens. It is, rather, the realm of perpetual change, of a ceaseless updating, of an incessant succession in real time, which produces this general equivalence, this indifference, this banality that characterizes the zero degree of the event....We have, then, to pass through the non-event of news coverage (information) to detect what resists that coverage. To find, as it were, the 'living coin' of the event. To make a literal analysis of it, against all the machinery of commentary and stage-management that merely neutralizes it. Only events set free from news and information (and us with them) create a fantastic longing. These alone are 'real,' since there is nothing to explain them and the imagination welcomes them with open arms". (Baudrillard, 2005, pp. 121–122, 133)

Baudrillard would thus have a very strong criticism of the mechanism of information presented in WikiLeaks' theory. Indeed, many of the authors cited in this chapter themselves make no distinction between *information* and knowledge. One of the problems that can present us with is that concerns focused on information as such—on data—serve to reduce knowledge, and the process of gaining knowledge, to an extractive process. In more extreme ways, this manner of thinking can be used to shut down debate—"don't tell me what you *think*, professor," the US student militarist tells the "radical" professor whose name is listed on Campus Watch, "just tell me what you *know*". In other words, give me information, quick, and hold the knowledge.

On another plane, in terms of conspiracy, the question that comes up is how much of a conspiracy is the phenomenon analyzed by Assange. Wedel argues that what we instead witness, in the case of the neoconservative flexians who penetrated deep into the George W. Bush administration, is not a conspiracy but rather a "coincidence of interests" and a "coordination of effort" (2009, p. 153)—where some activities and information are kept secret, but much else is made public, including the identities and networks of association of those Assange would call the conspirators. Yet, if they were conspirators in the commonly-understood sense, and if secrecy was really secret, we might not even know who they were in the first place. However, given what was outlined in the Introduction to this volume, certain US diplomats and military strategists themselves choose to write in conspiratorial terms, which tend to validate Assange's approach.

What is particularly interesting about Assange's theory and practice is the extent to which it virtually annuls Foucault's work on governmentality, rendering it both less useful and less interesting. Foucault tends to minimize state violence and state coercion. Foucault typically locates surveillance outside of the state, positing surveillance as something that is distributed, which takes the form of self-monitoring and compliance. If Foucault de-centres the state, then Assange has fully re-centred it. Assange is not alone in doing so of course; among those in agreement is the US military itself, which in its recent *National Military Strategy* asserts: "states remain the international system's dominant actors. They are preeminent in their capability to harness power, focus human endeavors, and provide security" (DoD, 2015, p. 2).

Lastly, it should be noted that very recently some of Julian Assange's analysis of secrecy has come to more closely resemble what is found in older anthropological treatments, especially on the question of "magic," the sacred and profane, and the rites of privileged access. For example, in his introductory chapter for *The WikiLeaks Files: The World According to US Empire*, Assange writes on the US state's religious approach to classification:

"Many religions and cults imbue their priestly class with additional scarcity value by keeping their religious texts secret from the public or the lower orders of the devoted. This technique also permits the priestly class to adopt different psychological strategies for different levels of indoctrination....

"The implication is that there is a non-physical property that inhabits documents once they receive their classification markings, and that this magical property is extinguished, not by copying the document, but by making the copy public. The now public document has, to devotees of the national security state, not merely become devoid of this magical property and reverted to a mundane object, it has been inhabited by another non-physical property: an evil one.

"This kind of religious thinking has consequences. Not only is it the excuse used by the US government to block millions of people working for the 'state within a state' from reading more than thirty different WikiLeaks domains—the same excuse that was used to block the *New York Times*, *Guardian*, *Der Spiegel*, *Le Monde*, *El País*, and other outlets publishing WikiLeaks materials". (Assange, 2015)

As Assange notes in the same text, the "religious hysteria" generated by the state might be "laughable," were it not for the fact that many US scholars take it seriously—seriously enough that, "the US-based *International Studies Quarterly (ISQ)*, a major international relations journal, adopted a policy against accepting manuscripts based on WikiLeaks material—even where it consists of quotes or derived analysis" (Assange, 2015).

The State as a Network

Through the conflict between WikiLeaks and the US, we also learn more about the actual expanse of state power, which embraces non-state actors and extra-legal means. As Benkler (2011, p. 18) put it: "The integrated, cross-system attack on WikiLeaks, led by the U.S. government with support from other governments, private companies, and online vigilantes, provides an unusually crisp window into the multi-system structure of freedom and constraint". Also interesting to note is how the state and pro-state actions were combined without being centrally coordinated, as if mimicking the decentralized structure of various counterattacks from Anonymous, consumer boycotts, and the distribution of WikiLeaks clone sites. As Benkler (2011, p. 26) observes, this is an "implicit alliance" (we might find some of Wedel's flexians here), "a public-private partnership between the firms that operate the infrastructure and the government that encourages them to help in its war on terror" which "was able to achieve extra-legally much more than law would have allowed the state to do by itself".

The Code of Silence

Perhaps one way to configure the results of this dual-focus analysis of secrecy from the perspectives of WikiLeaks and anthropology would be to consider how "code" is understood by each side. For WikiLeaks, code essentially has to do with data, with cryptographic codes, with breaking through the electronic walls that form the infrastructure of secrecy. These things exist, Assange has personally done battle with them, and there is no denying the validity of his experience and the logic of his understanding.

For anthropologists, there is another kind of "code" that they instead emphasize. This is the code of conduct—code in terms of the rules, personal loyalties, the sociolinguistic code of discretion in speech, and the political code of privilege that governs who gets to divulge certain information. These two codes are not entirely dissimilar. We may or may not gain from combining our diverse understandings of code into one unitary, synthetic approach. But perhaps the more immediate and less abstract lesson to learn here is that just as Assange has mastered the art of electronic hacking (information is power), anthropologists have mastered another hacking, that which exposes the meanings, rituals, and bonds that construct certain ideas as sacred information (the power that creates information).

Information Supremacy?

Finally, and returning to some of the US military's assumptions of "full-spectrum dominance" addressed in the Introduction, which to some extent are shared yet more maturely developed by Assange, we have reason to be sceptical about the power of information, especially information assumed to be "the truth". Information is not power, nor is it knowledge, let alone a philosophy of knowledge. It is, at best, raw material for potential knowledge. Nor does everyone have access to the same information, as some netizens would flatter themselves in thinking. There are still numerous paywalls and firewalls, and even having physical access ensures neither *use* nor the ability to *understand*, that is, the ability to access intellectually. Greater access to information then is literally meaningless. In the absence of motivation, the right questions, and the skills needed to make meaning out of information, leaks only have symbolic value.

There are many criticisms of WikiLeaks, and Assange's theory, criticisms that are sometimes based on tenuous foundations: that if the imperial state continues in spite of the leaks, then Assange has failed, and his theory is a failure. That is a bit too hasty. First, real history does not move at the speed of Twitter, and we are not yet in a position to ascertain the full outcome of the now regular publication of leaks, large and small. Our theories and descriptions will largely determine how we discern the outcome. Second, there is a mistake made in concluding that because WikiLeaks failed to disrupt the flexians' order, that it is not a threat. Clearly, WikiLeaks does undermine the social relationships of power constructed around the management of information, while undermining the ability of the US to effectively use "soft power" on issues of press freedom, government transparency, and individual civil liberties, which are also core areas of the neoliberal agenda. We would have been mistaken to assume that dramatic, earth-shattering consequences would arise from the publication of so many leaks. However, what damage there has been to the imperial order has been significant in terms of the erosion of the propaganda produced by key states such as the US and its allies, at a time when they are desperate to salvage credibility following the invasions and occupations of Afghanistan and especially Iraq (and now Libya). The government of the UK specifically identifies the risk of "political harm or embarrassment" that can arise from the leak of classified documents—as we learn from a document leaked to WikiLeaks (Ministry of Defence [MoD], 2001, p. 2-26). In a wide definition of what constitutes a "threat," the UK's MoD explains that "the 'enemy' is unwelcome publicity of any kind, and through any medium" (MoD, 2001, p. 17-3). Anthropologists would well understand the significance and value of symbols, public image management, credibility/credulity, and reputation, all of which are involved in the latter statement. Also noteworthy is the number of times that MoD lists "investigative journalists" along with "terrorist groups," often placing these two together in the same sentence (see WikiLeaks, 2009).

Others have also convincingly laid out a series of WikiLeaks' successes that I need not recite here (see Hawley, 2011), with some insisting that, "the world has changed in major ways for democratic possibilities, with WikiLeaks as a catalyst" (Solomon, 2015). The fact that Assange is so consistently rebuked, reviled, and demonized by government officials, political elites, and members of the corporate media, is taken as evidence of the power of WikiLeaks' sting. More than that, it is evidence of how much we are intended not to know, while being asked to continue supporting the dominant classes. As Solomon (2015) explains, "in acute contrast to so many at the top of the corporate media and governmental food chains, Assange insists that democracy requires the 'consent of the governed' to be *informed* consent. While powerful elites work 24/7 to continually gain the uninformed consent of the governed, WikiLeaks has opposite concerns".

This is a critical revelation in itself that WikiLeaks has helped to magnify, one that should cause us to debate to what extent hegemony is really based on the "consent" of the governed—as so many adaptations of Gramsci would have us believe, thereby implicating the dominated in their own domination. It is also a strong blow to the "democracy" myth reproduced in Western, namely US international propaganda campaigns. Ours is shown to be a democracy that daily operates on the basis of lies, secrets, and mass ignorance. That reminders of this fact are constantly needed, only reaffirms the value of WikiLeaks' continued work.[5]

On the other hand, there are clearly flaws with the assumptions at the base of Assange's theory of information freedom. We are daily proving ourselves to be better informed than ever and yet somehow more powerless and passive than ever. A more visible imperial state is not one that is less imperial. The "shadow elite" continues in its daily operations *seemingly* unruffled by the all too rare examples of a Manning or Snowden. Their position is even more of an open secret, in the words of one reviewer of this chapter. Spectacular disclosure has annoyed the imperial state, but *apparently* it has not disrupted it—however, this may also be due to the fact that the disclosures have not been as regular or as extensive as they might yet be.

However, it would still be a mistake to believe that the shadow elite can function without some expectation of secrecy, especially given the extent to which regime change is tied to market considerations and converted into insider trading schemes—all of which require a tight and exclusive control over information:

"Since corporate property was always restored after a successful regime change [with 24 national leaders installed by the CIA], these operations were potentially profitable to nationalized companies. If foreknowledge of these operations was truly secret, then precoup asset prices should not have reflected the expected future gains. However, this article shows that not only were U.S.-supported coups valuable to partially nationalized multinationals, but in addition, asset traders arbitraged supposedly 'top-secret' information concerning plans to overthrow foreign governments". (Dube, Kaplan & Naidu, 2011, pp. 1375-1376)

What we learn is that some of the top US-based transnational corporations benefited "from top-secret events, suggesting information flows from covert operations into markets" (Dube, Kaplan & Naidu, 2011, p. 1376).

What does anthropology have to learn from the experience and practice of WikiLeaks? For an anthropology of international relations, for the study of imperialism, for more documentary depth on the US and NATO occupations of Afghanistan and Iraq, for critical analysis of the foreign policy realities shielded by diplomats, and to develop a stronger realization of how mass media are manipulated as instruments of elites that form part of the military-industrial complex, then the study of WikiLeaks itself, and the documents it has released, are indispensable. As a mode of research that differs from Western anthropology's current ethnographic fetishism, WikiLeaks shows exactly how "studying up" can mature and expand in practice. From these vantage points, I believe that WikiLeaks has had more to teach anthropology about both research methodology in the context of contemporary geopolitics, than vice versa.

Acknowledgements

This chapter has an unusual history. Beginning first as a series of essays published online, primarily in *CounterPunch* and *Zero Anthropology*, it then became a paper presented at a conference; then it became a book chapter for a volume that the editor chose to leave behind, even though contributors were told it had been awarded an advance contract from Oxford University Press; and, more recently, it was developed into an article for a special issue of *Anthropologie et Sociétés*, which furnished three reviews from peers.

Though the article passed peer review (but with many inconsistent, contradictory, and deeply problematic comments and recommendations for revision), I chose to withdraw it from publication in *Anthropologie et Sociétés*. Unfortunately, apart from lacking time to do the requested revisions in short order, I had several serious reservations about the nature of some of the comments. Rather than allow the work to continue to languish in oblivion, or sequester it behind a paywall, I decided to make it freely available to a wider audience. I am generally thankful to both the editors, issue editors, and three anonymous reviewers, some of whose comments were useful for developing the updated and revised final version that appears here.

This is also an unusual chapter because though ostensibly self-published, it has probably been kicked around more than most papers, after several stages of peer review and revision, over a period of years. However, as an elder colleague once said, "you only get to kick the cat so many times before it runs away". Hence, here is my cat.

I am thankful to the organizers of "Leaks, Lies, and Red Tape: State Secrecy and its Discontents," for inviting me to participate in the session which took place at the conference of the American Anthropological Association, held in Montreal on November 18, 2011. In addition, I wish to thank several WikiLeaks supporters, for their numerous leads, suggestions, debates, and analyses, in particular some of those who were once involved with writing for WL Central, but who remain anonymous. A fair portion of the documents and news articles which initially formed the foundation for this research came thanks to their recommendations. None of these acknowledgments are meant to imply any sort of endorsement for the contents of this chapter.

Notes

1   The three persons in question are Laurie Rush (Cultural Resource Management at Ft. Drum, NY), Kerry Fosher (affiliated with Syracuse University and the Marine Corps Intelligence Activity [MCIA]), and Laura McNamara (Sandia National Laboratories)—see the CEAUSSIC page at:
http://web.archive.org/web/20081121014400/http://www.aaanet.o
rg/cmtes/commissions/CEAUSSIC/index.cfm.

2   To allay the concerns of one reviewer, it is doubtful that Wedel is referring to Foucault's treatment of the concept of *governmentality*, or whether she means that in government circles themselves "governance" is only recently the new buzzword. I suspect it is the latter, and that what she describes is how government insiders use the term *governance*, which is not the same idea as governmentality.

3   It was interesting to watch some US anthropologists discussing WikiLeaks on Twitter in 2010, sharing inchoate gripes about the organization and Assange personally, while endorsing an incompetent and collaborationist rival, OpenLeaks, whose founder actually destroyed thousands of Afghan war documents. To date, not only has OpenLeaks never published anything (but has erased a lot), it is no longer even open, having surrendered even its Internet domain name. I suspect that the fact that most US anthropologists vote Democrat, have known sympathies for Obama, and retain some margin of patriotism, likely motivated them to join the media-orchestrated chorus of denunciation of WikiLeaks, without a gram of their much vaunted "reflexivity" ever on display. On the other hand, I am not a neutral party either—more than once I have donated funds to WikiLeaks, published articles in its defence, and used *Zero Anthropology* as a part-

ner website that hosts WikiLeaks documents so as to ensure access during numerous distributed-denial-of-service attacks against WikiLeaks' websites. As a result, I was publicly listed as a "media contact" by WikiLeaks. Nonetheless, on numerous points of political theory and practice, I depart significantly from WikiLeaks, including its past anarcho-libertarian messaging; the convictions it sometimes shares in common with the US State Department; the manner it can soften itself to appeal to mainstream media; and, its sometimes naive analysis and resultant enthusiasm for the regime change extravaganza that delighted Western cyber-spectators, known as the "Arab Spring," among other differences in perspective and practice. Assange's theory, however, is a work in progress.

4   For a much more in-depth view of WikiLeaks self-descriptions as an activist organization around issues of freedom of information, see the organization's older "About" page on its former website, now archived at:
      http://web.archive.org/web/20080328010014/www.wikileaks.org/w iki/Wikileaks:About.

5   It may be disappointing, but nonetheless important to note that none of the anthropologists who reviewed an earlier version of this chapter seemed to have any concern for this question of democracy, when accusing WikiLeaks of having achieved so little.

References

Appadurai, A. (1990). Disjuncture and Difference in the Global Cultural Economy. *Theory, Culture & Society*, 7(2), 295–310.

Arthur, C. (2010/12/7). WikiLeaks under Attack: The Definitive Timeline. *The Guardian*, December 7.
      http://www.guardian.co.uk/media/2010/dec/07/wikileaks-under-attack-definitive-timeline

Assange, J. (2010). Presentation at "The State of Play," the Fourth Annual Reva and David Logan Investigative Reporting Symposium, Berkeley Graduate School of Journalism, April 16–18.
      http://fora.tv/2010/04/18/Logan_Symposium_The_New_Initiatives#chapter_12

——————— . (2011). Conspiracy as Governance. *Frontline Club*, June 28.
      http://www.frontlineclub.com/blogs/WikiLeaks/2011/06/julian-assange-the-state-and-terrorist-conspiracies.html

——————— . (2015). Exclusive: Julian Assange's Introduction to The Wikileaks Files. *Gizmodo*, August 26.
      http://gizmodo.com/gizmodo-exclusive-read-julian-assanges-introduction-to-1726605781

Baudrillard, J. (2005). *The Intelligence of Evil or tile Lucidity Pact*. Oxford: Berg.

Bellman, B. (1984). *The Language of Secrecy: Symbols and Metaphors in Poro*

Ritual. New Brunswick, NJ: Rutgers University Press.

Bendix, R. (2003). Sleepers' Secrets, Actors' Revelations. *Ethnologia Europaea*, 33(2), 33-42.

Benkler, Y. (2011). A Free Irresponsible Press: Wikileaks and the Battle over the Soul of the Networked Fourth Estate. *Harvard Civil Rights-Civil Liberties Law Review* (working draft).

http://www.benkler.org/Benkler_Wikileaks_current.pdf

Branigan, T. (2009/11/16). Barack Obama Criticises Internet Censorship at Meeting in China. *The Guardian*, November 16.

http://www.guardian.co.uk/world/2009/nov/16/barack-obama-criticises-internet-censorship-china

Brenneis, D., & Myers, F. (Eds.). (1984). *Dangerous Words: Language and Politics in the Pacific.* New York: New York University Press.

Davies, N. (2010/7/25). Julian Assange Profile: Wikileaks Founder an Uncompromising Rebel. *The Guardian*, July 25.

http://www.guardian.co.uk/media/2010/jul/25/julian-assange-profile-wikileaks-founder

Dortch, D.T. (2010/12/9). Job Hunters Should Steer Clear of WikiLeaks Site. *The Washington Post*, December 9.

http://www.washingtonpost.com/wp-dyn/content/article/2010/12/08/AR2010120806796.html

Ellsberg, D. (2011/1/24). Daniel Ellsberg: We Need Whistleblowers to Stop Murder [transcript]. *The Real News*, January 24.

http://therealnews.com/t2/index.php?option=com_content&task=view&id=31&Itemid=74&jumival=6132

Feldman, G. (2003). Breaking our Silence on NATO. *Anthropology Today*, 19(3), 1–2.

——————— . (2011). If Ethnography is more than Participant-Observation, then Relations are more than Connections: The Case for Nonlocal Ethnography in a World of Apparatuses. *Anthropological Theory*, 11(4), 375–395.

Fulton, R.M. (1972). The Political Structures and Functions of Poro in Kpelle Society. *American Anthropologist*, 74(5), 1218–1233.

Gable, E. (1997). A Secret Shared: Fieldwork and the Sinister in a West African Village. *Cultural Anthropology*, 12(2), 213–233.

Gilens, M., & Page, B.I. (2014). Testing Theories of American Politics: Elites, Interest Groups, and Average Citizens. Pre-publication draft.

https://politicalanthro.files.wordpress.com/2014/09/gilens-and-page-2014-testing-theories-3-7-14.pdf

González, R.J. (2012). Anthropology and the Covert: Methodological Notes on Researching Military and Intelligence Programmes. *Anthropology Today*, 28(2), 21-25.

Goodman, A. (2011/7/5). Watch: Full Video of WikiLeaks' Julian Assange & Philosopher Slavoj Žižek with Amy Goodman. *Democracy Now!* July 5.

http://www.democracynow.org/blog/2011/7/5/watch_full_video_of_wikileaks_julia

n_assange_philosopher_slavoj_iek_with_amy_goodman

Grinberg, E. (2010/12/8). Will Reading Wikileaks Cost Students Jobs with the Federal Government? *CNN*, December 8.

http://articles.cnn.com/2010-12-08/justice/wikileaks.students_1_wikileaks-security-clearance-students?_s=PM:CRIME

Guerin, M. (2014). Life, Liberty and the Pursuit of Wage Labour: The American Legislative Exchange Council and the Neoliberal Coup. In Maximilian C. Forte (Ed.), *Good Intentions: Norms and Practices of Imperial Humanitarianism* (pp. 121–145). Montreal: Alert Press.

Hawley, M. (2011). Transparency Shift: An Overview of the Reality of WikiLeaks. In Maximilian C. Forte (Ed.), *Interventionism, Information Warfare, and the Military-Academic Complex* (pp. 129–144). Montreal: Alert Press.

Kapferer, B. (2005). New Formations of Power, the Oligarchic-Corporate State, and Anthropological Ideological Discourse. *Anthropological Theory*, 5(3), 285–299.

Kasfir, S.L. (2010). Review of Masquerades of Modernity: Power and Secrecy in Casamance, Senegal by Ferdinand De Jong. Bloomington: Indiana University Press, 2007. *African Arts*, 43(2): 81–85.

Keller, B. (2011/1/30). Dealing With Assange and the WikiLeaks Secrets. *The New York Times Magazine*, January 30.

http://www.nytimes.com/2011/01/30/magazine/30Wikileaks-t.html?pagewanted=all

Kessler, G. (2010/11/30). Clinton, in Kazakhstan for Summit, Will Face Leaders Unhappy Over Wikileaks Cables. *The Washington Post*, November 30.

http://www.washingtonpost.com/wpdyn/content/article/2010/11/30/AR201011300 1095.html

la Fontaine, J. (1977). The Power of Rights. *Man*, 12(3–4), 421–437.

Levine, A. (2010/10/16). Gates: WikiLeaks don't Reveal Key Intel, but Risks Remain. *CNN*, October 16.

http://articles.cnn.com/2010-10-16/us/wikileaks.assessment_1_julian-assange-wikileaks-documents?_s=PM:US

Little, K.L. (1949). The Role of the Secret Society in Cultural Socialization. *American Anthropologist*, 51(2), 199–212.

——————— . (1966). The Political Function of the Poro, Part 2. *Africa*, 36(1), 62–72.

Luhrmann, T.M. (1989). The Magic of Secrecy. *Ethos*, 17(2), 131–165.

Marcus, G.E. (1995). Ethnography in/of the World System: The Emergence of Multi-Sited Ethnography. *Annual Review of Anthropology*, 24, 95–117.

Ministry of Defence (MoD). (2001). The Defence Manual of Security (Volumes 1, 2 and 3, Issue 2). London: Ministry of Defence.

Moynihan, D.P. (1999). The Science of Secrecy. Delivered at MIT, Cambridge, Massachusetts, March 29.

http://www.aaas.org/spp/secrecy/Presents/Moynihan.htm

Mueller, M. (2010/12/7). Why Wikileaks Polarizes America's Internet Politics. *Internet Governance Project*, December 7.
http://blog.internetgovernance.org/blog/_archives/2010/12/7/4698146.html

Murphy, W. (1980). Secret Knowledge as Property and Power in Kpelle Society: Elders versus Youth. *Africa*, 50(2), 193–207.

Nader, L. (1972). Up the Anthropologist: Perspectives Gained from Studying Up. In Dell Hymes (Ed.), *Reinventing Anthropology* (pp. 284–311). New York: Pantheon Books.

Obirst, H.U. (2011). In Conversation with Julian Assange, Part I. *E-flux*, 25, May.
http://www.e-flux.com/journal/view/232

Ottenberg, S. (1989). *Boyhood Rituals in an African Society*. Seattle: University of Washington Press.

Piot, C.D. (1993). Secrecy, Ambiguity, and the Everyday in Kabre Culture. *American Anthropologist*, 95(2), 353–370.

Politact. (2010/12/2). The Secrets of Wikileaks: Impact on International Relations and the Role of Media. *Politact: Strategic-Intel*, December 2.
http://politact.com/af-pak-and-fata-situation/the-secrets-of-wikileaks-impact-on-international-relations-and-the-role-of-media.html

Price, D.H. (1998). Gregory Bateson and the OSS: World War II and Bateson's Assessment of Applied Anthropology. *Human Organization*, 57(4), 379–384.

——————. (2008). *Anthropological Intelligence: The Deployment and Neglect of American Anthropology in the Second World War*. Durham, NC: Duke University Press.

Rappaport, R.A. (1979). *Ecology, Meaning, and Religion*. Richmond, CA: North Atlantic Books.

Rosaldo, M. (1984). Words that Are Moving: The Social Meanings of Ilongot Verbal Art. In Don Brenneis & Fred Myers (Eds.), *Dangerous Words: Language and Politics in the Pacific* (pp. 131–160). New York: New York University Press.

Ross, C. (2010/11/30). The End of Diplomacy as We Know It. *The Huffington Post*, November 30.
http://www.huffingtonpost.com/carne-ross/the-end-of-diplomacy-as-w_b_790128.html

Schorr, D. (2009/9/23). Obama Feels Pressure on Leaked McChrystal Report. *NPR*, September 23.
http://www.npr.org/templates/story/story.php?storyId=113130422

Simmel, G. (1950). The Secret and the Secret Society. In K.H. Wolff (Ed.), *The Sociology of Georg Simmel* (pp. 330–344). Glencoe, IL: The Free Press.

Smith, B. (2009/9/22). A D.C. Whodunit: Who Leaked and Why? *Politico*, September 22.
http://www.politico.com/news/stories/0909/27414.html

Solomon, N. (2015). Subverting Illusions: Julian Assange and the Value of

WikiLeaks. *CounterPunch*, August 17.
http://www.counterpunch.org/2015/08/17/subverting-illusions-julian-assange-and-the-value-of-wikileaks/

Stark, H., & Rosenbach, M. (2010/12/20). WikiLeaks Is Annoying, But Not a Threat. *Spiegel Online International*, December 20.
http://www.spiegel.de/international/germany/0,1518,735587,00.html

Stiglitz, J.E. (1999). On Liberty, the Right to Know, and Public Discourse: The Role of Transparency in Public Life. Oxford Amnesty Lecture, Oxford, U.K., January 27.
http://derechoasaber.org.mx/documentos/pdf0116.pdf

Taussig, M. (1999). *Defacement: Public Secrecy and the Labor of the Negative*. Stanford, CA: Stanford University Press.

————— . (2006). *Walter Benjamin's Grave*. Chicago: The University of Chicago Press.

US Department of Defense (DoD). (2010a). DOD News Briefing with Secretary Gates and Adm. Mullen from the Pentagon, November 30. Washington, DC: US Department of Defense, Office of the Assistant Secretary of Defense (Public Affairs).
http://www.defense.gov/Transcripts/Transcript.aspx?TranscriptID=4728

————— . (2010b). DOD News Briefing with Geoff Morrell from the Pentagon, August 5. Washington, DC: US Department of Defense, Press Operations.
http://www.defense.gov/transcripts/transcript.aspx?transcriptid=53001

————— . (2015). The National Military Strategy of the United States of America. Washington, DC: Joint Chiefs of Staff, US Department of Defense.

Watkins, M.H. (1943). The West African 'Bush' School. *American Journal of Sociology*, 48(6), 666–675.

Weber, M. (1968). *Economy and Society: An Outline of Interpretive Sociology*. Gunther Roth and Claus Wittich (Eds.). Berkeley: University of California Press.

Weiner, A. (1984). From Words to Objects to Magic: "Hard Words" and the Boundaries of Social Interaction. In Don Brenneis & Fred Myers (Eds.), *Dangerous Words: Language and Politics in the Pacific* (pp. 161–191). New York: New York University Press.

Wedel, J.R. (2009). *Shadow Elite: How the World's New Power Brokers Undermine Democracy, Government, and the Free Market*. New York: Basic Books.

WikiLeaks. (2009). UK MoD Manual of Security Volumes 1, 2 and 3 Issue 2, JSP-440, RESTRICTED, 2389 pages, 2001. *WikiLeaks*, October 4.
https://wikileaks.org/wiki/UK_MoD_Manual_of_Security_Volumes_1%2C_2_and_3_Issue_2%2C_JSP-440%2C_RESTRICTED%2C_2389_pages%2C_2001

Wilkinson, W. (2010/11/29). Overseeing State Secrecy: In Defence of WikiLeaks. *The Economist (Democracy in America blog)*, November 29.
http://www.economist.com/blogs/democracyinamerica/2010/11/overseeing_state_secrecy

Wolf, E.R. (1990). Distinguished Lecture: Facing Power–Old Insights, New Questions. *American Anthropologist*, 92(3), 586–596.

CONTRIBUTORS

Chloë Blaszkewycz grew up in Montréal. She graduated from a BAC in anthropology at Université de Montréal in 2014. Her interests are grounded in critical and political anthropology, gender issues as well as documentary.

Mandela Coupal-Dalgleish is from Mont-Saint-Grégoire, Québec. He is currently an undergraduate student at Concordia University in the Joint Specialization in Anthropology and Sociology where his particular area of interest lies in agriculture. He also spends much of his time working on his family farm.

Maximilian C. Forte is a Professor in the Department of Sociology & Anthropology at Concordia University in Montréal, Canada, where he directs the New Imperialism seminar. He specializes in the political economy, media, and cultural dimensions of US imperialism.

Iléana Eilis Sóley Gutnick is an anthropology student at Université de Montréal. She served as secretary general of the Association Étudiante d'Anthropologie de l'Université de Montréal. A radical feminist, she is interested in bottom-up anthropology and anticolonial movements. She wishes to continue her travels and studies.

Robert Majewski is an alumnus of the Honours program in Anthropology at Concordia University, Montréal. Though he was born in Montréal, both of his parents are from Częstochowa, Poland. His main areas of interest and research are migration, sexuality (queer issues in particular), political anthropology and anthropology of food.

Leah Marinova arrived from Bulgaria as an immigrant, at the age of 17. Attracted by the arts, she began to study cinema. Soon the documentary form brought her to question ethics and to study the significance of cultural contexts. Thus Lea undertook her studies in anthropology. Marinova's research and films have taken many forms and have tackled very different subjects, but most recently an interest towards her own region is increasing. Born during the rise of "democracy," just one year after the fall of the Berlin Wall, Marinova is acquainted with the qualities of this so-called "democracy". Raised with the stories of her family chased by the socialist government for generations, she is now investigating the cultural, historical and presently-political contexts to understand the reasons of her own uprooting.

John Talbot, originally hailing from Edmonton Alberta, is completing his BA Specialization in Anthropology at Concordia University in Montréal, Québec. His primary interest is political anthropology, with focuses on direct action, empire, and politicized concepts of posthumanism such as deep ecology.

www.ingramcontent.com/pod-product-compliance
Lightning Source LLC
Chambersburg PA
CBHW030006290326

41934CB00005B/242